Protectors of Pluralism

Why do some religious groups protect victims of genocide while others do not? This book argues that local religious minorities are more likely to save persecuted groups from purification campaigns. Two reinforcing mechanisms link minority status to rescue operations. First, religious minorities are better able to setup clandestine organizations because their members are more committed and inward looking. Second, minority elites empathize with targets of purification campaigns, imbuing their networks with preferences that lead them to resist genocide. A geo-referenced dataset of Jewish evasion in the Netherlands and Belgium during the Holocaust is deployed to assess the minority hypothesis. Spatial statistics and archival work reveal that Protestants were more likely to rescue Jews in Catholic regions of the Low Countries, while Catholics facilitated evasion in Protestant areas. Postwar testimonies and secondary literature demonstrate the importance of minority groups for rescue in other countries during the Holocaust as well as other episodes of mass violence, underlining that it is the local position of church communities – and not something inherent to any religion itself – that produces networks of assistance to threatened neighbors.

Robert Braun is an Assistant Professor of Sociology and Political Science at the University of California, Berkeley. His research focuses on civil society and intergroup relationships in times of social upheaval. He has been published in several esteemed journals, including the *American Journal of Sociology* and the *American Political Science Review*, and has received more than twenty scholarly awards.

Cambridge Studies in Contentious Politics

General Editor

Doug McAdam *Stanford University and Center for Advanced Study in the Behavioral Sciences*

Editors

Rina Agarwala, *Informal Labor, Formal Politics, and Dignified Discontent in India*

Ronald Aminzade, *Race, Nation, and Citizenship in Post-Colonial Africa: The Case of Tanzania*

Ronald Aminzade et al., *Silence and Voice in the Study of Contentious Politics*

Javier Auyero, *Routine Politics and Violence in Argentina: The Gray Zone of State Power*

Phillip M. Ayoub, *When States Come Out: Europe's Sexual Minorities and the Politics of Visibility*

Amrita Basu, *Violent Conjunctures in Democratic India*

W. Lance Bennett and Alexandra Segerberg, *The Logic of Connective Action: Digital Media and the Personalization of Contentious Politics*

Nancy Bermeo and Deborah J. Yashar, editors, *Parties, Movements, and Democracy in the Developing World*

Clifford Bob, *The Global Right Wing and the Clash of World Politics*

Clifford Bob, *The Marketing of Rebellion: Insurgents, Media, and International Activism*

Charles Brockett, *Political Movements and Violence in Central America*

Marisa von Bülow, *Building Transnational Networks: Civil Society and the Politics of Trade in the Americas*

Valerie Bunce and Sharon Wolchik, *Defeating Authoritarian Leaders in Postcommunist Countries*

Lars-Erik Cederman, Kristian Skrede Gleditsch, and Halvard Buhaug, *Inequality, Grievances, and Civil War*

Continued after the index

Protectors of Pluralism

*Religious Minorities and the Rescue of Jews
in the Low Countries during
the Holocaust*

ROBERT BRAUN

University of California, Berkeley

CAMBRIDGE
UNIVERSITY PRESS

CAMBRIDGE
UNIVERSITY PRESS

University Printing House, Cambridge CB2 8BS, United Kingdom

One Liberty Plaza, 20th Floor, New York, NY 10006, USA

477 Williamstown Road, Port Melbourne, VIC 3207, Australia

314–321, 3rd Floor, Plot 3, Splendor Forum, Jasola District Centre,
New Delhi – 110025, India

79 Anson Road, #06–04/06, Singapore 079906

Cambridge University Press is part of the University of Cambridge.

It furthers the University's mission by disseminating knowledge in the pursuit of
education, learning, and research at the highest international levels of excellence.

www.cambridge.org
Information on this title: www.cambridge.org/9781108471022
DOI: 10.1017/9781108633116

© Robert Braun 2019

First published 2019

Printed in the United Kingdom by TJ International Ltd, Padstow Cornwall

A catalog record for this publication is available from the British Library.

ISBN 978-1-108-47102-2 Hardback
ISBN 978-1-108-45697-5 Paperback

Een Driewerf Hoera voor de Barmhartige Samaritaan!

Contents

Figures

Tables

Acknowledgments

Studying genocide is intriguing but challenging. It poses the ultimate puzzle: it feels impossibly far removed from our daily lives, but it is actually extremely close. Only two generations ago collective killings organized by the Nazis threatened the lives of ancestors on one side of my family, while other members of my family saw the killing machine roll out its tentacles yet decided to do nothing. How could all of this happen to people very much like myself in the streets that I know so well?

The main challenge of genocide studies is trying to remain excited and non-cynical about the academic enterprise of answering a research question without losing sight of the fact that "your empirical puzzle" involved the suffering of thousands and thousands of innocent people. This became crystal clear to me eight months into my fieldwork when, on a Monday morning, I arrived in the archives to see stacks of Jewish registration cards waiting for me on my desk. My first thought was one that blended demoralization and frustration, a feeling very similar to the one I had when a waiter in the restaurant where I was employed as a dishwasher at a university loaded yet another pile onto my workstation. I was living the banality of evil. Was this the same feeling that Hitler's bureaucrats – who had written these registration cards in the first place – had when they arrived in the office after the weekend? This realization disturbed me, as it stood in stark contrast with how I came to think about genocide early on in life.

My first exposure to the Holocaust came in elementary school when my teacher decided to dedicate an afternoon session to a discussion on the destruction of Dutch Jewry. This decision was taken in response to something that had happened during the morning break. Several Dutch kids had beaten up a Turkish boy. When the teacher stepped in to end the assaults, the main instigator legitimized his behavior by accusing the victims dad of stealing his father's job. The teacher explained to us that this was a typical case of racism. This brief introduction to the Holocaust in the Netherlands drove home the point that racism was dangerous and should be fought with any means necessary. Having done nothing to end the fight myself, I remember feeling embarrassed after class ended. Especially since the Turkish boy was one of my best friends at the beginning of the school year. Ever since, the relationship between the protection of pluralism and the Holocaust has been edged in my soul, although the words I used back then were very different.

I started thinking about these issues in more depth for the first time as an undergrad in the back row of KC-07, the main lecture hall of the Vrije Universiteit Amsterdam. Here, Geert de Vries, a bowler hat and suspenders–wearing sociologist, introduced me and many others to the ideas of Durkheim, Weber, Goffman and Elias. His extraordinary lectures changed my life and turned me into a social scientist (although he would probably not like this term). Under the wings of Harry Ganzeboom, Ruud Koopmans and Rens Vliegenthart, who all happened to be at the Vrije Universiteit Amsterdam at the time, I published my first papers on racist violence. Ruud and Harry taught me how to think systematically and urged me to apply for grad school in the United States.

As a result, this book started as a doctoral dissertation in government at Cornell University. Cornell provided a wonderful environment to develop my ideas; my experiences in classes that I took with David Patel, Jessica Weeks and Patrick Sullivan are imprinted in the following pages. I owe a substantial intellectual debt to my advisors, Sidney Tarrow, Christopher Way, Alex Kuo and Kevin Morrison. Alex and Kevin had the rare ability to tear my work apart constructively and supportively. And, as junior faculty, I thank them for having been so forthcoming with professional advice as I navigated the often ambiguous social cues that dominate academia. Chris is arguably Cornell government's most valuable player: his advice improves the quality of your work almost instantly. The fact that his students have won best dissertation awards in international relations, comparative politics, American politics and sociology is indicative of the quality of his graduate student training. Professor Tarrow is a superb advisor and role model. He influenced me intellectually, professionally and personally. I hope, but highly doubt, that I will be able to live up to his standards. As such, I guess I will always remain a Tarrow student.

Most parts of this book were written while I was a predoctoral fellow and assistant professor at Northwestern University. The Department of Sociology provided me with a warm and intellectually stimulating home. Although people say that all departments have their problems and discontents, I am not able to name a single one for Northwestern Sociology. Its weekly colloquium turned me into a better sociologist and showed me what it means to be a good colleague. Northwestern's Comparative-Historical Social Science and War and Society Programs are the most interesting intellectual communities I have encountered to date. Its interdisciplinary focus and emphasis on contextualized knowledge fit me like a glove. I would like to thank the groups' core members, Bruce Carruthers, Dan Krcmaric, Jim Mahoney, Ann Orloff and Monica Prasad, for being fantastic colleagues and wonderful intellectuals. Outside of these programs, I also thank Ben Frommer and Jörg Spenkuch, who were both always available for much appreciated interdisciplinary exchanges.

Both the Netherlands and Belgium are home to extraordinarily strong academic communities, and I was lucky to have interacted with many members of both. My work on the Netherlands would not have been possible without input from Marnix Croes, Fred Cammaert, Froukje Demant, Bert-Jan Flim, Pim Griffioen, Jan Ramakers, Herman van Rens, Ton Salemink, Annika Smits, Wout Ultee, Hans de Vries and Ruud Weissmann. Dirk Luyten, Lieven Saerens, Laurence Schram and Aline Sax helped me find my footing in Belgium. During my time in Belgium, Peter van Aelst generously hosted me at the University of Antwerp's M2P program, while Bert Klandermans from the Sociology Department at the Vrije Universiteit Amsterdam did the same when I was doing archival work in Amsterdam.

A scholar of history is worth nothing without the help of archivists. I had the pleasure to work with some of the best and most dedicated archivists in the world, from whom I learned more than I can ever repay. In the Netherlands, Michiel Schwartzenberg, Marieke Bos and, particularly, Raymund Schutz from the Netherlands Red Cross, Lonnie Stegink from the Dutch Jewish History Museum, Jose Martin from Kamp Westerbork, Lodewijk Winkeler from the Katholiek Documentatie Centrum in Nijmegen, Aike van der Ploeg from DOCDIRECT Winschoten, and Sierk Plantinga and Gijs Boink from the National Archives provided me with invaluable assistance throughout the process. For Belgium, the same can be said about Dorien Styven and Laurence Schram from the Kazerne Dossin in Mechelen and Joris Colla at the KADOC in Leuven.

Along the way, I benefited enormously from feedback from participants who attended presentations hosted by Yad Vashem, the United States Holocaust Memorial Museum, the Buffett Institute for Global Studies at Northwestern, the Sia Chaou-Kang Center for International Security and Diplomacy at the University of Denver, and from the Departments of Sociology at the University of California, Berkeley, Harvard University, the University of Chicago, Northwestern University, the University of Pittsburgh and Tulane University. Likewise, I am grateful for feedback from the Departments of Political Science at the University of Amsterdam, the University of Essex, Leiden University, the University of New Mexico, Ohio State University, Princeton University, University of California, Los Angeles and Yale University as well as the Department of Justice, Law and Criminology, at American University, the Institute for Political Economy and Governance at Pompeu Fabra University, the Joint Speaker Series Department of Political Science & the Graduate School of Public & International Affairs at the University of Pittsburgh and the Program on Order Conflict and Violence at Yale University. On these occasions, I was particularly grateful for feedback from Mark Beissinger, Carles Boix, Lisa Brush, Ruben Enikolopov, James Evans, Jude Hayes, Mala Htun, Stathis Kalyvas, Orlando Patterson, Maria Petrova, Grigore Pop-Eleches, Burcu Savun, Stephan Skowronek and Tim Snyder. In addition to the useful critiques offered by participants in these seminars, I received important comments and suggestions from Sheri Berman, Michael Bernhard, Nancy Bermeo, Daniel Blocq, Ivan Ermakoff, Chad Goldberg, Brandon Gorman, Patrick Kuhn, Andrew Little, Aliza Luft, Harris Mylonas, Laura Nelson, Jensen Sass, Charles Seguin, Evgeny Finkel and Jason Wittenberg. The latter two have been instrumental for the development of my research agenda. I thank them for having blazed the trail by demonstrating the important lessons that the Holocaust provides for mainstream social science in two spectacular books (Evgeny Finkel, *Ordinary Jews: Choice and Survival during the Holocaust*, Princeton University Press, and Jeffrey S. Kopstein and Jason Wittenberg, *Intimate Violence: Anti-Jewish Pogroms on the Eve of the Holocaust*, Cornell University Press, respectively).

I would also like to thank Marnix Croes, Bert-Jan Flim, Hans Knippenberg, Paul Pennings, Peter Tammes, Herman van Rens, the late Jan Sonneveld, the Dutch Museum for Jewish History, Kamp Westerbork, the CEGESOMA, LOKSTAT at the University of Ghent the Kazerne Dossin

Memorial and the Netherlands Red Cross for sharing data. Onno Boonstra, Gijs Boink, Laurence Schram, Raymund Schutz, Dorien Styven, Peter Tammes, Jean-Emile Veth and Sven Vrielinck provided invaluable help in accessing the digital material. Shapefiles of administrative boundaries were provided by NLgis and LOKSTAT. The Belgium Topographic Map 1939 and the Dutch TMK 1830 are used as backgrounds in most figures. These maps are provided by ESRI Nederland, NGI-IGN and the Kadaster. I would also like to thank Elias Passas for his assistance in finalizing the manuscript.

Financially, this project has been made possible by the National Science Foundation (grant #1122985), the Council For European Studies, the Reppy Institute for Peace and Conflict Studies, the Kellogg School of Management, the Cornell Institute for European Studies and a Saul Kagan Fellowship in Advanced Shoah Studies. The latter fellowship, in particular, enriched my intellectual life by embedding me in a truly global community of scholars working on the Holocaust.

Earlier versions of this book project were published in "Religious Minorities and Resistance to Genocide: The Collective Rescue of Jews in the Netherlands during the Holocaust," *American Political Science Review* 110.1 and "Minorities and the Clandestine Collective Action Dilemma: the Secret protection of Jews in Nazi-Occupied Europe," *American Journal of Sociology*, 124.2. I am grateful to Cambridge University Press and the University of Chicago Press for its permission to integrate part of these articles here. The former press also served as a wonderful home for this book. I would like to thank Robert Dreesen and the editors of the Contentious Politics series as well as two anonymous reviewers for their insightful feedback and efficiency.

My family, most importantly Riekje, Rob, Jiska and Bink, have always had my back. Although, they may not always have fully understood what I was up to as I trekked from university to university, archive to archive, their support and love has always been unconditional. The same can be said for Jeff, Lori, Peter and Mandy who were my American family. Lastly, I would like to thank Martha. She is my best friend, confidant, colleague and, most importantly, love of my life. We have always done everything together. I hope this will stay this way for the rest of our lives.

Notes on the Text

- In this manuscript I make use of testimonies collected in light of an honors pension program. Following an agreement with the Social Insurance Bank, the institution storing and maintaining these files, I will refer to these testimonies anonymously. Detailed information on the individual files can be obtained from the author upon request.
- Names of locations are translated into English. If an English translation is lacking, the name in the original language is used.
- All quotations from written sources in French, German or Dutch are translated into English by the author.
- With a few exceptions in Chapters 5 and 9, visualizations of statistical models are presented in the main text, while regression tables and descriptives are presented in appendices at the end of the chapter.

1

Introduction

It is sometimes hard to escape the dark side of religion. The support for aggressive nationalism by Orthodox Church leaders during the Balkan Wars (Sells 1996), Islamic nationalists during the Armenian Genocide (Bloxham 2005) and Christian bishops during the massacres in Rwanda (Des Forges 1999) all draw attention to how robust religious networks, in combination with absolute truth claims and tight authority structures, can produce devastating outcomes for outsiders. The Divine also has a brighter side, however. Islamic, Buddhist, Jewish and Christian leaders alike have combatted racism, created humanitarian assistance movements for excluded groups and produced some of the most influential pioneers of tolerance and empathy within nations (Allport 1966; Philpott 2007).

This book aims to shed light on this "ambivalence of the sacred" (Appleby 1999) by studying religious assistance to threatened neighbors in times of social upheaval. Why do some religious groups provide protection to victims of mass persecution while others passively condone or even support such attacks? I aim to answer this question by looking at how the Holocaust, one of the most gruesome and intellectually challenging episodes of mass persecution, played out in the Low Countries, a laboratory of denominational diversity spanning several religious fault lines. I argue that it is the interplay of church and community – and not something inherent to any individual, group or denomination itself – that determines which side of the sacred prevails. In doing so, I aim to illuminate the robustness of pluralism and inter-group relationships more broadly.

Throughout this study, I shed new light on abstract concepts such as empathy, civil society and collective action, trace the roots of intergroup solidarity back to the Reformation in the sixteenth century and discuss the argument's extension to different episodes of mass killing such as the Armenian and Rwandan genocides. However, it was in my home country where I stumbled over an empirical puzzle that formed the starting point of this research project.

1.1 PUZZLE AND RESEARCH QUESTION

About 200 kilometers from the Dutch capital Amsterdam, in the region of Twente, lie the medium-sized towns Almelo and Borne. Before the outbreak of World War II, Almelo and Borne had a similar sociocultural outlook. The population in both towns was relatively prosperous and labored in local textile factories. Ever since the turn of the nineteenth century, the towns were home to sizable Jewish communities. During the German occupation, both communities faced similar challenges and underwent identical structural transformations. From 1941 onward, Jews were no longer allowed to take part in public life. After being segregated socially and spatially, German officers, helped by local policemen, started organizing roundups to track down Jewish inhabitants and send them to the infamous extermination camps in Eastern Europe (Presser 1965). Despite the sociocultural similarity of the two towns, outcomes of these roundups differed fundamentally, as we can see in Figure 1.1. In Almelo, numerous Jews were able to evade deportation with the help of Catholic Church chaplains Bodde and Middelkoop, who temporarily sheltered Jews in Saint Gregorius Church before housing them with loyal members of their parish. As a result, 42 percent of the Jews in Almelo survived the war. Despite the presence of three Catholic congregations, no successful Catholic rescue network emerged in neighboring Borne. Consequently, only 22 percent of the Jewish population escaped deportation (Weustink 1985).

If we step back and look at the Netherlands as a whole, depicted in the back panel of Figure 1.1, we see that this pattern is not unique to Almelo and Borne. Throughout the country we can discern fine-grained pockets of evasion. This raises an important question. Why are some Christian communities willing and able to protect victims of mass persecution while others are not? It is important to note that this question is not only pertinent to how the Holocaust played out in the Netherlands. Throughout occupied Europe, Church leadership proved crucial for

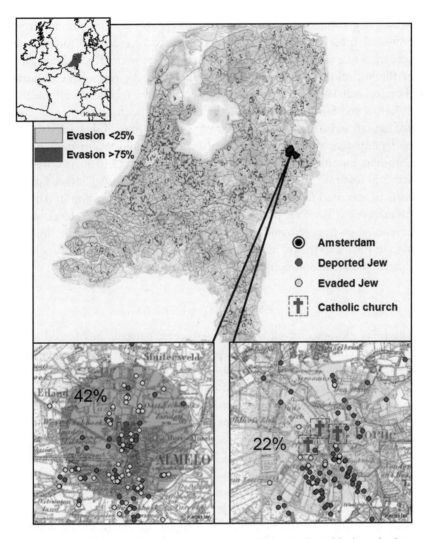

FIGURE 1.1 Evasion in Almelo, Borne and the Netherlands. A black-and-white version of this figure will appear in some formats. For the colour version, please refer to the plate section.

the emergence of defense movements that arrested the Holocaust by enabling Jewish evasion (Fein 1979). Needless to say, the Holocaust's 11 million victims attest to the reality that religious help was far from universal.

The importance of this question also travels well beyond the borders of Holocaust studies, as puzzling variation in religious resistance to violence abounds within conflicts, nations and denominations across time and space. While clerics were key in creating defense movements that tried to protect Tutsis from Hutu massacres in the Rwandan region of Bigihu, religious help was almost absent in the rest of the country (Longman 2010). Christian protests prevented the escalation of violence in Kenya and South Africa, while the absence of such protests facilitated killings of Serbs in Bosnia and Croatia (Sells 1996). Likewise, Islamic leadership was a mobilizing force of genocide against Christians in the Ottoman Empire and Darfur, but it created pockets of protection for Tutsis in Rwanda (Ternon 2008; Viret 2008). In the United States, Protestantism was used to both legitimize and oppose the repression of African Americans (Miller 1957; Foner 2015). Even on an individual level, social psychologists have shown that religious inspiration can provide the normative justification for humanitarian assistance, passivity and violence (Fogelman 1994; Staub 2003).

1.2 EXISTING RESEARCH

The mere existence of all these contradicting patterns has forced some authors to conclude that religious protection is purely driven by idiosyncratic accidents of history or randomly distributed personality traits that fall outside the explanatory realm of the social sciences (Gilbert 2010). Indeed, existing explanations of political violence, altruism, religion and genocide seem to fall short in explaining the emergence of religious assistance to threatened neighbors.

Dominant theories of political violence focus on territorial control (Kalyvas 2006), electoral dynamics (Kopstein and Wittenberg 2011) and cross-cutting civic organizations (Varshney 2003), yet these fail to explain subnational variation in Jewish rescue within the Netherlands; Nazi authority was not seriously challenged anywhere in the country, party politics were neutralized during the war, no Jewish political parties existed and interreligious associations were extremely rare (Lijphart 1968). This lack of explanatory power is due to the fact that scholars of violence prioritize the role of warring parties, rarely theorizing the capacity of local civilian bystanders to protect human rights (O. Kaplan 2013).

Although existing theories on religion, altruism and genocide recognize the importance of bystanders, they do not fare much better, because their focus is either too micro or too macro. On the macro-side of the spectrum, researchers tend to focus on how broad social environments such as religious communities or nations produce norms that motivate rescue. Often these branches of theory treat nations and denominations as monolithic entities driven by inherent doctrines or national leaders exploiting strong hierarchies (Fein 1979; Croes and Tammes 2004). On the micro-side, scholarship focuses on how religion triggers a wide range of individual-level dispositions such as altruism, compassion, inclusive identities (Fogelman 1994), obedience (Waller 2007), conformity and antipathy toward outsiders and adventurousness (Adorno et al. 1950), which either motivate or discourage help to those in need.

The first branch of research is too broad and overlooks subnational variation in resistance altogether. Inherent doctrines, overarching institutions and national leaders are not able to explain why two nearby churches in Borne and Almelo, belonging to the same denomination and diocese, diverged completely in their response to the deportations. Work focusing on how broad environments produce the norms to rescue ignores the fact that orders by leaders are not automatically followed by everyone and that doctrine is interpreted differently by different people.

The micro branch implicitly assumes the existence of a universal religious disposition that operates the same for everyone regardless of social position, while failing to link individual dispositions back to community-level outcomes. Furthermore, this line of work is indeterminate, expecting both negative and positive effects from religion. To make this concrete, it is not clear why religion would create altruism and not xenophobia in Almelo, while the opposite would happen five kilometers to the east in Borne.

Instead of focusing on how individual dispositions, nations and denominations operate in isolation of each other, this book looks at how the interplay of all three enables the appropriation of existing networks for assistance to threatened neighbors. As such, I explore how national and religious norms, local community structures and individual dispositions interact to produce resistance by weaving together elements from the different approaches outlined earlier. In particular, I show that the ways in which environmental norms and individual dispositions shape resistance to genocide is contingent on how religious communities are embedded locally vis-à-vis other communities.

1.3 THE ARGUMENT

The central argument of this book is that local religious minorities[1] are more likely than their majority counterparts to protect victims of mass persecution, because they have both the willingness and the capacity to do so. Two distinct, but partly reinforcing, mechanisms link minority status to rescue operations.

The first mechanism focuses on the capacity to rescue. Minorities are better equipped to translate opposition to genocide into action because they have an advantage in setting up clandestine networks that are immune to individual betrayal (Brewer and Silver 2000; Berman and Laitin 2008). As a result, minorities mobilize more and are discovered less often. Throughout the book, I refer to this process as the capacity mechanism. This mechanism derives from the fact that minority enclaves are embedded in isolated hubs of commitment which:

- assure members that mobilization is possible (Elster 1979)
- make it easier for organizers to select good and diverse recruits (Marwell and Oliver 1993)
- reduce the chance that a movement gets dismantled by security forces (Aldrich 1999).

The second mechanism involves the willingness of local leaders to resist genocide. Aristotle, Homer and Rousseau taught us long ago that compassion is largely a function of understanding the shared vulnerability of human beings and recognizing that what happens to others can easily befall ourselves (Nussbaum 1992a). As leaders of religious minorities themselves depend on pluralism for group survival, they will be more likely to empathize with those targeted by violent purification campaigns, imbuing their networks with preferences to oppose genocide (Hoffman 2001). Throughout the book I refer to this process as *the empathy mechanism.*

Hence, the convergence of clandestine capacity and empathy with outsiders turns minority enclaves into bulwarks of resistance against genocide. Consequently, it is the local position of faith-based communities –

---

[1] Local religious minority status is produced by the intersection of denominational and spatial boundaries. I define denomination as a subgroup within a religion that operates under a common name, tradition and organizational infrastructure. Local minority denominations are all denominations within a local politically relevant space, except the largest one. Politically relevant spaces are those around which political parties and civil society are organized.

and not something inherent to any local community, individual or religion itself – that produces networks of assistance to threatened neighbors.

1.4 THE HOLOCAUST

Covert resistance poses enormous obstacles for empirical investigation. Gaining direct access to contemporary clandestine cells is next to impossible, exactly because these cells need to reduce exposure in order to survive. Archival work on historical cases can alleviate this challenge, because it enables the study of groups that are no longer under immediate threat, reducing the urgency of secrecy. Moreover, when political structures open and regimes change, former clandestine networks sometimes go public in order to gain recognition for their activities against foes from the past. This often opens up a wide array of archives and testimonies. Instead of focusing on contemporary cases, this study, therefore, focuses on an historical episode of resistance against violence: the protection of Jews in the Low Countries during the Holocaust.

The Holocaust is without doubt the most well-documented episode of mass killing. Exploiting the extraordinary array of largely unused historical sources presented by the Holocaust enables me to trace the capacity and willingness of religious actors to resist genocide on an extremely fine-grained level. In addition to secondary literature and preexisting data, I rely on:

- A unique geocoded database of German administrative records detailing the victimization of 123,000 Dutch and 52,000 Belgian Jews to explore whether Jews living close to minority churches were more likely to evade deportation.
- A content analysis of more than 1,700 prewar claims by opinion leaders to explore attitudes of different religious and secular groups toward Jews between 1930 and 1939.
- A semi-automatic content analysis of 905 clandestine Dutch newspapers that explores attitudes of different religious and secular groups toward Jews during World War II.
- An underutilized collection of postwar testimonies collected in light of an honors pension program to investigate whether and, more importantly, why minority churches in the Netherlands were better able to provide assistance to Jews.

- A collection of postwar trial data to explore why majority rescue networks were not able to stay underground and got infiltrated by the security forces.
- A collection of Nazi archives to gauge the number of police officers who did not collaborate with German security forces.
- A postwar survey conducted among Protestant and Catholic clerics in Belgium to ascertain why some church communities did provide assistance to Jews.
- Existing collections of testimonies collected by Yad Vashem from twenty-one countries to assess whether geographical patterns of evasion can be plausibly linked to church communities that form local minorities beyond the Low Countries.

Of course, the use of postwar testimonies and archival material has serious limitations as well. These data points do not throw a spotlight on a random or representative sample of war experiences as a whole, but instead overrepresent the stories of winners and survivors. Furthermore, interpretations of events are likely to be influenced by an extremely powerful post-Holocaust commemoration culture. During my archival work, several people hinted at the fact that some materials were not stored or were even destroyed when they did not fit the national narrative that the institute in question aimed to convey. Although we will probably never find out whether this is true, the possibility merits pause.

However, it is unlikely that this study is reproducing an intentionally crafted narrative as my findings go against the strains of immediate postwar discourse. Right after the war, Belgian Catholics prided themselves for protecting so many Jews, while the emphasis in the Netherlands was on how resistance transcended existing social boundaries in Dutch society and formed the starting point for a breakthrough movement that tried to overthrow religious and political segmentation (Lagrou 1997). My research, on the contrary, highlights the *relatively* limited role of the Catholic Church in Belgium and emphasizes the salience of denominational differences on a local level in the Netherlands.

1.5 THE LOW COUNTRIES

The Holocaust took place in a wide range of contexts over a relatively long period of time, enabling systematic comparative research on group-level variables and resistance. The Shoah in the Low Countries provides a particularly unique, albeit tragic, opportunity to investigate whether religious minority status affects the production of rescue networks.

Looking to the Low Countries allows me to test the minority hypothesis in a research design that complements the strengths of a most similar systems research design (Lijphart 1975) with elements of a research design that is most different in scope conditions (Przeworski and Teune 1970). The former, employed in a subnational study of the Netherlands, compares cases that are as similar as possible, except on the key explanatory variable, enabling me to carefully investigate causal relationships while keeping alternative factors constant. The latter matches more diverse cases, here drawn from Belgium, to assess whether similar causal processes operate the same way in different contexts.

This research design makes use of the fact that the Low Countries were located at the frontline of the Reformation and Counter-Reformation. As a consequence:

1. the northern part of the Netherlands is dominated by Protestantism
2. the southern part of the Netherlands is dominated by Catholicism
3. Belgium is completely dominated by Catholicism.

Despite these overarching patterns, however, missionary activities, interregional migration (of both Protestants and Catholics) and disputed scripture (mostly within the Protestant Church) created a dynamic religious landscape, resulting in pockets of religious minority communities in both Catholic and Protestant parts of the Low Countries (see Figure 1.2a). Importantly, Jews lived throughout both countries (see Figure 1.2b). This mixed landscape allows me to assess whether religious minority positions affected mobilization for both Protestant and Catholic communities, while keeping inherent characteristics of nations, local communities and religions constant. This is done by comparing the same religious groups in both minority and majority environments within the same country and different countries. In particular, if the minority thesis holds, we would expect Catholics to be more likely to rescue in Protestant parts of the Low Countries (1), while Protestants should be more likely to rescue in Catholic parts of the Low Countries (2 and 3).

This book first examines resistance activities of religious groups within the Netherlands (1 and 2) before moving on to Belgium (3). The initial focus on the Dutch case has the advantage that it controls for potentially confounding variables. First, top–down enforcement of

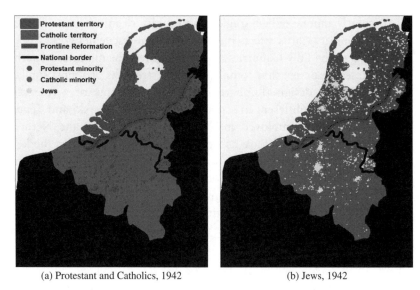

(a) Protestant and Catholics, 1942   (b) Jews, 1942

FIGURE 1.2 Religious minorities in the Netherlands and Belgium. A black-and-white version of this figure will appear in some formats. For the colour version, please refer to the plate section.

mobilization between congregations was kept constant as Protestant and Catholic leaders in the Netherlands protested anti-Semitic legislation collaboratively at the national level (Snoek 2005), providing all Christians, regardless of congregation, with the same moral message of how German persecutions went against the tenets of their faiths. Second, minority and majority congregations in Protestant and Catholic parts of the Netherlands were exposed to the same occupation regime and Jewish population.

At the same time, comparisons of religious rescue activities in Belgium (3) provides variation in potential scope conditions and enables us to investigate whether the minority hypothesis operates the same in diverse political contexts. Like the southern part of the Netherlands, Belgium was home to sizable Protestant minority enclaves living in the vicinity of Jews. However, there were fundamental national-level differences between the Netherlands and Belgium in occupation regime, political cleavages, religious diversity, national religious elites and Jewish populations (Kossman 1986). If religious minorities were more likely to rescue Jews in Belgium as well as the Netherlands, we can be certain that the minority mechanisms operate independently of these contextual differences.

1.6 CONTRIBUTIONS

This project calls for a multilevel perspective on humanitarian movements that interrogates the interactions between individual dispositions, community structures, nations and denominations. As such, it makes an important contribution to the study of intergroup relationships in times of social upheaval. Most notably, it draws attention to the fact that if we want to understand intergroup solidarity and conflict we should not study group dyads in isolation from each other. Although, scholars have repeatedly stressed the importance of crosscutting identities *between* insiders (e.g., Christians) and outsiders (e.g., Jews) for intergroup conflict, solidarity and mobilization (Coser 1956), this study shows that we should also pay attention to intersections *within* insider groups alone as they produce empathy and condition the appropriation of networks for collective action. By situating intergroup dynamics in the context of broader cleavage structures, this study has important implications for the study of civil society, altruism, social movements, political violence, intergroup relationships, humanitarian intervention and scholarship on the Holocaust.

The arguments put forward in this project lie at the heart of two intersecting debates about the role of civil society during times of social upheaval. The first debate revolves around the question of whether civil society improves the coordination of opposition against repressive authorities or, to the contrary, begets acquiescence (Gramsci 1935). The second debate centers on the relationship between civil society and pluralism. Following Tocqueville, scholars have argued that through associational life the "heart is enlarged" (Tocqueville 1840, p. 201) and violent conflict can be contained (Varshney 2003), at least according to some, because "joiners become more tolerant [....] and more empathetic to the misfortune of others" (Putnam 2000, p. 288). Yet Tocqueville himself was the first to admit that civil society could be perverted into a "cause of destruction" (p. 220), and it has been shown to sometimes legitimate participation in violent attacks on pluralism (McDoom 2014). The theoretical argument put forward in this book qualifies the relationships between civic life, coordinated opposition and ethnic violence by identifying important structural conditions at the local level under which relations between subgroups of civil society produce both the norms and the networks necessary to resist attacks on pluralism.

Second, while the micro literature on rescuers has helped us to better understand how compassion and altruism motivate (some) individuals to help (Monroe 2001), the equally important collective capacity to actually rescue has received less attention. Even if individuals are willing to save Jews, their environment does not always provide them with the protective shell needed to reduce risk, impeding the impact they would want to have on evasion. This book suggests that whether religious altruists can turn into heroes depends on the local networks in which they are embedded, linking micro motives to community outcomes (M. Gross 1994).

Third, and relatedly, micro studies mainly provide insight into proximate causes of rescue. This book furthers this literature by suggesting that individual-level motivations and networks to rescue are not distributed randomly, but, in part, reflect the underlying relational structures of civic life, as members of groups are more likely to display empathy and be embedded in subgroups capable of clandestine collective action when they have a distinctive relationship with the local community.

Fourth, this project highlights that, even when national elites consistently protest genocidal policies, the actual willingness and capacity of constituents to resist mass killing depends on subnational networks and norms. It therefore urges (macro) scholars of conflict to move beyond the study of bishops and other high-level national officials and dig deeper into localized patterns of evasion to understand in what ways national forces of restraint are conditioned by local-level relationships (Straus 2012). Fifth, traditional arguments on religion and genocide have focused on doctrines of different congregations (Kuper 1990). The central finding of this book is that it is the local position of church communities that, regardless of doctrine, produces collective networks of assistance to threatened neighbors (Longman 2010).

Sixth, this book strengthens the links between literatures on social movements and political violence by investigating how outcomes of mass killing are contingent on localized forms of clandestine mobilization by bystanders. Scholars of political violence traditionally depict civilians as powerless pawns in the hands of warring parties who either support rebels or are coerced to provide local intelligence (Kalyvas 2006). More recently, scholars of social movements have looked at the mobilization of killers (Y. Su 2011) and victims (Einwohner and Maher 2011). This book demonstrates how and where empathetic or adventurous bystanders can also mobilize in secret to condition the local impact of political violence.

In doing so, this book sheds light on the root causes of clandestine mobilization. Clandestine movements have played a crucial role in the instigation of revolutions (Lenin 1970), resistance movements (Finkel 2017), guerrilla groups (Viterna 2006), terrorism (Shapiro 2013) and rescue operations for victims of mass persecution (Foner 2015). When talking about revolutions, Lenin, one of the more successful movement organizers in world history, identified secrecy as the most important constraint on success (Lenin 1970; Erickson 1981; Finkel 2015). Despite the importance of clandestine collective action, we lack a complete understanding of why some local communities are able to produce and sustain clandestine operations while others are not. In addition to obvious data collection problems, this is, according to some, due to a scholarly focus on public claim making (Zwerman, Steinhoff and della Porta 2000). Understanding how violence is conditioned by clandestine operations forces movement scholars to move away from public claim making and highlight, like I have done in this project, the specific and understudied challenges of organizations that prefer to remain invisible.

The few studies that do look at secretive movements explicitly focus on network recruitment and have revealed that participation in different forms of clandestine collective action depends on strong personal and organizational ties between nascent organizers and potential members (McAdam 1986; della Porta 2013). Yet, strong organizational networks and personal ties abound, while clandestine mobilization is rare. This book shows that the network configuration facilitating this distinctive type of mobilization is not distributed randomly, but, in part, reflects the underlying structure of civic life, as members of minority groups are more likely to be embedded in communities capable of secretive collective action. Dense networks need to be structured in a particular way to facilitate underground collective action. As such, the minority hypothesis put forward in this book qualifies the relationship between dense networks and coordinated opposition by identifying an important condition under which network configurations produce clandestine networks capable of resisting attacks by much stronger opponents. The theory put forward here underlines that how groups are locally embedded determines the feasibility of this distinctive and important type of mobilization, and provides insight into the roots of resistance and transformation, both of which initially require pockets of covert mobilization embedded in minority enclaves (Smelser 1962).

In explaining clandestine collective action, the minority thesis also sheds new light on the secrecy–efficiency trade-off studied by network analysts, criminologists and scholars of terrorism. On the one hand, scholars working on terrorism assert that covert networks necessarily sacrifice collective capacity for secrecy and are characterized by low density, the exact reverse of a network structure conducive to high-risk mobilization (Raab and Milward 2003; Enders and Su 2007; Crossley et al. 2012). Studies of criminal networks, on the other hand, show that underground organizations often rely on dense networks for complicated tasks, because denser networks increase solidarity and consequently enhance the quality of mobilization (Baker and Faulkner 1993; Morselli, Giguère and Petit 2007; Crossley et al. 2012). The minority thesis combines insights from scholars arguing in favor and against the secrecy–efficiency trade-off as isolated hubs of commitment are locally dense clusters located in a broader network that is sparse (Crossley et al. 2012), revealing a non-linear relationship between network density and clandestine collective action (Gould 1993).

The minority thesis pushes forward the literature on local structure and mobilization. Where earlier work has focused on how structural position affects the mobilizing capacity (Gould 1993), grievances (Gould 1996; Barkey and Van Rossem 1997) and boundaries of identity groups (Gould 1995; Bearman 1995), my argument shows that it also has an influence on the actual content of mobilizing identities by shifting norms toward outsiders.

This project also reveals the Reformation's lasting impact on clandestine resistance to political violence centuries later. In doing so, this book joins a small body of work that reveals how protective mobilization not only affects victimization directly, but is itself shaped by historical legacies of long-gone political movements. These legacies of contention introduce a new set of historical variables understudied by the movement scholars and highlight the importance of embedding the study of both political violence and collective action in the broader historical context of contentious politics (Clemens 2007).

Although further research is required to fully assess the ability of my argument to travel to these contexts, it nonetheless holds potentially important implications for foreign interventions in mass conflicts and other humanitarian crises. When resources are scarce, targeted campaigns to bolster minority groups might be a successful means by which to impede the spread of mass killings in the short run. In addition, building bridges between different minority groups might produce large-scale interregional resistance movements against violence in the long run, which could enable interveners to stop the violence altogether. It is important to highlight that the fruitfulness of such an approach depends on the overall prevalence of minority groups. In regions where minority congregations are too tiny to have an impact, other approaches are probably more successful.

More generally, the project draws attention to the role that local faith-based actors can play during humanitarian crises. My argument finds support, for example, in the aftermath of the tsunami emergency in Indonesia, where local religious groups were among the first to provide assistance to threatened neighbors. While these organizations are instrumental for humanitarian assistance, because they have large local constituencies on the ground that are well positioned to respond promptly (Ferris 2005), they seldom get the same amount of scholarly and public attention as foreign interventions by the United Nations and international nongovernmental organizations (Autesserre 2010).

Finally, and most specifically, this book also contributes to debates on religious rescue during the Holocaust. Most scholarship focuses on inherent doctrine (Blaschke 1997) or church hierarchy (Croes and Tammes 2004) to explain why only some church communities stepped up to protect Jewish victims of mass persecution. The main argument advanced in this book is that it was the local position of church communities – and nothing inherent to any religion itself – that produced networks of assistance for Jewish neighbors. To be sure, this is not the first book that draws attention to the positionality of religion. Other researchers suggest that adherents of *national* minority religions, often exposed to state persecution in the past, were most likely to protect Jews during the Nazi period (Hallie 1979; Cabanel 2008). My book qualifies this perspective in claiming that it is local, and not national, minorities that anchored resistance activities.[2]

1.7 A BRIEF NOTE ON EFFECTS OF CAUSES

Quantitative (Holland 1986) and qualitative methodologists (Mahoney 2010) alike have long recognized that it is important to distinguish between approaches that seek to find *effects of causes* and those that aim to find the *causes of effects*. Whereas the latter are interested in establishing the most important conditions that need to be present for certain outcomes to occur, the former are interested in how certain factors affect the likelihood of something happening. My work falls in the "effects of

---

[2] In the Dutch context, Houwink ten Cate (1999) has alluded to the importance of local minority groups. He based his suspicion on personal conversations with the late Van Der Leeuw, one of the co-founders of the Dutch Institute of War Documentation. This book is the first to systematically investigate the local minority hypothesis in the Low Countries. Earlier researchers have pointed out that Protestant outsiders were prominent rescuers in the Catholic province of Limburg (Cammaert 1994; Bronzwaer 2010; Van Rens 2013).

causes" category. For scholars outside of the social sciences, work in this category can, quite understandably, lead to confusion. To clear things up it can be useful to explicitly state what I am and what I am not arguing. This book demonstrates that minorities are more likely to protect victims of mass persecution than majorities. This, of course, does not imply that majorities never conducted rescue operations. Under certain conditions, it also does not imply that minorities do more rescuing in absolute numbers. In cases where minority groups are very small, they might – despite a strong overrepresentation among rescuers – still play a minor role in the overall rescue process.

1.8   ROAD MAP

This book is organized as follows. Chapter 2 presents a multilevel theory of religious resistance against mass persecution. Building on a long tradition in political thought and more recent insights about empathy, it argues that church–community relationships shape the preferences of religious elites to resist violent attacks on outsiders (Nussbaum 1992a). For religious majorities, religion and locality fuse, boundaries are strengthened, and solidarity with outsiders is weaker. In minority congregations, however, support for pluralism prevails, imbuing religious networks with empathy for other minority groups. Still, once empathy and support for pluralism are present, resistance to genocide does not come about automatically. Pluralism only gets translated into resistance if local factors allow for a solution to the clandestine collective action dilemma: the dual challenge of coordination and secrecy. Local minorities have the capacity to translate pluralist norms into clandestine collective action, because they form isolated hubs of commitment that are insulated from potential snitches.

In Chapter 3, I detail how the religious landscape of the Low Countries evolved from the Reformation to the Holocaust. By combining this religious landscape with the theory developed in the previous chapter, I derive four empirical implications, which are assessed in the following chapters. The chapter also presents statistical data, showing that minority congregations were more likely to form isolated hubs of commitment.

The remaining empirical analysis is structured in two separate parts. Whereas the first part focuses on the empathy with Jews among religious minorities in the Netherlands before the deportations started, and explores whether minority empathy was translated into actual resistance during the war, the second shifts its focus to investigate the scope conditions of and exceptions to the minority hypothesis, introducing the Belgian case in the process.

Chapter 4 traces the prewar evolution of empathy with Jews. It reports the results of a comparative content analysis of prewar newspapers and clandestine wartime publications published by minority and majority communities. Regardless of congregation, Christian minority elites were more likely to display empathy and defend pluralism when debating Jewish issues and, as a result, more pro-Semitic than leaders of majority groups. As a result, religious minority networks were imbued with preferences to resist genocide. Focusing on the occupation period when deportations started, Chapter 5 addresses the question of whether religious minority leaders were able to translate their empathy into action. The chapter establishes that they indeed had the capacity to do so. It pairs German registrations of Jews with commemoration books to construct a unique geo-coded database of Jewish victimization in the Netherlands. Spatial regression models of 93 percent of all Dutch Jews demonstrate a robust and positive correlation between the proximity to minority churches and evasion. While proximity to Catholic Churches increased evasion in dominantly Protestant regions by more than 20 percent, proximity to Protestant Churches had the same effect in Catholic parts of the country. County fixed effects (FEs) and the concentric dispersion of Catholicism from missionary hotbed Delft are exploited to disentangle the effect of religious minority groups from preexisting differences in tolerance and other omitted variables.

Statistical evasion patterns alone do not tell us whether clandestine mobilization of minority communities was driving the differential survival of Jews. In Chapter 6 I explicitly focus on religious rescue activities to assess whether minorities were indeed better able to set up clandestine missions to protect threatened neighbors. For this purpose, I zero in on the region of Twente in the Netherlands, which encompasses the villages of Almelo and Borne discussed at the start of this chapter. Importantly, Twente is an economically and socially integrated region that is located across the Catholic–Protestant fault line that divided Western Europe, allowing me to keep important economic and social factors constant when comparing Protestant and Catholic groups in minority and majority contexts. The extraordinary availability of unused postwar testimonies and trial data surrounding the Holocaust in Twente enable me to study clandestine collective action in an extremely detailed fashion.

In support of the minority thesis, the data reveal that a) religious minority leaders were able to exploit the mobilizing capacity of committed members to overcome the clandestine collective action dilemma; b) majority leaders that tried to do this were more likely to get denounced early on; c) religious mixing undermined the minority advantage by undercutting isolation; and d) as a result of this, insulated pockets of Protestants were more successful in protecting Jews in areas dominated by Catholics, while the same was true for Catholic enclaves in Protestant regions. This structured comparison also exposes an unanticipated advantage that minority leaders had when setting up rescue operations. Dovetailing with existing work on the important role that small religious groups play in creating and sustaining long-distance economic collaboration (Weber 1985; Greif 2006), postwar testimonies show that minority congregations were better at fostering interregional ties that helped Jews escape to other parts of the country.

Chapter 7 uses the same data sources to assess whether the minority advantage also travels beyond the borders of Twente. Statistical analysis of the whole country and case studies of four different provinces (two homogeneously Catholic and two homogeneously Protestant) back up the findings from Twente. In addition to providing support for the minority hypothesis, Chapters 6 and 7 also help me link deeply structural factors to actual outcomes by suggesting three feedback mechanisms that translate the (somewhat) abstract minority advantage into actual higher levels of clandestine mobilization. Whereas the first two hinge on the recognition of opportunities by forward-looking actors, the final mechanism, selective survival, is evolutionary in logic. Group commitment assures leaders that mobilization is possible (Elster 1979), helps leaders to recruit the right operatives (Marwell and Oliver 1993) and improves the selective survival of groups by reducing infiltration from outsiders (Aldrich 1999).

Chapters 8 and 9 and the Conclusion form Part III of this book, which looks at the exceptions to and scope conditions of the minority hypothesis. Although Chapters 6 and 7 largely confirm the minority hypothesis, they also revealed some rescue missions conducted by majority groups. These and other "off-the-line" cases are explored in Chapter 8. The empirical anomalies suggest that majority groups were able to mobilize whenever residential isolation or interregional entrepreneurs compensated for a lack of empathy, group commitment and interregional ties. In addition, the chapter demonstrates the important role that small left-wing groups played in protecting Jews. Often these groups, which had many Jews among their members, functioned as religious sects in that they combined strict discipline with a solemn commitment to the group

(Coser 1974). A recalibration of the statistical models presented in Chapter 6 confirms that evasion was higher in communities that were home to small factions, relatively isolated and exposed to interregional networks. In brief, the data suggest that communities were able to motivate and sustain clandestine collective action if they were rooted in small insulated enclaves or were part of interregional networks – in other words – if their social structure resembled that of minority groups.

Chapter 9 explores religious assistance to Jews in neighboring Belgium. A geo-coded database of Jewish victimization, secondary literature, a survey conducted among clerics and postwar testimonies highlight two empirical patterns. First, in line with the theory outlined in this book, Protestants, who formed local minorities everywhere, were strongly overrepresented among rescuers. As a result, Jews living in the vicinity of Protestant enclaves had a 5 percent higher chance of evading deportation. This shows that the minority mechanisms operated in both Belgium and the Netherlands, despite large differences between the two countries in terms of occupation regime, levels of resistance and religious climate.

For their part, Catholic rescue operations, inspired by leaders who saw the Holocaust as a opportunity to convert Jewish children, were most likely to succeed in places where the Roman Church was weak because of secularization. In these localities, conversion-related motives in conjunction with local isolation due to localized waves of secularization produced assistance to threatened neighbors. Similar to what we saw in Twente, therefore, an alternative form of isolation in combination with non-pluralistic motives combined to instigate rescue among majority groups.

To further identify the scope conditions of my theory, I investigate whether the minority hypothesis travels to other countries under Nazi occupation and other episodes of mass killing in the concluding Chapter 10, which draws on secondary literature and postwar testimonies from about 6,500 rescuers in twenty-one different countries collected by Yad Vashem. Although minorities are overrepresented among rescuers almost everywhere, the theory does not seem to travel to places where rescue missions were highly individualized or where the persecuting regime permitted national elites to openly cooperate with leaders of majority congregations to resist the Nazi occupation in general. Put otherwise, the theory does not work in cases where resistance to genocide is either not collective or not clandestine. In line with the minority proposition, Pentecostals in Abarokore, Muslims in Catholic Rwanda, Kurdish sects, Western missionaries and small patches of Syriac Christians in Armenia and the Quaker congregations that formed the backbone of Underground Railroad to Canada, suggest that the minority hypothesis travels to other episodes of mass persecution, as long as genocidal regimes did not actively lure minority groups into the killing machine with economic or political rewards. Finally, comparisons between rescue operations in bi-ethnic Belgium provide suggestive evidence that the minority mechanisms also operate for nonreligious groups.

PART I

THEORY AND CONTEXT

2

Theory

2.1 INTRODUCTION

Until 1926, the careers of Reverends Nanne Zwiep and Leendert Overduin followed a strikingly similar path to the city of Enschede, a regional and Protestant hub in the Twente region. Both men received their religious education at elite universities and aimed to become ministers in the mainstream Dutch Reformed Church. But, whereas Zwiep led small Dutch reformed congregations in the Catholic city of Hoorn before coming to Enschede, Overduin decided to switch to the minuscule and more orthodox "Reformed Church in Restored Dependency," founded in 1926, after an intense scriptural debate about whether man was able to hear the snake speak in the Garden of Eden.

Their intellectual differences notwithstanding, the two men, perhaps driven by their (past) experience of minority leadership, came together in September 1941 to file a complaint against early deportations of Jews with the local authorities. On multiple occasions Zwiep and Overduin delivered anti-Nazi sermons in which they tried to convince people to resist anti-Jewish legislation (Bekkenkamp 2000). Despite their similar actions, their faiths diverged dramatically on April 20, 1942; Zwiep was arrested and eventually died in Dachau, while Overduin became the most successful rescuer of Jews in the whole of the Netherlands.

What explains this difference? Overduin's congregation consisted of fewer than fifty souls, all of whom he knew personally. Consequently, his sermons were only heard by loyal people he could trust. Zwiep, on the other hand, lectured in the main church of Enschede and sometimes drew crowds of 1000 people, some of whom had never seen each other before. At numerous points in time, Zwiep was cautioned and asked to tone it down: "Reverend watch out, they are watching you! Your enemies do not sleep. They will be in the church this very morning" (De Wolf 1947). His sacristan told him that he had seen the organist, whose son was a Nazi, take notes while Zwiep was preaching (Bekkenkamp 2000). Zwiep's biographer, De Wolf, was probably right when he observed that "the church has a holy call but in order to fulfill it she needs to be able to rely on the love and strength of her members" (De Wolf 1947).

While Zwiep was denounced by a disloyal member of his congregation, Overduin was able to exploit the dense networks of his community to save over 700 Jews. His organization grew rapidly as his followers "always said yes," and he knew exactly whom to trust. Much like himself, his followers were often driven by "the desire to help those in danger" and the commandment to love thy neighbor.[1] Dressed up as a baker or chimney sweep, Overduin traveled between different members of his organization while hiding secret documents in his umbrella (Weustink 1985). The core of this organization consisted of twenty operatives, most of whom were recruited from the tiny Reformed Church in Restored Dependency.[2]

From within his parish Overduin was able to recruit helpers with diverse skill sets. One of his main helpers was the head of the council of aldermen of his church. He was employed in a wood factory and could therefore provide both the resources and skills to build secret hideouts and storage rooms in homes.[3] Other members of his parish were painters who helped to camouflage shelters,[4] typographers who delivered paperwork[5] and a graphic specialist who forged documents.[6]

This book argues that in order to understand why groups provide humanitarian assistance to threatened neighbors it is important to distinguish between willingness and capacity to protect. Leaders like Nanne Zwiep are willing to shelter Jews, but unable to translate their motives into action because they lack the networks and resources to setup the clandestine operations required to keep potential victims out of the hands of their oppressors. Communities that have the ability to keep victims of

---

[1] *Yad Vashem file A. Ten Tije in Michman et al.; SVB-file 55, DOCDIRECT, Winschoten.*
[2] *SVB-file 23, DOCDIRECT, Winschoten.*
[3] *SVB-file 23, DOCDIRECT, Winschoten.*
[4] *Yad Vashem file J. Hofstra in Michman et al.*
[5] *SVB-file 51, DOCDIRECT, Winschoten.*
[6] *SVB-file 23, DOCDIRECT, Winschoten.*

persecution underground, on the other hand, may never be motivated to do so. As the example of Zwiep and Overduin reveals, protecting victims of mass persecution requires both empathy and clandestine capacity. The minority enclave led by the latter possessed both.

Historians and social scientists working on humanitarian assistance, however, almost always start with the question of who is *willing* to rescue, drawing attention to the motivations of potential helpers. Scholars have focused on individual dispositions, nations and denominations. These approaches fail to shed light on why subnational variation in protection exists, for two reasons. First, all three approaches are conceptualized at the wrong level of analysis. Whereas the dispositional approach fails to link individual motivations to local structural factors, the national and denominational approaches ignore subnational variation in motivation altogether. Second, all three approaches overlook the importance of mobilizing capacity. In times of mass killing, nascent protectors face a much stronger opponent, whom they cannot exclude from their territory. As a result, they often need to rely on underground organizations to save threatened neighbors, and some communities are better at producing illicit networks than others. Whether motivations translate into help thus depends on the extent to which they are anchored in communities capable of clandestine collective action.

In this book, I take a multilevel perspective to explain how the interplay between local community and denomination shapes the willingness and capacity to resist genocide. In particular, I argue that local religious minorities are more likely to protect victims of mass persecution. This is the case because minority status produces both 1) empathy with outsiders that are under attack among elites and 2) isolated hubs of commitment that can be exploited for clandestine–movement building. Whereas the former mechanism motivates resistance among leaders, the latter makes it possible.

The next section discusses existing research on rescue and protection and distinguishes between dispositional and macroenvironmental theories. I highlight how neither of these approaches can provide a satisfactory account of protection because they ignore how subnational forces shape both the motivation and capacity to resist. Following this critique, I introduce the first mechanism, outlining how a local minority position affects antigenocidal motivations by creating attachment to pluralism and empathy with other outsider groups. I then build on existing collective action theories that recognize the importance of local capacity to develop the second mechanism. Although, these theories form important building blocks for my own argument, they fall short, either by focusing on public claim making as opposed to secrecy or by failing to identify where local capacity actually comes from. To drive this point home, I continue by introducing the *clandestine collective action dilemma* – the trade-off between coordination and increased exposure – to explain why minority communities have an advantage in overcoming this dilemma as their members form isolated hubs of commitment. In the last section, I outline three submechanisms through which nascent resistance organizers embedded in minority communities recognize their advantage and act upon it.

2.2 EXISTING RESEARCH

There is a vast literature on the pro-social protection of threatened neighbors during times of mass persecution. Scholars from across the social sciences have interrogated the root motivations behind those who display restraint and remain resilient to genocidal impulses. Most of these studies, however, tend to focus on how inherent characteristics of individuals (microlevel), nations and denominations (both macrolevel) affect the willingness to protect. Whereas the first approach is too narrow and fails to link individual motivations to local community relationships, the latter two are too broad and ignore how the impact of broad norms is conditioned by local relationships.

On the micro-side of the spectrum, historians and psychologists alike have tried to reveal the cognitive and emotional sources of altruism. For a large part, these studies aim to identify personality traits that are overrepresented among those who protect victims of mass persecution. All the usual suspects of demographic research, such as gender, religion, class, occupation and age have been assessed (Wolfson 1975; Tec 1987; Oliner and Oliner 1992; Fogelman 1994). Others have looked at how individual adventurousness (London 1970), individuality (Tec 1987) or a lack of time constraints (Nyseth Brehm 2018) push nascent rebels into clandestine operations. The results of these studies, however, often remain inconclusive, urging scholars to look for more complex interactions between factors (Viterna 2006; Fox and Nyseth Brehm 2018).

Maintaining an individual-level focus but moving away from standard variables, other scholars have focused on the ways in which identities and norms shape morals. Building on social psychological studies of pro-social behavior (Dovidio et al. 2006), Monroe, for instance, suggests that those who resist mass persecution see themselves as part of "a common humanity" (Monroe 2001). Along the same lines, others have tried to incorporate altruism into a (very) soft rational choice framework. This approach is exemplified by the work of Opp, who suggests that individuals are more likely to rescue Jews if they have internalized prosocial norms (Opp 1997). Combining both rationality and norms into a framing perspective, others argue that altruism and rational decision making are conditioned by situational triggers (Varese and Yaish 2000; Kroneberg, Yaish and Stocké 2010). The most recent wave of microresearch problematizes the category of rescue by highlighting that over time killers sometimes transform into rescuers and vice versa, suggesting that resistance to genocide is more dynamic than previously acknowledged (Fujii 2008; Campbell 2010; Fujii 2011; Luft 2015).

Religion features quite prominently in most microlevel scholarship. It has been argued that religiosity or membership in a religious community shapes pro-social norms and attitudes toward outsiders (Gushee 1993). In general, the conclusions of individual-level studies are deemed tautological (Gushee 1993). The claim that altruistic people with inclusive identities are more likely to display altruism and save persecuted outsiders is not particularly insightful. I argue that micro approaches do not shed much light on the question of why rescue is more common in some localities than in others because they fail to link individual dispositions, cognition and traits to local conditions. This accords with a general tendency in the social sciences and history to depict the Holocaust as a story in which heroes exemplify universal values that do not vary from one place to the other and that are juxtaposed against the extraordinary evil of the Nazis. This approach, however, provides no explanation for why certain individual traits, cognitive biases, internalized norms, identities or religious sources of inspiration are present in one village (e.g., Almelo) and not in another (e.g., Borne). In addition, they assume that motivation in and of itself is sufficient to create mobilization.

A smaller body of work focuses in on how macroenvironmental factors produce norms of resistance among bystanders. Instead of looking at individual dispositions, these scholars shift their focus to how widely carried norms produced by broad macroenvironments motivate the protection of threatened neighbors. Two social environments in particular feature prominently in this line of work: nations and denominations. Helen Fein's work exemplifies the nation-centered approach. In her comparative study of Jewish survival across Nazi-occupied countries, she finds that the destruction of Jews was less complete in countries where Jews were considered part of "the universe of obligation," that is, the circle of citizens who deserve state protection (Fein 1979). In a similar vein, Yahil has found that free social structures and democratic norms in society can restrain the impact of mass persecution (Yahil 1983), while Straus, in a recent comparison of Rwanda, Cote d'Ivoire, Mali and Sudan, stresses the importance of inclusive founding narratives of nations for the de-escalation of mass violence (Straus 2015).[7]

These nation-centered studies demonstrate the crucial importance of responses by governments and other national elites to human rights transgressions. Similar to what we saw with individual-level scholarship, religion plays an important role in this line of work. Fein conceives of national religious leaders as "keepers of the key" who are instrumental in facilitating resistance against genocide. If national representatives of a church opposed the Nazis, their flock would automatically follow. Similar arguments have been made about faith-based elites in Kenya, South Africa and Rwanda (Longman 2010).

However, only rarely do we see that national elites save persecuted populations as a whole. More frequently, protection varies from village to village. While illuminating important elements of their context, national-level analyses cannot explain why collective rescue operations emerge in certain localities and not others. Again, we saw in the Introduction that Catholics in Borne and Almelo received identical messages from their bishops but that their response to the Holocaust varied dramatically. As with the microlevel perspective, scholars working in this tradition ignore the fact that motivation is not enough to create rescue operations.

The idea that inherent attributes of different denominations explain the rise of norms that motivate protection is particularly well represented in Holocaust studies. It has been argued that religious doctrine shapes antipathies to persecuted groups, the acceptance of violence and the willingness to resist repressive authorities. For Catholics, it has been argued that their religion reduced solidarity with Jews because of its reactionary tendencies and the traditional Jewish–Christian Schism (Blaschke 1997). The hierarchical structure of the Catholic Church has been claimed to be a detriment to as well as a catalyst for resistance (Croes and Tammes

---

[7] Other cross-national studies highlight how natural environments (Blom 1987), repressive capacity of persecutors (Lammers 1994) and relationships between neutral civilians and rulers (Moore 2010) indirectly impact the opportunities for rescuers to mobilize (Griffioen and Zeller 2011).

2004). Orthodox Protestantism has been linked to fascism as it hinges on biblical racism (Scholder 1977), while others claim that Orthodox Protestants were willing to defy German authorities because of their individualistic traditions and emphasis on the Old Testament in which the Jews were depicted as the chosen people (Moore 2010). The opposite has been said about Lutherans, who, the conventional wisdom goes, blindly accepted any form of secular political authority (1972). In general, the results of studies that focus on religious doctrine are mixed and their implications indeterminate (Gushee 1993). Why, for instance, does Catholicism in one place result in support for national socialism, while generating resistance elsewhere?

Inspired by scholarship on contentious politics (Su 2011), criminology (Hagan and Rymond-Richmond 2008; Nyseth Brehm 2017) and political violence (Kopstein and Wittenberg 2011; King 2012), a recent wave of studies on genocide tries to transcend micro- and macro-level explanations by focusing on community-level variation in killing (Verdeja 2012; Owens, Su and Snow 2013). So far this very productive line of research has mainly focused on killers (McDoom 2014), victims (Einwohner and Maher 2011; Finkel 2017), foreign intervention (Autesserre 2010) and the aftermath of violence (Berry 2017), while resistance by neighbors has been left largely unexplored. Two European exceptions, however, deserve to be mentioned. First, at the University of Nijmegen a group of researchers organized by Ultee have explored how municipality-level demographics are related to rescue (Flap, Geurts and Ultee 1997; Croes and Tammes 2004). Second, at Sciences Po in Paris, Semelin and colleagues have looked at how mesolevel networks and frames translated into unarmed resistance against Hitler (Semelin 1993; Semelin, Andrieu and Gensburger 2008). My work builds on these two European traditions.

In summary, existing scholarship mostly focuses on how inherent traits of individuals, nations and religions shape the motivation to protect victims of mass persecution. These studies suffer from two shortcomings. First, the theories cannot account for local-level variation in motivations to resist genocide. Whereas the latter two branches of scholarship are too broad and ignore subnational variation altogether, the first is too narrow and fails to link individual motives to differential mobilization on a local level. In this light, scholarship on faith-based resistance in particular is problematic in its assumption that religion is monolithic and operates the same for everyone regardless of local position and mobilization opportunities. Second, by solely focusing on motivation, both branches of theory also overlook the fact that people who are willing to act do not always have the capacity to do so. In the following sections I will outline how the interplay of individual dispositions, local community structures, nations and denominations and a focus on capacity and empathy simultaneously can help us understand when and where altruistic motivations emerge and are able to manifest themselves, linking and macro- and micro-forces to subnational variation in mobilization.

2.3 EMPATHY

Ancient political thought provides a promising starting point for understanding the ambivalent relationship between religion and empathy. In order to comprehend compassion with others, Greek thinkers such as Sophocles distinguish between *agnōmosunē* and *suggnōmosunē*. Whereas the former refers to a lack of concern for others that is natural to those who do not share or cannot conceive themselves sharing related forms of suffering, the latter describes pity in humans that is driven by the acknowledgment that the possibilities of impairment are very similar for the pitier and the pitied. In short, it is the recognition of the shared vulnerability of human beings, understanding that what happens to others can easily befall ourselves, that generates empathy with those in need (Nussbaum 1992b). Aristotle makes clear in *Poetics* that similarity plays a crucial role in who we see as fellow humans and who not. Alikeness creates a bond and engenders identification that makes us see that what happens to others can also happen to us personally. Yet, at the same time, we do not care about the fortunes of the wicked as we fail to see them as alike (Kenny 2013).

Centuries later, the relationship between shared vulnerability and empathy was also recognized by Rousseau when he discussed morality in *Emile*: "Why are the rich so harsh to the poor? It is because they have no fear of becoming poor. Why does the noble have such contempt for a peasant? It is because he will never be a peasant. It is the weakness of the human that makes it sociable, it is our common sufferings that carry our heart to humanity; we would owe it nothing if we were not humans" (Rousseau [1889] 1979, p. 224).

Social psychology has blended these insights, reformulating them into the *empathy–altruism nexus*, which positions empathy as the primary driver of altruistic behavior (De Waal 2008). When individuals know that hardship and trauma can befall themselves, their capacity to empathize with others increases, especially for those who suffer in similar situations to one's own. These feelings of empathy transcend identity boundaries and thereby motivate altruistic behavior toward in-group, but especially out-group, members (Krebs 1975; Batson 1991). Experimental research backs up the notion that perceived similarity with those affected by hardship is crucial for the creation of empathy (Staub 2003). It compellingly shows that when subjects perceive another as similar, they are more likely to feel sympathy and provide assistance, even in emergency situations (Karylowski 1976). This is partly due to enhanced perspective taking and the greater capacity for a cognitive understanding of another's condition, which in turn activates vicarious arousal and sympathy (Dovidio 1984).

But what creates similarity, identification and empathy with those who are actually considered different? If similarity triggers empathy, ethnic outsiders are most likely to find support among other minority groups. This is the case because these groups themselves depend on pluralism (i.e., peaceful coexistence of different groups) for group survival (Verkuyten and Yildiz 2006) and can conceive of themselves as being discriminated against if pluralism comes under threat (Staub 2003).[8]

These effects are particularly strong among those who possess the abstract reasoning skills, responsibility, autonomy and moral reasoning aptitude required for perspective taking and cognitive flexibility (Staub 2003). We would therefore expect leaders, who often combine these competencies (Morris and Staggenborg 2004), to recognize, before their followers do, the link between one's own minority position and that of others (Hoffman 2001).[9]

Max Weber was probably one of the first to recognize the importance of a minority position for empathy among religious elites: "A fully developed church – advancing universalist claims – cannot concede freedom of conscious for others; wherever it pleads for this freedom it is because it finds itself in a minority position [...] However if they are strong enough, neither the Catholic nor the (old) Lutheran church, and, all the more so, the Calvinist and Baptist old church recognize freedom of conscious for others" (Weber [1968] 1978, p. 1209).[10]

---

[8] Exploiting this idea, scholars of immigration in the United States have indeed observed that non-dominant groups are significantly more likely to side with minority detainees and support pro-civil rights policies for communities different than their own (Sirin, Villalobos and Valentino 2016).

[9] This is not surprising given that Rousseau, Aristotle and Sophocles hardly ever had the average man in mind when producing their writings.

[10] To be precise, this argument goes one step further than the one put forward by Weber. Whereas Weber emphasizes rationality and opportunism, I suggest that over time the attachment to pluralism sticks and becomes sincere.

Hence, religious minority leaders are more likely to empathize with outsiders because they recognize the vulnerability they share with those in danger. They themselves depend on pluralism for group survival and will perceive an imminent threat of persecution if this form of political toleration is in danger. When denominational lines cross or fall outside the national community, the mystical unity of church and nation is undermined, and religious elites become accustomed to defending pluralism and empathy. Put otherwise, when religious dominance is not possible, pluralism and ecumenical policies toward those who are different are the next best things and need to be cherished by religious elites (Gill 2007; Wilde 2007).

As Sophocles, Rousseau and Aristotle taught us long ago, compassion is largely a function of understanding the shared vulnerability of human beings and recognizing that what happens to others can also happen to us (Nussbaum 1992b). When other outsiders are under attack and pluralism comes under fire, leaders of minority communities will empathize, while elites in majority communities will often refrain from doing so. To use the words of the ancient Greeks, dominant group leaders have *agnōmosunē*, while their minority counterparts have *suggnōmosunē* when confronted with the persecution of outsiders.

2.4 CAPACITY

Certainly, local differences in empathy among leaders are crucial to understanding responses to genocide. However, an exclusive focus on motivations that overlook local constraints to mobilization fails to fully account for local-level variation in rescue operations. If we cannot explain collective outcomes as the cumulative effect of individual interests (Hardin 1982) and if national-level factors hardly ever have universal effects, it is wrong to assume that motivations are sufficient for rescue operations to emerge. The explanation of pro-social mobilization must be augmented by an analysis of the conditions that turn empathy into successful mobilization against genocide. This requires a shift toward the local and social infrastructure of rescue operations (McCarthy and Zald 1977; Klandermans and Tarrow 1988).

2.4.1 Resource Mobilization and Insurgency

This idea dovetails nicely with theories of resource mobilization (Jenkins 1983), which claim that whether the motivation to engage in collective action translates into behavior is conditioned by the resources available to movement entrepreneurs.[11] This perspective draws attention to how movement organizers exploit social networks for collective action (Snow, Zurcher and Ekland-Olson 1980).

Empirical studies of mobilization have similarly revealed that participation in different forms of high-risk collective action depends on strong personal and organizational ties between nascent organizers and potential recruits (McAdam 1986). Often, these scholars look at successful instances of mobilization and observe that participants are more likely to be embedded in dense networks than nonparticipants (Snow, Zurcher and Ekland-Olson 1980). The fact that mobilization is embedded in networks that facilitate collective action is in itself not informative as these networks are inherently part of the mobilization process. At the same time, strong organizational networks and personal ties abound, while resistance and collective action is both rare and diverse. This literature is therefore not able to explain why some dense networks produce different forms of high-risk mobilization while others remain unmobilized altogether (Darden 2015).

Related branches of social movement scholarship have tried to answer this question but tend to overlook mobilization done in secret. Instead, they focus on groups that aim to bring about social change by making themselves heard, that is, by becoming visible. They show that reactive networks get activated when they are embedded in broader political opportunities, broader institutional coalitions or broader issue networks (Loveman 1998). All three of these are less useful to understand clandestine organizations that purposively stay within the narrow confines of underground communities and actively avoid broader opportunities, coalitions and issue networks in order to reduce exposure.

Scholars of insurgency and terrorism encounter this very problem when examining secretive forms of collective action at length (Shapiro 2013; della Porta 2013). These scholars analyze how underlying social bases of mobilization shape insurgent success. This line of work, however, does not delve into the question of where distinctive networks structures actually come from, and, as such, only provides insight into the proximate causes of collective action. The few studies that do address the roots of clandestine collective action tend to focus on legacies of state repression in authoritarian settings. Finkel, for instance, powerfully

---

[11] Some go even further and state that motivations are actually transformed by the available resources (McCarthy and Zald 1977).

shows how Jewish underground movements were more likely to emerge in ghettos where a significant proportion of the population had been targeted by selective repression before World War II (Finkel 2017). Although insightful, this analysis provides less information about how underground mobilization emerges in historically pluralist states with strong civil societies. This project furthers this literature by suggesting that networks that facilitate clandestine mobilization are not randomly distributed but reflect the underlying structure of civic life as members of minority groups are more likely to be embedded in subgroups capable of clandestine collective action. It not only points out that resources are needed for mobilization, it also locates mobilization's underlying sources.

2.4.2 The Clandestine Collective Action Dilemma

Underground mobilization poses two interrelated challenges that together constitute what I call the *clandestine collective action dilemma*. First, one needs to mobilize. This involves the well-studied high-risk collective action problem. A secret organization requires the establishment of communication lines, safe houses, forged documents, infiltration into the persecuting apparatus and the procurement of sufficient food for its members (Finkel 2017, Parkinson 2013). This is too much work for one person or family alone, necessitating cooperation and delegation. Yet, attracting people to participate is far from easy. Engagement in any of these illegal activities entails enormous personal risks as both the costs and odds of getting caught are often high. Numerous scholars have shown that dense organizational structures as well as dense interpersonal networks are key in solving these types of high-risk collective action problems (Lenin 1970; McAdam 1986; Morris 1986; della Porta 2013).

Second, in addition to solving the high-risk collective action problem, resistance networks need to be sustained. This requires secrecy because movement organizers cannot exclude oppressors from the areas in which they operate (Shapiro 2013). Indeed, becoming known to the persecuting power not only leads to operational failure, but also results in further security threats as persecutors try to arrest associates of captured individuals (Sullivan 2016). The secrecy challenge is related to the high-risk collective action problem, because more secrecy reduces the odds of getting caught and makes participation more attractive for forward-looking actors. However, underground mobilization faces a unique trade-off that distinguishes it from other forms of high-risk collective action (Morris 1981): mobilization requires dense networks for recruitment, coordination and communication (Loveman 1998), all of which increase the chances of a group being detected and compromised (Goffman 1970; Baker and Faulkner 1993).

Hence, the tools needed to increase the collective capacity of a group are the very tools that put the group at risk (Shapiro 2013), a dilemma that network analysts commonly refer to as the secrecy–efficiency trade-off (Morselli, Giguère and Petit 2007; Crossley et al. 2012). Advocates of this trade-off assume that covert networks necessarily sacrifice collective capacity for secrecy and consequently are characterized by low density, the exact reverse of a network structure conducive to high-risk mobilization (Raab and Milward 2003; Enders and Su 2007; Crossley et al. 2012). Studies of criminal networks have challenged this assumption, revealing that underground organizations do sometimes rely on dense networks for complex tasks, because denser networks increase solidarity and facilitate careful recruitment and coordination, thereby reducing the risk of exposure by enhancing the quality of mobilization (Baker and Faulkner 1993; Morselli, Giguère and Petit 2007; Crossley et al. 2012).

The sociology of secrecy suggests that dense networks need to be structured in a distinct way in order to facilitate clandestinity. More explicitly, networks need to be both dense and isolated. On the one hand, secrecy, just like high-risk mobilization, requires strong group commitment, cohesion and dense internal networks (Simmel 1906; Fine and Holyfield 1996). On the other hand, underground groups also need to exclude uncommitted outsiders (Herdt 1990) in order to create barriers that prevent the leakage of secrets to the outside world (Gibson 2014). Whereas the classic collective action problem requires creating a core of committed partners that are willing to mobilize, overcoming the secrecy challenge necessitates that information actually stays within this core and does not spread to undedicated outsiders who could potentially reveal clandestine activities (Herdt 1990).

Overcoming both challenges at once requires isolated hubs of commitment without weak ties that could potentially transmit secrets to the uncommitted (Herdt 1990). The same process that makes weak ties strong when looking for jobs, that is, the flow of new information, turns them into a liability for clandestine collective action (Granovetter 1995) and explains why covert organization often emerge within segregated groups of like-minded individuals (Raab and Milward 2003). This notion combines insights from scholars arguing both in favor and against the secrecy–efficiency trade-off: isolated hubs of commitment are locally dense clusters located in a broader network that is sparse (Crossley et al.

2012), revealing a nonlinear relationship between network density and clandestine collective action more (Gould 1993).

2.4.3 The Minority Advantage

This high premium on commitment and secrecy restricts recruitment. Because it is easier to generate group commitment between similar actors already engaged in frequent interaction, recruitment into illicit collective action often proceeds through existing bonds of trust, typically resting on kinship ties or other strong relationships. As a result, clandestine collective action in times of upheaval often inherits group structures present in uneventful times (Erickson 1981; Fine and Holyfield 1996); thus, group relationships during regular times create the confines within which clandestine mobilization emerges in times of crisis. Indeed, several studies indicate that participation in different forms of secretive collective action such as criminality, terrorism and resistance depends on strong personal network ties between recruiters and the recruited, with the former appropriating existing social bases in service of emerging movements (McAdam, Tarrow and Tilly 2001). Chains of heroin traffickers tend to be embedded in family ties (Bruinsma and Bernasco 2004), a large majority of recruits in the Italian Red Brigades had friends within the movement already (della Porta 1988), and 75 percent of early mujahideen had close relationships with insiders before they joined (Sageman 2004).

Minority groups are not only more motivated by their leaders to resist genocide, they also have a natural advantage in producing and sustaining the clandestine networks that are required to turn antigenocidal motives into results. Differences in epistemology, ontology and methodology notwithstanding, researchers across the social sciences agree that minorities form isolated hubs of commitment that provide relatively safe places for illicit mobilization. At least three reinforcing processes increase isolation and commitment of minorities: distinctive identification, exclusionary pressures and, in some cases, membership screening. Building on the distinctiveness postulate, social psychologists have revealed that people rely on perceptual selectivity to make sense of who they are and what groups they are willing to commit to (McGuire and Padawer-Singer 1976). Individuals tend to be willing to base commitment on characteristics that are relatively rare in their social environments, because these rare traits provide the most unique and important information about their bearers. In line with the distinctiveness postulate, social psychologists studying collective action have demonstrated that minority groups – groups organized around relatively rare traits – display strong group identification and are more likely to invest in within-group networks. These network choices and levels of identification in turn increase internal cohesion, compliance with group norms, overall loyalty and voluntary self-sacrifice among members (Brewer and Silver 2000), as well as social isolation (Mehra, Kilduff and Brass 1998).

Sociologists, for quite some time, have recognized that isolation is not always driven by the behavior of the minority itself. Dominant groups see the practices and beliefs of minorities as strange and deviant, producing perceptions of threat and prejudicial attitudes, which, in turn, results in avoidance. Exclusion by the majority reinforces isolation from mainstream society for minority groups while at the same time increasing cohesion and the importance of formal institutions (Coser 1956; Turner and Killian 1957).

Economists, for their part, assume that every form of group membership is voluntary. Under this assumption, exclusion also creates isolated hubs of commitment and trust by changing the membership profile of minority groups. Whenever social life is segregated by group membership, a minority position acts as a natural screening device, because it imposes unproductive costs on members by inhibiting participation in dominant political, economic and social networks. If one is not allowed to interact with out-group members in a region where everyone belongs to the same community, membership costs are marginal. However, if on a local-level one group decreases in size relative to another community, prohibitions start to matter. For members of a minority, the costs of limited interaction become enormous as they exclude themselves from a large part of the population. At the same time, these costs subsequently screen out potential free riders and increase the importance of the collectivity for everyone (Iannaccone 1994).

Distinctive identification, exclusion and membership screening turn minorities into dense networks of committed individuals (Coleman 1988) that are insulated from undedicated outsiders (Granovetter 1995; Portes 1995). These isolated hubs of commitment in turn create an opportunity to overcome the dual challenge of high-risk collective action and secrecy.

It is important to emphasize that the processes underlying the minority advantage are driven by relative, not absolute, size. Even if a minority group is large, it can still be excluded by the majority and membership can still be costly. Indeed, small groups (in absolute numbers) are better at producing collective action because they are better at monitoring members and suffer less from the diffusion of responsibility (Olson 1965). However, throughout this book, I will present evidence that it is indeed relative size the produced rescue operations. In some of the statistical analysis in Chapters 5 and 7, I find an effect for relative size while keeping absolute size constant. Moreover, Chapters 6 and 7 reveal that minority thesis also operates for large congregations in big cities such as Amsterdam, Groningen, Leeuwarden, Enschede, Den Bosh and Heerlen.

2.4.4 From Isolated Commitment to Clandestine Mobilization

As outcomes cannot be explained by their consequences, the minority advantage in clandestine capacity does not manifest itself automatically (Elster 1989). Reliable and committed volunteers who happen to be embedded in isolated networks cannot simply walk to a recruiting office, nor do all organizers automatically possess the cognitive skills and information to seize the opportunity provided by social enclaves (Simon 1982). This study exposes three feedback mechanisms that translate the abstract minority advantage into higher levels of clandestine mobilization among minority enclaves: selective retention, organizers' assurance and organizers' selectivity.

First, selective retention refers to the process through which entities with favorable traits perpetuate themselves because they are more likely to survive environmental conditions (Aldrich 1999). Selective pressures for resistance groups are severe, as repressive authorities have consistent strategies to detect, infiltrate and uproot clandestine networks (Sullivan 2016). These strategies depend on intelligence about where illicit activities take place. Given their isolated nature, minority groups are less likely to reveal this information than majority groups and are consequently less likely to see their mission interrupted by intelligence agents. Selective retention also amplifies the overall segregation of clandestine organizations. Expansion of recruitment outside the confines of existing groups is appealing to some because it can enlarge an organization's impact and scope, but, unfortunately, networks that scale outward often create internal differences in ideology, strategy or style, triggering innate strife and increasing the demand for coordination. As such, expansion reduces the likelihood that a rescue organization can keep intelligence out of the hands of its much stronger opponent.

Second, the importance of a minority position for clandestine collective action reveals itself to forward-looking organizers and recruiters via an assurance mechanism. As followers embedded in minority groups are more willing to take on risks for the group and the leadership, organizers recognize that clandestine coordination is possible within the confines of their enclave. The mere assurance that fellow church members would cooperate in this way increases the overall motivation among group members to setup and engage in clandestine missions (Elster 1989).

Third, organizers' selectivity refers to the leaders' ability to distinguish individuals who are valuable from those who are not. Compared to their majority counterparts, it is easier to acquire this internal intelligence for minority leaders. In part, this ability derives from deep inside knowledge of the community. Due to the isolated nature of enclaves, minority organizers take up more central network positions. Centrality allows leaders to better tap into information flows and increases the number of signals available so that they can recognize the preferences, trustworthiness and capacities of different followers (Marwell and Oliver 1993). Networks in which close primary relationships were provided in this way not only assure leaders of the feasibility of mobilization, but also produce an inventory of the different skills and resources available within the group, all of which could be accessed without having to leave the enclave of trust. The network closure of minorities, as a result, cuts across individuals with different skill sets, allowing for coordinated action among actors who can be trusted (Burt 2009).

Taken together, the assurance, retention and selectivity mechanisms activated by a minority position provide empathetic elites with the knowledge (Nepstad and Bob 2006), networks (Morris and Staggenborg 2004) and skill sets (Ganz 2000) to produce rescue networks for threatened neighbors. When facing strong persecuting forces, minorities mobilize with more vigor and are more resistant to being dismantled.

2.5 CONCLUSION

Existing work on the protection of threatened neighbors suffers from two shortcomings. First, it focuses on micro- and macro-level factors at the expense of subnational processes and outcomes. Second, it focuses solely on motivations and overlooks the necessary capacity to translate motivations into action.

I depart from existing research by emphasizing how subnational relations simultaneously affect the willingness and capacity to resist genocide. The convergence of willingness and capacity makes religious

minorities particularly likely candidates to provide protection to persecuted neighbors. Two distinct mechanisms link minority status to rescue
operations. First, minorities are better able to provide shelter because
they can more easily overcome the clandestine collective action dilemma
– the need to coordinate collective action while reducing exposure. A
combination of group commitment and isolation is required to transcend this dual problem. Minorities are embedded in self-segregated hubs
of commitment and, as a result, have a structural advantage to setup
secretive operations. Through selective survival, organizers' assurance
and organizers' selectivity, this structural advantage manifests itself in
increased mobilization for those in need.

Minority leaders are, secondly, more willing to protect victims of
mass persecution because they empathize with persecuted outsiders
and because they themselves depend on pluralism to survive. Whereas
the latter mechanism imbues minority networks with the motivations
to resist, the former enables the translation of these motivations into
action. Durkheim is arguably the most famous scholar who anticipated
the important role of minority churches: "Obviously, the less numerous confessions facing the hostility of the surrounding populations, in
order to maintain themselves are obliged to exercise severe control over
themselves and subject themselves to an especially rigorous discipline.
To justify the always precarious tolerance granted them, they have to
practice greater morality" (Durkheim 1897).

To test the minority hypothesis, one would want to reveal differences between empathy, networks and commitment of recruits active in
minority, majority and mixed groups and link these to higher rates of
mobilization and lower rates of denunciation. Leaders of minority groups
should display more empathy with Jews, while their followers should be
easier to mobilize and have fewer ties with potential snitches compared
to their counterparts in majority or mixed groups.

However, the same problem that hinders clandestine collective action
makes it difficult to do clean empirical research: who is committed
and who is not cannot be observed directly. Nevertheless, the minority
hypothesis outlined earlier suggests a number of empirical patterns to
look for when analyzing rescue attempts. Specifically, I expect that 1)
minority leaders are more willing to setup clandestine rescue networks
because they identify with victims of mass persecution; 2) minority
leaders are more successful in mobilizing in general and in setting up
clandestine rescue networks in particular; and 3) whenever they mobilize,

majority groups are less likely to sustain minority operations because they suffer from denunciation by marginal members or bystanders. As we will see in the next chapter the Low Countries provide a unique opportunity to investigate this while keeping constant the micro- and macro-level factors suggested by previous research.

3

Religious Minorities in the Low Countries:
From the Reformation to the Holocaust

3.1 INTRODUCTION

I substantiate the claim that minorities are more likely to protect victims of mass persecution by utilizing evidence drawn from the religious rescue of Jews in the Low Countries during the Holocaust. Religious rescue of Jews in the Netherlands and Belgium provides a unique, albeit tragic, opportunity to investigate the minority hypothesis for four reasons.

First, there is sufficient variation on the minority variable. The Low Countries were at the frontline of the Reformation, Counter-Reformation and Protestant secessions. Missionary activities (of both Protestants and Catholics) and disputed scripture (mostly within the Protestants Church) created a religiously pluralist society and resulted in pockets of minority communities in both Catholic and Protestant parts of the region (Rogier 1964). This mixed landscape allows me to assess whether religious deviance affected mobilization for both Protestant and Catholic communities while keeping ideology constant. Second, comparisons within the Netherlands allow me to keep constant both top–down enforcement of mobilization and cross-national differences. Protestant and Catholic leaders alike protested anti-Semitic legislation collaboratively at the national level, providing all Christians with the same moral message of how German persecutions went against the tenets of their faiths regardless of congregation (Snoek 2005). Third, there is enormous variation on the dependent variable. As Jews lived spread out over the Low Countries, both Protestant and Catholic congregations were presented with the challenge to provide protection. How they responded however, varied from one place to another. Fourth, a comparison of subnational patterns between the Netherlands and Belgium enables me to explore whether the minority hypothesis operates similarly in places where the Holocaust evolved differently.

In the next section, I briefly describe the religious landscape of the Low Countries leading up to World War II, highlighting the enormous religious diversity of the region. I then discuss the similar ways in which religious diversity was managed by political elites in both countries. This involves a brief discussion of what Arend Lijphart dubbed pillarization. Next, I describe the Jewish community in the Low Countries at the onset of World War II, before moving on to outline how the Holocaust played out in both countries. In the last section, I discuss the specific empirical implications of the minority hypothesis in the context of the Low Countries.

3.2 FRONTLINE BETWEEN ROME AND REFORMATION

In 1506, about a decade before becoming both the king of Spain and the emperor of Germany, Charles V inherited large parts of the Netherlands and Belgium from the Duke of Burgundy. Exploiting his powerful position, Charles brought together a territory he referred to as the Seventeen Provinces, or the Low Countries, an area to the north of France locked in between the Rhine and Meuse rivers, which corresponded to present-day the Netherlands and Belgium (Blom 2006).

The Low Countries had historically been a breeding ground for new religious movements. While traditions of tolerance attracted religious dissenters from all over the world, the expansive trade system, advanced printing industry, waterways and high levels of urbanization created fertile soil for different streams of Lutheranism, Anabaptism and Calvinism, with the last denomination becoming the most dominant during the Reformation (Van Eijnatten and van Lieburg 2005).

Together with urban patricians and lower nobility, who were attracted to more fiscal autonomy, Calvinists organized an insurgency against the Catholic King Phillip, who had inherited the Seventeen Provinces from his father Charles and who pursued intense anti-Protestant policies. Compared to other dissenting religions, Calvinism formed the most natural ideological underpinning for this revolution given its belief in bottom–up reform (differentiating it from Lutheranism) and emphasis on a public display of identity (as opposed to Baptism). In addition, its international infrastructure and organizational structure provided a strong backbone for the independence movement (Van Eijnatten and van Lieburg 2005).

After the uprising, the Seventeen Provinces were cut in half in 1579. Whereas large parts of the south were reattached to Phillip's territory, the northern parts broke away from the Spanish crown, forming the Republic of the United Provinces. These political processes had an enormous impact on the effectiveness of the Reformation as well as Catholic reconversion policies. While the Catholic Church could uproot newly founded Protestant communities and reinstate Catholicism in the southern Netherlands as well as Belgium under the reign of the Spanish king, the reestablishment of Catholicism in the north was largely impaired and depended heavily on the passion of individual missionaries (Rogier 1964). Here, the Protestant Church could establish a unified religious infrastructure (Van Eijnatten and van Lieburg 2005). As we can see in Figure 3.1a, this resulted in Protestant territory in the north and Catholic territory in the south of the Low Countries.

In 1648, Dutch troops reconquered some southern provinces from the Spanish crown (Blom 2006). This military development proved to be a defining moment in the history of the Low Countries. For the next century, Catholic Belgium and the religiously mixed Netherlands, separated by a national border, would follow different paths both politically and culturally (see Figure 3.1b).

In the Netherlands, the constitutional protection of religious pluralism prevented the complete conversion to Calvinism. For the same reason, the Netherlands never became religiously homogenous, despite Calvinist privileges in education and politics in the north. Instead, local elites in the southern provinces were granted autonomy in religious affairs, sustaining Catholic dominance in these areas (Van Eijnatten and van Lieburg 2005). Being literally at the fault line between Rome and Reformation, the Netherlands now became a hotbed of missionary activity as both Protestants and Catholics started to make inroads into each other's territories. These activities created religious enclaves on both sides of the religious boundary. While the Catholic mission in the north was more successful than its Protestant counterpart in the south, small pockets of Protestantism were able to grow over the years due to economic integration of industrialized regions near the Belgian border (Rogier 1964).

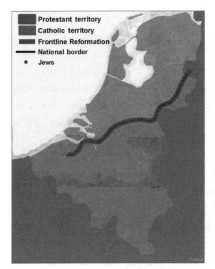

(a) Frontline insurgency 1579

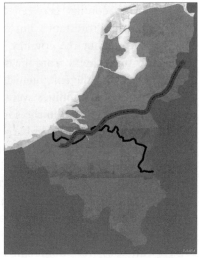

(b) Conquest of the southern Provinces and national split, 1648

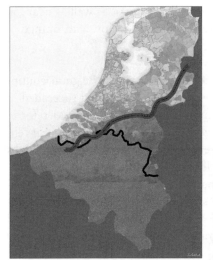

(c) Religion in the Low Countries before outbreak of World War II

(d) Jews in the Low Countries, 1942

FIGURE 3.1 Evolution of religion in the Low Countries, 1579–1945. A black-and-white version of this figure will appear in some formats. For the colour version, please refer to the plate section.

Apart from conflict between Protestantism and Catholicism, conflicts within the Protestant Church added to the emergence of minority enclaves throughout the country. In the nineteenth century, Orthodox Protestants broke away from the dominant Dutch Reformed Church out of discontent with the enlightened undertones of modern Protestantism. Although these communities were spread out all over the country, they were more concentrated in the southwest and center, an area known as the Dutch Bible Belt (Knippenberg 1992).

Figure 3.2 shows the relative strength of Catholicism versus Protestantism and the strength of Orthodox Protestant movements per municipality, a geographic unit roughly comparable with a U county, in 1930. Whereas completely red municipalities were dominated by Catholics, green municipalities were dominated by Protestants. The political geography of three centuries was still visible in the interwar period (CBS 1931). Catholics were dominant in the south, while Protestants dominated the north. In addition to the Orthodox Protestant churches that were spread throughout the country, minority enclaves of Protestants and Catholics also emerged in the east and northwest as well as near the religious fault line (municipalities represented in yellow and orange in Figure 3.2).

Under Habsburg rule, the Counter-Reformation in Belgium continued with success. The Spanish king rejected pluralism and succeeded in completely restoring Catholic hegemony. Through educational reform, theological centralization, clerical oversight and the mobilization of religious orders, Protestantism was largely weeded out, with only small hubs of Protestantism remaining. Ironically, the Reformation had historically been strongest in Belgium (Van Eijnatten and van Lieburg 2005). Dedicated hubs of Protestants therefore sustained themselves at the margins of society. These small pockets of religious dissent were strengthened throughout the centuries by immigrants from nearby, France, Germany and Holland (Dhooge 1985).

Right before the German invasion, Catholic Belgium was home to twelve different Protestant denominations. Although it is not possible to retrieve census data on religion, estimates based on subsidization requests suggest that around 50,000 Belgian citizens belonged to one of these twelve communities during the interwar period (Saerens 2007a).[1]

---

[1] For an overview see (Dhooge 1985).

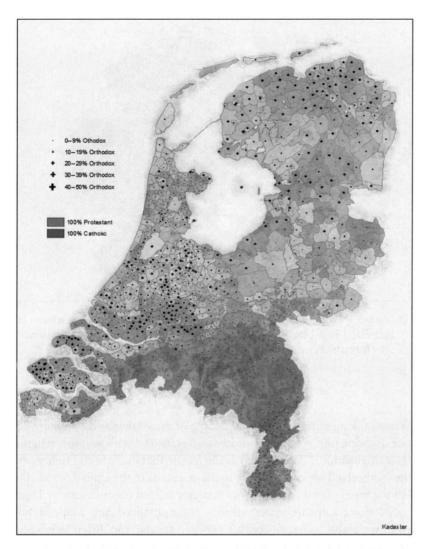

FIGURE 3.2 Protestants, Catholics and Orthodox Protestants in the
Netherlands, 1930 (CBS 1931). A black-and-white version of this figure will
appear in some formats. For the colour version, please refer to the plate section.

According to the 1950 yearbook of the Catholic Church, these Protestant
churches were organized into 248 congregations spread out through the
country, as is displayed in Figure 3.3.[2]

---

[2] *Katholiek jaarboek van Belgie. 1950. Brussels.*

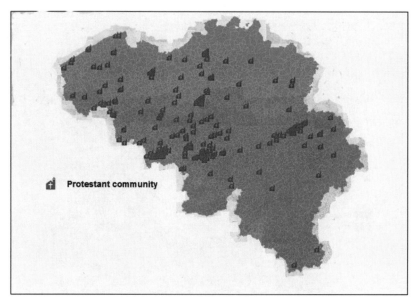

FIGURE 3.3 Protestant communities in Belgium, 1950 (Katholiek jaarboek van Belgie 1950). A black-and-white version of this figure will appear in some formats. For the colour version, please refer to the plate section.

3.3 PILLARIZATION

When looking at the religious landscape of the Netherlands in Figure 3.2, one question jumps out: how did a small state deal with so much religious fractionalization?[3] This exactly is the puzzle that made both Lijphart and the Netherlands famous among social scientists in the United States. Following more casual and often normatively loaded observations by Dutch sociologists, Lijphart systematically conceptualized and mapped how elites were able to pacify conflict between secular and different religious groups (Rigthart 1986). According to Lijphart's theory, Protestant and Catholic leaders alike stabilized society by preventing members of different religious communities from interacting with each other at a local level, while allowing for elite cooperation on a national level (Lijphart 1968). As Lijphart would soon find out, this strategy was not unique to the Netherlands (Lijphart 1981). In neighboring Belgium, religious elites

[3] Dutch political scientist Daalder famously wrote that an American colleague had once remarked that given its combination of religious diversity and strong democratic institutions the Netherlands should in theory not exist (Daalder 1974).

organized society along similar lines. Here, self-segregation was used not as a way to prevent interaction between followers of different congregations, but solely as a protection mechanism against the rise of the secular forces of socialism and liberalism (Hellemans 1988).

In both countries religious leaders build impermeable walls of associations to seclude the different groups and strengthen ties between leaders and followers. Most importantly, both Catholics and the different Protestant communities were encouraged to build their own churches and schools and were prohibited from participating in religious and educational activities of other groups. In response to the growth of civil society, religious leaders in both countries, regardless of denomination, established parallel organizations under exclusive clerical control. In addition to schools, church communities maintained youth organizations, sport teams, mass media and labor unions as well as associations for highly specific activities, such as goat breeding or homing pigeons, to make sure that interdenominational contact as well as contact with seculars was limited to a bare minimum (Rigthart 1986).

It has been argued that pillarization in and of itself reduced help for Jews as local-level segregation inhibited interaction between Jews and gentiles (Croes and Tammes 2004) and its hierarchical setup induced obedience to authority (Blom 1987). The central argument advanced here refines this thesis by revealing that whether pillarization had a positive or negative impact on evasion opportunities depended on how a pillar was embedded in local communities. Whereas a majority pillar induces passivity and reduces empathy with outsiders, the opposite is true for local minority pillars, where identification with fellow minorities is stronger and leaders are able to exploit tight authority structures and group commitment to setup rescue operations.

3.3.1 Minorities, Commitment and Isolation

According to the theory outlined in the previous chapter, local minority communities are not only more empathetic, but also better able to translate pluralist norms into action as their members form isolated hubs of commitment. These hubs can be exploited in times of crisis to produce the clandestine collective action required to protect those in danger. Needless to say, commitment and isolation should also manifest themselves in the absence of upheaval. If the capacity mechanism holds true, we would expect minority enclaves to display more group isolation and commitment than majorities before the outbreak of World War II. It would therefore follow from the minority argument that members of minority enclaves would be more likely to listen to appeals from religious elites to self-organize into insulated pillars as they are more committed to the group and leadership.

Based on historical census data obtained from the Institute of Human Geography at the University of Amsterdam, I compiled a database of religious groups, nested in counties. For each of these groups, the original file provides county-level information of the size of Protestant and Catholic communities. I created five proxies to assess whether minority groups were indeed more committed than their majority counterparts. In particular, I looked at the number of church buildings per 1,000 members in 1942 (IKGN 2011), the percentage of members voting for the political party with corresponding religious affiliation in the years 1918, 1922, 1925, 1929, 1933 and 1937 (CBS 1937), the percentage of members going to religiously segregated schools in 1910, 1920 and 1930 (De Kwaasteniet 1990),[4] the percentage of members who joined religiously segregated labor unions (Pennings 1991)[5] and the percentage of members that were leading members of their respective national religious organization in 1948 (Duffhues, Felling and Roes 1985).[6]

The results of a series of ordinary least squares (OLS) models with county clustered standard errors that condition on absolute size and include county and year FE are presented in Figure 3.4.[7] In line with the central hypothesis of this book, minority communities were considerably more likely to form isolated hubs of commitment measured in many different ways. A one standard deviation increase in relative size leads to three fewer churches per 1,000 followers, a 3.5 percent decrease in religious voting, a more than 4 percent decrease in segregated school attendance, a 2 percent decrease in union membership and a 0.5 percent decrease in the production of national leaders.[8]

---

[4] I would like to thank Peter Tammes for sharing this data.

[5] I would like to thank Paul Pennings for sharing this data.

[6] I would like to thank the Catholic Documentation Center in Nijmegen for sharing data.

[7] This analytical strategy is not possible for the leadership data as we only have information on one religious group (Catholics) per county at our disposal. When analyzing the production of leadership I therefore rely on the inclusion of province FEs and province-level clustered standard errors. No year dummies were included for the church analysis as information on only one time point was used.

[8] Although the local-level FEs powerfully address issues of omitted variable bias there might still be within locality confounders that are driving the results. To test for the plausibility of such confounders I follow the approach suggested by Oster (Oster 2014)

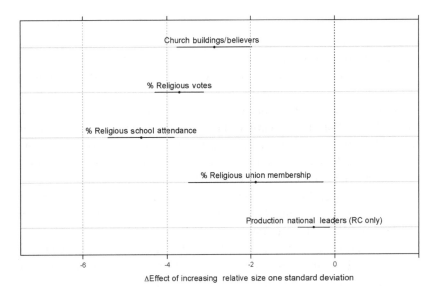

FIGURE 3.4 Effect of relative size on religious commitment.

3.4 JEWS IN THE LOW COUNTRIES

The Jewish community hardly registered as an independent pillar in the Low Countries (Romijn 2002). Despite the emergence of some smaller Jewish associations, attempts to setup distinct unions or schools largely failed. Numbers were too small, identification too low and internal divisions too large to constitute a cohesive and independent community (Wasserstein 2012).

This was the logical outcome of a long history of Jewish migration. Jews had already established themselves permanently in the region around the turn of the sixteenth century when the Counter-Reformation

to estimate corrected bounds on the coefficients. These conservative bounds are created by allowing all the variation in the dependent variable of concern to be explained (hence $R^2=1$), while assuming that the potential confounders have the same explanatory power as county-level fixed effects FEs, a plausible assumption given the already high R^2 of the estimated models. The bounds are presented in the bottom panel of Table 3.A1 and 3.A2 in the Appendix. The implied bounds of the first three models are very close to the normal estimates, while the corrected estimate in the fourth model even exceeds the original coefficient. This suggests that including omitted variables will either strengthen or not affect the findings. The lower panel of Table 3.A2, however, suggests that the significant correlation between a minority position and the production of national leaders is likely to be driven by one or more omitted variables, as the conservative bound of the effect is positive while the original coefficient was negative.

was unfolding. Large groups of affluent, highly educated Sephardic Jews, fleeing the Catholic Inquisition, arrived in the Low Countries that had recently introduced freedom of worship (Israel 1989).

The contrast with the Ashkenazic Jews who entered the country around the same time was stark. This Yiddish-speaking group from Eastern Europe was driven to the West by extreme levels of poverty and the Thirty Years' War. For a century, the Ashkenazic Jews from the east and the Ladino-speaking Sephardic Jews from the south enjoyed religious freedom and formed communities that were separate both from each other and from gentile society (Kaplan 1989; Abicht 2006).

This all changed with the French Revolution, the core values of which were imposed on the Dutch and Belgians directly through the Napoleonic occupation. From that point forward, foreign rulers and subsequent native governments actively pursued integration of Jews into their host societies (Michman, Beem and Michman 1999). These policies proved to be quite successful. Both Yiddish and Ladino slowly disappeared, and Jewish elites from both subgroups started aligning themselves with neutral or secular organizations, minimizing the influence of organized Zionism and Orthodoxy. The gradual disappearance of a distinctive Jewish identity was enhanced by the fact that anti-Semitism was mild and had never been an obstacle to social assimilation (Blom and Cahen 2002).

Among the lower classes, Jewish identification remained somewhat stronger, expressing itself through low intermarriage rates and more residential segregation, mainly in Amsterdam, Brussels and Antwerp. This continued with the 79,000 Jews who came as refugees from Nazi Germany and Eastern Europe in the 1930s. These recent arrivals formed their own separate group who leaned toward more culturally distinct practices than did those born in the Low Countries (Houwink-ten-Cate 1989).

At the onset of the German occupation in May 1940, the Netherlands had a Jewish population of about 140,000, of whom 56 percent lived in Amsterdam. Still, due to their long history in the Netherlands, Jews lived throughout the country in both Catholic and Protestant regions, as we can see in Figure 3.1d. This is important because it urged minority and majority congregations on both sides of the religious fault line to engage in rescue activities when the German Wehrmacht invaded and the Final Solution started unfolding.

Belgium was home to between 66,000 and 70,000 Jews right before the outbreak of World War II. By the time that the deportations started, this number had fallen to 52,000, as several thousand Jews were able to escape the country. These 52,000 Jews are mapped in Figure 3.1d and lived throughout Belgium, with large concentrations in Antwerp and Brussels (Saerens 2006a). When we compare Figures 3.3 and 3.1d we can see that residencies of Jews and Protestants largely overlapped. As a result, like their Dutch counterparts, minority Protestant enclaves in Belgium were exposed to the plight of the Jews throughout the twentieth century.

It is important to highlight that despite historical similarities, the Jewish populations in the two countries were not completely comparable at the onset of the war. The biggest difference was that only 10 percent of all Dutch Jews were foreign nationals, while this was true for 90 percent of all Belgian Jews. This discrepancy was driven by three processes. First, early pluralist traditions in the religiously mixed Netherlands made the country more attractive than homogeneously Catholic Belgium for Jews in the nineteenth and twentieth centuries. Second, economic differences between the two countries in the nineteenth century triggered substantial migration of well-integrated Jews from Belgium to the Netherlands. Third, Belgium was more attractive for refugees in the 1930s because its ports provided better access to countries overseas (Caestecker 1993; Griffioen and Zeller 2011; Abicht 2006).

3.5 THE HOLOCAUST

The Nazis invaded the Low Countries in 1940. Contrary to what happened in Eastern Europe, which was ruled through terror, plunder and exploitation, German occupation policy in the Netherlands and Belgium was aimed at preserving public order and integrating the national economies into the war effort. This resulted from the fact that Germany did not have enough man power and resources to administer all foreign territory directly. Instead, they established supervisory administrations (*Aufsichtsverwaltungen*), leaving day-to-day matters, whenever possible, to native authorities and local civil servants (Griffioen and Zeller 2011).

When implementing the Final Solution, the two countries, together with France, were considered to be a single unit by central planners in Berlin. With help from domestic institutions, the Nazis isolated Jews socially, economically and administratively (Herzberg 1978; Steinberg 2004). When the major deportations started in June and July 1942, Jews were no longer allowed to travel without a permit, enter public spaces or possess more than 250 guilders. More importantly, the Nazi institutions responsible for Jewish persecution had been able to exploit lower echelons of local bureaucracies, which had remained intact, to obtain detailed residential information on all Jews living in the countries (Wielek 1947; Van Doorslaer et al. 2004).

In both countries, the Nazis tried to deport Jews to extermination camps under the guise of work. At first they hoped all Jews would obey orders and show up for deportation themselves after receiving a call. When this did not work for large portions of the Jewish population, the German security forces started organizing roundups in collaboration with either local police forces or new native volunteer troops. In the last stage of the deportation, between October 1943 and September 1944, the Nazis, helped by newly established police units and bounty hunters, started tracking down Jews who had gone underground (Meershoek 1999; Saerens 2000; Van Liempt 2002; Croes and Tammes 2004; Saerens 2007b; Van Liempt 2013).

At the end of 1944, the Netherlands was declared "freed of Jews." The result of the preceding years was nothing less than a disaster: more than 70 percent of the Jews were killed (Hirschfeld 1991). Jews fared much better in neighboring Belgium where 60 percent were able to survive the war (Steinberg and Schram 2008). This considerable difference can be largely explained by three factors: Jewish responses, the autonomy of persecuting agencies and, most important for this book, resistance by the gentile population (Griffioen and Zeller 2011).

First, the Jewish populations in the two countries reacted differently to anti-Jewish legislation. These differences largely reflected demographic differences between Belgian and Dutch Jews. Jews in the Netherlands, a large majority of whom were well-integrated Dutch citizens, had a tendency to trust local institutions and rely on legal ways that (falsely) appeared to enable escape (Blom 1987). The importance of the Jewish Council in implementing anti-Jewish legislation was indicative of this process. This representative body was imposed on the Jews by the occupying forces and was completely subordinated to the SIPO-SD, the persecuting agency in the Netherlands. Members of the council were highly regarded Jewish leaders who participated in the hope that they could limit the damage for their followers. Unintentionally, however, they legitimized and streamlined the registration and deportation process by collecting information and inducing Jews to cooperate with the authorities (Michman 1992).

In Belgium, a large majority of the Jews were of foreign descent and had witnessed violent persecution before. As a result, they were defiant when faced with deportations and were more inclined to turn to underground movements in order to escape (Moore 2010). With the establishment of the Association for Jews in Belgium (AJB), the Nazis hoped to create a tool similar to the Dutch Jewish Council. However, the AJB lacked legitimacy and was immediately contested by Jewish underground councils. The Nazi police was never able to attain full control over this Jewish body as it had to share authority with other German agencies (Van Doorslaer and Schreiber 2004).

This brings us to the second difference between the Netherlands and Belgium: the autonomy of the persecuting police agencies. Following the quick capitulation by the Dutch armed forces, a Nazi civilian government led by Reich Commissioner Seyss-Inquart, gave carte blanche to the SIPO-SD. The German persecutors in the Netherlands created a system that enabled them to organize and implement the deportations seamlessly. The SIPO-SD had around 5,000 German police officers at its disposal and was given full control over the newly centralized Dutch police forces that had been wrestled from the control of Dutch authorities (Griffioen and Zeller 2011).

Initially, Belgium was considered a launch pad for attacks on Germany's nemesis Great Britain. The Nazis therefore ruled the country through a military government, which had to let defense interests prevail over purely ideological goals. Within this government the agencies in charge of deporting Jews were among many authorities vying for influence. The 2,000 German police officers in the country could in principle be used for arresting Jews, but they were also needed for other tasks. Except for some roundups in Antwerp, the Nazis could also not exploit the man power of the local police apparatus. As a result, the Nazis had to rely on relatively chaotic and brutal arrests, which soon alienated everyone (Meinen 2009).

This alienation in part explains the third important difference between the Netherlands and Belgium: mobilization by the gentile population. As crossing the national border was extremely difficult, Jews who wanted to escape deportation had to find hiding inside the country, which depended heavily on the aid of others, whether through sharing of resources, providing shelter or allowing mobility (Varese and Yaish 2000). How did gentiles in both countries respond? After some smaller ad hoc roundups in the spring of 1941, civil servants in the Dutch capital of Amsterdam instigated in protest a furious strike that diffused to surrounding cities and private industries, paralyzing the economic center of the country for a few days (Sijes 1954). This rebellious attitude, however, dissolved after the strike was brutally repressed by German security forces. Although most gentiles were aggrieved about what happened to the Jews, they remained inactive in the face of repressive threats. Feelings of power-lessness and fear dominated as helping Jews entailed the risk of getting deported oneself (Van Der Boom 2012). Occasionally, isolated altruists were able to assist Jews, but more often sheltering was too much work for one or two people alone (Flim 1998). With the exception of some stu-dent networks, most rescue activities remained geographically isolated and disjointed (De Jong 1969–1991). It was not until late 1943, when forced labor was extended to include gentiles as well, that the willingness to provide shelter started to grow, and something resembling a national rescue movement emerged. By then it was "too little too late" (Moore 1997) as most Jews had already been rounded up or lived in Amsterdam and The Hague, strongholds of German security forces that were difficult to escape (Presser 1965).

After a short period of indifference among gentiles, help was more readily available in Belgium. In addition to the outrage over police bru-talities and willingness of Jews to ask for help, this was largely due to discontent among the gentile population with general Nazi politics. Unhappiness was driven in particular by the early and more radical introduction of compulsory labor for gentiles in October 1942. As a consequence, the availability of escape opportunities exploded nine months earlier than in the Netherlands, when both non-Jewish and Jew-ish citizens were forced to participate in working programs (Moore 2010).

Despite overall passivity in the Netherlands, one group of actors that did openly stand-up for the Jews, protesting anti-Semitic policies early on, were national church leaders. Contrary to almost all other organiza-tions, such as political parties and labor unions, church networks were never dismantled because the occupiers were afraid to alienate religious elites. Their denominational differences notwithstanding, the three major religious groups – Protestants, Orthodox Protestants and Catholics – all saw anti-Semitism as being in conflict with the inclusive underpinnings of Dutch society (Braun 2016).

Motivated by this fear, Protestant leaders were the first to protest discriminatory Nazi policy. The Dutch Reformed Church and the two smaller Orthodox churches (Reformed and Christian Reformed) col-lectively sent an open petition to Reich Commissioner Seyss-Inquart in

October of 1940 to denounce the declaration of Aryan ancestry that civil servants had to sign in order to stay employed (Touw 1946). The petition was also delivered from the pulpit in all Dutch Reformed churches. In the meantime, the Reformed and Christian Reformed Protestants also organized fundraisers "to support their Jewish brothers" (Delleman 1949). Over four years, all Protestant churches openly protested anti-Semitic legislation twenty-two times, five of which involved statements being read from the pulpit during public sermons across the whole country. Four of these acts of defiance explicitly rejected the deportations of Jews; others targeted prohibition signs, sterilization measures or persecutions more generally (Croes and Tammes 2004).

The Roman Catholic bishops expressed their outrage with anti-Jewish measures for the first time in September 1941. In response to legislation that forbade Jews to attend Christian schools, the Catholic leaders openly challenged German authorities for stripping Dutch citizens of their civil rights (Aukes 1956). This protest was followed by sixteen others, two of which were read out during mass (Tammes and Smits 2005). In addition, Archbishop De Jong donated 12,000 guilders to an organization that provided shelter to Jewish children (De Jong 1969–1991) and secretly encouraged local clergy to help Jews "by any means possible" (Stokman 1945).

From January 1942 onward, leaders of the three churches, for the first time in Dutch history, combined forces. In an unprecedented display of interreligious solidarity, Christian clergy agreed to read joint statements from their pulpits during local services throughout the whole country in July 1942 and February 1943, declaring the culpability of anyone who contributed to the deportations of Jews (Snoek 2005). In line with the moral impetus sent out by their superiors, local clergymen (and women) and other religious opinion leaders played a key role in instigating the small assistance networks that were so crucial for evasion early on (Michman et al. 2004). However, protests and sermons told congregants what not to do rather than what to do. As a result, religious help to Jews was far from universal. At a local level, some religious groups produced rescue networks while others did not.

Interestingly, although overall resistance to the Nazis was more widespread in Belgium, the country's church leaders did not stage open protests against anti-Jewish legislation on a national level. Although some claim that this had to do with anti-Semitic traditions within the dominant Catholic Church (Saerens 2006b), others suggest that the churches remained silent so as to not attract attention and, as such, to be able facilitate clandestine rescue operations (Gevers 2006). Indeed, both Bishop Van Roey and Protestant leaders expressed their indignation about the deportations in private correspondences. Moreover, local clerics and believers seem to have played an important role in providing assistance to Jews. Again, as we saw for the Netherlands, this varied from one place to another (Saerens 1998).

Although the Nazi security apparatus suspected that religious leaders played an important role in producing resistance against the Holocaust on a local level in both countries, the Nazi's never seemed to have identified religious minorities in particular as their prime target. In security reports sent back to Berlin, no distinction between religious minorities and majorities was ever made.[9] Inspection of collaboration files suggests that minorities were slightly underrepresented among bounty hunters (Van Liempt 2013), suggesting that the Nazis penetrated majority and minority communities almost equally. Given the inclusive nature of consociationism in both countries, it is also unlikely that local government society relationships drove differential protection. How then can we explain this variation in religious rescue operations? The minority hypothesis introduced in the preceding chapter sheds light on this question.

3.6 EMPIRICAL IMPLICATIONS

In the previous chapter I outlined why religious minorities are at the same time more willing and better able to protect victims of mass persecution. While group isolation provides the capacity to stage clandestine collective action, shared dependency on pluralism creates empathy with other outsiders among elites, inculcating networks with the preference to resist genocide.

When we combine the mixed religious landscape of the Low Countries with the minority hypothesis, we end up with the following empirical implications:

1. Catholics were more likely to protect Jews in Protestant parts of the Netherlands because their members had more empathy with Jews and formed isolated hubs of commitment; taken together,

---

[9] *NIOD 020, 2122: Uitreksels Meldungen aus den Niederlanden; NIOD 077, 353–357: Meldungen aus den Niederlanden.*

this enabled them to both initiate and sustain clandestine rescue networks.

2. Mainstream Protestants were more likely to protect Jews in Catholic parts of the Netherlands because their members had more empathy with Jews and formed isolated hubs of commitment; taken together, this enabled them to both initiate and sustain clandestine rescue networks.

3. Orthodox Protestants were more likely to protect Jews throughout the Netherlands because their members had more empathy with Jews and formed isolated hubs of commitment; taken together, this enabled them to both initiate and sustain clandestine rescue networks.

4. All Protestants were more likely to protect Jews in Belgium because their members had more empathy with Jews and formed isolated hubs of commitment; taken together, this enabled them to both initiate and sustain clandestine rescue networks.

To test these implications, this book first examines subnational rescue patterns within the Netherlands before moving on to Belgium. The first three empirical implications about the Netherlands together constitute a tailored, most similar case research design that keeps constant numerous confounding variables, including any inherent characteristics of religions and cross-national variation.

Comparing the same religious groups in areas of different religious composition within one country achieves three goals. First, it provides variation in minority/majority status for both Protestants and Catholics. Second, it allows for comparisons between minority and majority groups in different geographic areas. Third, national level differences in deportation policies, Jewish populations and top–down mobilization are kept constant. The latter is unique to the Netherlands, where religious leaders, regardless of congregation, collectively and consistently protested anti-Semitism, providing all Christians with the same message about how the Holocaust went against the tenets of their faith.

The fourth empirical implication allows me to explore whether the minority hypothesis operates in a completely different national context. The Netherlands and Belgium differed fundamentally in occupation regime, Jewish population, overall levels of resistance, Nazi strength, religious pluralism, and religious protests. If the minority hypothesis operates in both contexts, we can be more certain that these powerful factors do not act as scope conditions for my theory.

3.A APPENDIX

TABLE 3.A1 *Commitment among religious communities in the Netherlands, 1900–1939: Effect relative size*

	OLS			
	(1) Churches/ believers	(2) % Votes	(3) % School attendance	(4) % Union membership
Relative size %	−0.011***	−0.101***	−0.117***	−0.582*
	(0.003)	(0.010)	(0.014)	(0.288)
Constant	0.009***	0.390***	0.160***	0.464*
	(0.001)	(0.006)	(0.010)	(0.210)
County FEs	Y	Y	Y	Y
Year FEs	N	Y	Y	Y
Counties	1024	1024	845	492
Religious communities	2883	10376	3111	1728
R^2	0.41	0.42	0.67	0.41
Relative size % (selection corrected)	−0.014	−0.088	−0.120	−1.343

Entries are unstandardized regression coefficients.
County clustered standard errors are in parentheses.
*p<0.05; **p<0.01; ***p<0.001.

TABLE 3.A2 *Commitment among religious communities in the Netherlands, 1900–1939: Effect relative size*

	OLS
	(5) Leaders/believers × 1000
Relative size %	−0.012**
	(0.005)
Constant	0.001
	(0.002)
Province FEs	Y
Controls	Y
Religious communities	804
R^2	0.06
Relative size % (selection corrected)	0.274

Entries are unstandardized regression coefficients.
Province clustered standard errors in parentheses.
*p<0.05; **p<0.01; ***p<0.001.

PART II

RELIGIOUS MINORITIES
IN THE NETHERLANDS

4

Minority Empathy 1900–1942

4.1 INTRODUCTION

Before the late 1800s, anti-Semitism, frequently religiously inspired, remained isolated and at the margins of Dutch society. Following the economic crisis of 1870, revolutionary developments across Western Europe and the infamous Dreyfus affair in France, anti-Semitism slowly gained traction in Christian circles. Catholics and Protestants alike started blaming Jews for secularization, economic windfall and political turmoil. Major international events such as the Spanish Civil War (in which some Jews chose to side with the Republicans), developments in Palestine, religious persecution in the Soviet Union and, of course, anti-Jewish legislation in Nazi Germany all made attitudes toward Jews more salient in the early twentieth century. This development touched Christian communities in particular because of the ancient Jewish–Christian schism (Griffioen and Zeller 2011).

Throughout the Netherlands, Christian magazines started blending religious, political and economic forms of anti-Semitism. According to a translation of the Jesuit magazine *Civilta Cattolica*, the Jew "invented the sectarian, Masonic, communist, socialist, international and nihilistic idea ... causing the total decay of Christian society" (Ramakers 2006). Although these types of statements were largely contained within small clerical communities, comparable sentiments started spreading slowly to more popular Catholic magazines throughout the country (Poorthuis and Salemink 2006). Still, the way in which Christian elites responded to the slow rise of anti-Semitism in Christian circles varied significantly between the north and south of the country.

This chapter presents a comparative content analysis of religious claim making about Jews in Catholic and Protestant parts of the country for the time period 1930–1939 to assess the empathy mechanism outlined in Chapter 2. If the minority hypothesis is true, religious minorities should be less anti-Semitic and show more empathy toward persecuted and stigmatized Jews than their majority counterparts. In particular, I analyze the frames and positions that majority and minority Christians as well as secular elites employed when talking about Jews. Following Habermas, I distinguish between first-order *identity-related frames* and second-order *utilitarian frames*. The former pinpoint how Jews were perceived in relation to society in general and Catholicism in particular. These perceptions in turn activate the latter type of frames, which justify different sentiments toward outsiders by emphasizing the importance of attaining specific goals. Based on the minority theory outlined in Chapter 2 and an extensive reading of secondary literature on anti-Semitism/philo-Semitism, I identify four identity and six utilitarian frames.

I code the frame, evaluation of Jews and the claimant for each public statement regarding Jews that appeared in two different news outlets using a semi-automatic content analysis. I compare a Catholic newspaper published in the Protestant north of the Netherlands with a Catholic newspaper in the Catholic south to allow for cross-group comparisons between minority and majority Catholics. Unfortunately, it was not possible to conduct a parallel analysis for Protestant newspapers as no Protestant newspapers were digitally available for the whole time period.

The main analysis underlines the importance of minority status for the formation of empathy toward Jews before the outbreak of World War II. In Protestant areas, Catholic leaders were more positive toward Jews than Catholics living in Catholic parts of the country. The content analysis suggests that this was due to the fact that minority Christians were more likely to perceive themselves as similar to Jews, highlighting the importance of pluralism when discussing anti-Semitism and Jewish rights. During these discussions, Jews were often conceived as a pious ally in the fight against secularism, deserving protection from religious persecution.

Catholic elites in Catholic Limburg, on the contrary, were more likely to represent Jews as religious deviants who needed to be assimilated. Majority Catholics frequently highlighted important differences between themselves and Jews, even going so far as to claim that Jews were given preferential treatment by international and Dutch elites. This focus on cultural contrast and assimilation occasionally kindled separate strands of religious anti-Semitism into a Christian discourse that was more hostile toward Jews. A similar pattern can be discerned when looking at Protestant sentiments toward Jews.

An additional semi-automatic content analysis of local clandestine resistance newspapers published during the war reveals that minority empathy with persecuted outsiders persisted during the German occupation. Illegal newspapers published by minority congregations were more likely to pay attention to the Jewish plight and display empathy with victims of mass persecution than those published by majorities. Taken together, these findings indicate that both before and during World War II minority elites in the Netherlands were more likely to imbue their networks with the pluralist values that led followers to resist anti-Semitism and attacks on pluralism, compared to their majority counterparts.

In the next section, I explain what is meant by a frame and introduce the aforementioned categorization. I then discuss the data sources and coding strategies. The discussion of results that follows is split into four parts. The first part compares the different ways in which minority and majority Catholics in the Netherlands evaluated Jews in public debates. The second provides a bird's-eye view of the argumentative structure underlying this difference by comparing the frames that minority and majority Catholics deployed. I then illustrate differences in framing by examining how Catholics and Protestants in both regions responded to the rise of anti-Semitic legislation and mobilization. The last section of this chapter presents a content analysis of clandestine resistance newspapers and shows that minority empathy persisted during the war.

4.2 FRAMES

In line with Entman's influential conceptualization, most scholars define a frame as a selection of perceived reality that emphasizes certain problem definitions, prognosis and causal chains over others (Goffman 1974; Snow and Benford 2000; Entman 2004) in order to justify certain moral evaluations (Ferree 2003). Frames are almost always attributed to actors, enabling researchers to see not only how the world is perceived and evaluated, but also by whom (Bail 2012). Despite this broad acceptance of what a frame is, no agreement has been reached about the best way to identify frames (Vreese 2005). On an epistemological level, little consensus exists about how abstract or specific identified frames need to be. Some scholars suggest that frames should be tailored to the actual problem and context under study (McCombs and Shaw 1993), while others argue in favor of more general categorizations that transcend a wide range of issues and contexts (Helbling 2014). Methodologically, scholars quibble about whether frames should be detected deductively or inductively. Whereas the former strategy investigates discourse with predefined and operationalized frames in mind to test already-formulated hypothesis (Vreese 2005), the latter allows frames to emerge during the course of analysis and is more descriptive in nature (Gamson 1992).

Instead of taking a strong stance in these debates, I mix and match elements of all the different approaches and tailor them to the specific analysis at hand. In this chapter I want to deploy frame analysis to assess the importance of the minority hypothesis across a wide range of different political issues that all involve one specific ethnic-religious group: Jews. I therefore use predefined general frames derived from the minority hypothesis in combination with more tailored frames established through extensive reading of secondary literature on attitudes toward Jews.

Following Habermas, I distinguish between Identity-related and Utilitarian frames. Identity-related frames highlight the inherent nature and values of the communities of which actors are part. They also demarcate different groups and specify relationships between them. Utilitarian frames justify positions based on whether that position may help an actor attain a specific goal or defend a particular interest. It is easy to see that utilitarian frames are largely shaped by identity-related frames as group boundaries, values and relationships shape the goals and interests of all actors involved. As such, utilitarian frames are activated by identity-related frames (Habermas 1993). In the next section, I focus on four identity-related frames before introducing the utilitarian frames.

4.2.1   Identity-Related Frames

The central hypothesis put forward in this book would lead us to expect that, compared to majority groups, religious minorities had different attitudes toward themselves and Jews and consequently embraced different identity-related frames when debating the role of Judaism. Religious minorities were historically dependent on pluralism to survive in the Netherlands. This should be reflected in the ways in which they perceived the ideal Dutch society that they wanted to be part off. In line with their own experiences as minorities, they should be attracted to the ideal of a pluralistic community that embraces diversity, exchange of ideas and the coexistence of various cultural and religious groups.

Inequalities in education, politics and the labor force should be reduced to foster diversity. I refer to this frame as the *pluralism frame*.

Religious majorities, conversely, should be more inclined to support a homogeneous society grounded in one dominant religion into which everyone else assimilates. Diversity should be depicted as a threat that undermines stability, while dialogue should be aimed at converting outsiders. Finally, institutions should work to benefit the dominant groups at the expense of those who refuse to adopt. I call this frame the *assimilation frame*.

Differences in religious demography are also likely to affect how religious elites present the relationship between Christians and Jews. For minority groups, other outsiders are kindred allies in defending (religious) group rights and pluralist values. This should result in empathy for and feelings of alikeness with fellow minorities. For religious majority groups, this motivation is absent, and ethnic as well as religious differences are reinforced (Zubrzycki, 2009). Therefore, I expect Catholics in Protestant areas to be more likely to identify with Jews and stress interreligous similarities, while Catholics in Catholic parts of the country should be more focused on differences with Jewish communities. I dub these frames *similarity* and *difference*, respectively. As previously explained, these four identity-related frames activate a series of utilitarian frames that will discussed now.

4.2.2 Utilitarian Frames

Because identity-related frames shape how religious elites perceived community values, relationships and boundaries, they also affect whether Jews posed a threat or opportunity for attaining specific group goals. As such, the four identity-related frames discussed earlier activate a series of utility frames that conceive of Jews as either threatening or contributing to group goals. Whereas *similarity* and *pluralism* frames are more likely to induce utilitarian frames that emphasize opportunities, *difference* and *assimilation* frames will induce threat-based frames.

Historical case studies of anti-Semitism and philo-Semitism make clear that attitudes toward Jews are and alway have been multifaceted. Evaluation of other minority groups often centers on religious, economic, political or racial cleavages. Interestingly, twentieth-century popular opinion toward Jews combined elements of all four of these dimensions (Brustein 2003). Depicting Jews as a *religious threat* is arguably the frame with the longest history in Western European thought. Religious anti-Semitism stems from Jewish refusal to give up their religion, which according to some was indicative of their association with Satan (Langmuir 1971), collective responsibility for the death of Christ (Lindemann 1997) and the perceived overrepresentation among secular movements such as socialism, liberalism, freemasonry and communism that aim to destroy religion altogether (Birnbaum 1992).

Christianity, on the other hand, also inspired a voluminous body of pro-Semitic thinking that considered Jews a *religious opportunity*. This view highlighted the notion that Christ himself was Jewish and that Judaism had formed an important stepping-stone from paganism and multitheism toward Christianity. In the twentieth century, this view was reinforced by the notion that Judaism functioned as a pious ally in the fight against the rise of godless ideologies. In addition, Jews, in line with the parable of the Good Samaritan, provided an opportunity to display Christian compassion (Carroll 2002).

While not as old as the *religious threat* frame, the portrayal of Jews as as an *economic threat* dates back to the early medieval period. Restrictions on property ownership and employment as well as widespread literacy within the Jewish community pushed Jews into urban middlemen positions that were looked down upon by Christian elites. As a result, over the centuries Jews came to be characterized as miserly manipulators of money and extremely materialist accumulators of wealth who engaged in unproductive and unethical business practices such as secondhand trade, petty commerce and moneylending (Weiss 1997). These sentiments surfaced especially in times of economic hardship as Jews were often held responsible for international financial crises (Friedlander 1997).

As we saw for religiously inspired attitudes, economic reasoning was deployed in defense of Jews as well. Economic skills, widespread literacy and financially motivated ambition could also be seen as providing an *economic opportunity*. This frame was commonly deployed when comparing the divergent economic faiths of territories populated by Jews and Muslims in Palestine. Whereas Muslims were said to squander their land, Jews turned the dessert into paradise (Gilman 1997).

At numerous points in modern history, ideologies that framed Jews as a *political threat* attracted adherents. Jews have been accused of undermining political order and taking over the world as well as founding subversive movements aimed at transforming the status quo (Bauer and Keren 2001). A combination of Jewish dispersion over the world and messianic tendencies in Judaism were often blamed for a Jewish lack of political loyalty and Jews' predisposition to join internationalist movements such as socialism and Zionism (Shatz 2004).

Other thinkers highlighted how this regime actually persecuted religious Jews and presented the sons of Abraham as an ally in a shared fight against communism (Golding 1939). This *political opportunity* frame often deployed by Christians frequently overlapped with the *religious opportunity frame*. Religious Jews and Christians together were fighting secular forces that were challenging the political order.

Finally, from the mid-nineteenth century onward, Jews were increasingly depicted as members of a separate race rather than as a religious community. Theories of scientific racism stressed that mankind could be divided into different groups based on physical characteristics. This notion challenged ideas of equality as it assumed a racial hierarchy in which some groups are superior and more deserving than others. The Jewish race, according to this line of thinking, constituted a lower strain that had only been able to maintain itself unnaturally through craftiness. As such, Jews were framed as a *racial threat* who by their mere and unnecessary existence degenerated racial pureness of societies. Unlike the religious, economic and political threat frames, this *race* frame did not have a positive, opportunity-oriented counterpart. However, the race frame met with so much resistance that *rejecting race* in and of itself became a powerful frame to defend Jews in public debates (Gilman and Katz 1991).

4.2.3 Data and Coding

To gain insight into elite attitudes toward Jews, I rely on a content analysis of news print media for the time period 1930–1939. During this decade Europe witnessed an enormous upsurge in anti-Semitism (Brustein 2003).

As other information-gathering tools such as surveys are rarely available before World War II, newspapers provide the most powerful instrument to trace elite opinions. During the 1930–1939 period, the newspaper was the most important medium though which average citizen were informed about their leaders' positions (Brustein 2003) and could make sense of the world around them (Gamson 1992). This was particularly true for the segmented societies of the Low Countries where religious and secular elites at the head of each political pillar deployed print media to control their base (Lijphart 1968; Lijphart 1981). Needless to say, newspaper data has its shortcomings when assessing elite discourse as only a small portion of all elite claims being made would be reported (Franzosi 1987). Moreover, newspapers tend to overreport the statements of influential actors. However, it is the exactly this publicly visible and prominent part of public discourse that interests us here as invisible claims by regular citizens will never affect public opinion of followers without media coverage (Koopmans and Statham 1999).

The data for this study was retrieved from *De Tijd*, the biggest Catholic news outlet published in the Protestant province of North Holland, and *Het Limburgs Dagblad*, the biggest Catholic news outlet in the Catholic province of Limburg. I used two criteria to select these newspapers. First, they had to be digitally available for the entire time period under study and, second, they had to have the broadest readership within their local pillar. The newspapers were accessed via computer portals available at the Royal Library in The Hague. Unfortunately, it was not possible to conduct a parallel analysis for Protestants as no mainstream Protestant newspapers are available for this time period.

The time period 1930–1939 is chosen for both pragmatic and substantive reasons. First, newspapers appearing before 1930 have not yet been fully digitalized, making a semi-automatic content analysis more difficult. Second, 1939 is the last year during which newspapers were not censored by the Nazis, providing a more truthful look into elite attitudes. Third, as was mentioned at the beginning of this chapter, Jewish persecutions in other parts of the world featured prominently in media debates during this time period. This provides ample opportunity to investigate how religious discourse evolved toward persecution elsewhere immediately before the Nazis started deporting Jews closer to home.

Based on a straightforward search string, I identified all newspaper articles that could potentially include information about Jewish issues.[1] Instead of taking the newspaper article as a unit of analysis, as is common in a lot of media analyses, this research focuses in on more fine-grained acts of public claim making (Koopmans and Statham 1999). This is done because one newspaper article often contains multiple actors from different political backgrounds making claims with separate and often contradicting frames.

---

[1] Joden* OR Joodsch* OR Jood* OR Israel*

An act of public claim making is defined as the public articulation of political demands, critiques, proposals and policies targeting specific collective actors (Koopmans and Statham 1999). This includes conventional forms of public claim making such as editorials, parliamentary statements, interviews, opinion articles, columns, protests and more indirect forms of claim making such as the introduction and implementation of policies. In particular, I coded all claims against, about or on behalf of Jews. For each claim I coded the claimant, issue, target of the claim, evaluation of Jews and the frame underlying this evaluation. I coded claimants as belonging to a particular group if they represented the official church, political party or organizations affiliated with either of the two.

To code the frames I made use of a series of sensitizing yes or no questions (Roggeband and Verloo 2007). Answering these questions enables me to assess whether a particular frame is present in a claim. The questions for each frame are depicted in Table 4.1. This study relied on only one coder. I used the percentage of agreement (Stemler 2001) to assess intra-coder reliability. The coder double-coded 100 claims at the beginning and end of the data collection process, a procedure that involved 600 coding decisions. The rate of perfectly matching decisions was 94 percent, almost 10 percent above the cutoff point suggested by Holsti (as described in Krippendorff 2004). A similar procedure was deployed with an outside coder to assess overall reliability of the coding scheme. This resulted in a level of agreement of 86 percent. This reasonable performance indicates that coding twelve different and partly overlapping frames is possible, but does involve complex coding decisions.

4.3 PRO-JEWISH CLAIMS

In total, I coded 1,797 claims. As a first step in the frame analysis, I compared the percentage of pro-Semitic claims by Catholics in both parts of the Netherlands. The results are visualized Figure 4.1. In line with the minority hypothesis, Catholics in minority Catholic areas were much more pro-Semitic than their majority counterparts. While close to 80 percent of all Catholic claims in majority Protestant areas were pro-Semitic, the same was true for less than 52 percent of all Catholic claims in majority Catholic parts of the country.[2] It is striking that secular claim making regarding Jews is relatively similar in both Catholic and

---

[2] Unpaired T-tests of these differences suggest that these differences are significant with P-value < 0.00001.

TABLE 4.1 *Sensitizing questions for coding of frames*

Frame	Does claim mention:
Pluralism	Group rights?
	Intergroup cooperation?
	Diversity as cultural enrichment?
Assimilation	Denial of group rights?
	Critical of diversity?
	Conversion?
Similarity	Jews as allies?
	Similarities in Jews and Christians?
Difference	Jews as opponents?
	Differences in Jews and Christians?
Religious threat	Jews as undermining Christianity?
	Jews as secular threat?
	Killing of Christ?
	Critique of Jewish religious practices?
Religious opportunity	Judaic roots Christianity?
	Critique of Jewish religious practices?
	Jews as a dam against secularism?
	Christian compassion?
	Praise Jewish religious practises?
Economic threat	Jews causing economic problems?
	Jews taking jobs?
	Malicious economic practices?
Economic opportunity	Jews strengthening the economy?
	Praise for economic practices?
Political threat	Jews as communists/socialists?
	Jews as revolutionaries?
	Jews as undermining society?
Political opportunity	Jews as a force against communism?
	Jews as good/loyal citizens?
Race	Racial distinctions?
Reject race	Rejection of racial distinctions?

Protestant areas. This indicates that the difference between minority and majority Catholics is not purely driven by general regional differences in anti-Semitism, but is instead created by the local minority position of the Catholic Church. This confirms the minority hypothesis as it shows that minorities were more likely to empathize with stigmatized outsiders than were majority groups.

Unfortunately, no major Protestant newspapers have been digitalized yet, inhibiting a parallel comparison for this religious group. However, if

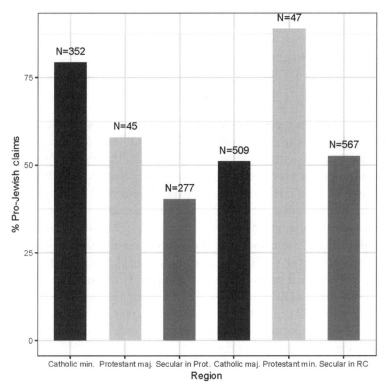

FIGURE 4.1 Pro-Jewish claims for Catholics and seculars in different parts of
the Netherlands, 1930–1939.

one codes the location of all Protestant claimants in Catholic newspapers,
it does become possible to conduct a small-scale comparison of Protestant minority and majority claims regarding Jewish issues. The outcomes
of this analysis mirror the patterning of Catholic claim making. Whereas
majority Protestants are pro-Jewish 58 percent of the time, this is the case
89 percent of the time for their minority counterparts. Hence, minorities
appear to have been more pro-Jewish compared to their religious fellows
living in majority areas. In addition, in Catholic areas of the country,
Protestants were more pro-Jewish than Catholics, whereas the reverse
was true in Protestant areas.[3] Where do these different patterns come
from? The next section investigates the different arguments religious
elites deployed to justify their positions toward Jews. In particular, it

---

[3] Needless to say, the outcomes for Protestant claims are tentative at best as the numbers
are too small for a serious statistical analysis.

will compare the identity-related and utilitarian frames discussed earlier. Are – as our theory would expect – alikeness, empathy and attachment to pluralism driving these results?

4.4 A BIRD'S-EYE VIEW OF FRAMES

Figures 4.2 and 4.3 describe the frames that made up Catholic discourse toward Jews in the Netherlands between 1930 and 1939. Each circle denotes a frame, with white circles representing frames that are positive toward Jews and gray ones representing frames that are negative in tone. The size of each circle reflects the overall influence the frame exerted on Catholic discourse.[4] Ties between frames depict the co-occurrence of frames in particular claims.[5] The frames are positioned using a statistical technique that clusters them based on overall co-occurrence (Bail 2012).

Figure 4.2 shows the framing environment of claims made by Catholic elites in Protestant parts of the Netherlands. Given the fact that more than 80 percent of all claims toward Jews were positive in tone, it is not surprising that all negative/dark frames take rather isolated positions and are smallest in size, indicating that they had only limited influence and rarely ever reinforced each other.

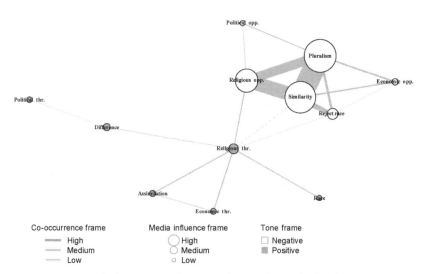

FIGURE 4.2 Catholic minority framing of Jews, the Netherlands, 1930–1939.

---

[4] Size is calculated by taking the percentage of claims deploying the frame in question.

[5] Thickness of the ties is calculated based on the percentage of all co-occurrences of frames.

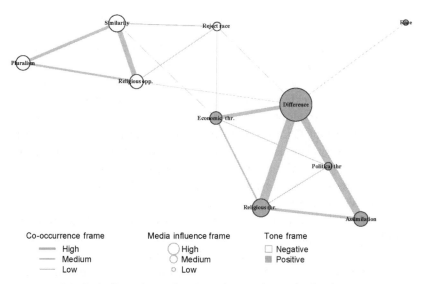

FIGURE 4.3 Catholic majority framing of Jews, the Netherlands, 1930–1939.

Only three frames obtained a prominent position in Catholic minority discourse. Together with the religious opportunity frame, the two positive identity-related frames highlighting pluralism and similarity take center stage. Together, they seemed to have activated a religious opportunity frame. The strong network ties between the three frames reveal that similarity, pluralism and religious opportunities mutually reinforced each other in public debates about Jews.

Figure 4.3 reveals that the contrast with discourse in Catholic majority areas is stark. Whereas the positive framing was dominant among Catholic minorities, the opposite is true for their majority counterparts. The religious opportunity, similarity and pluralism frames that formed the self-perpetuating center of Catholic discourse in Protestant areas remained relatively isolated in majority claim making. Instead, the negative identity-related frames emphasizing difference and assimilation exerted strong media influence. Together they created room for a religious threat frame to emerge.

Hence, whereas potential sources of anti-Semitic discourse remained isolated and disconnected among Catholic minorities due to a strong emphasis on pluralism and similarity, Catholic majorities were more likely to stress cultural differences and, to a lesser extent, assimilation. In the next section, I explore debates on anti-Jewish persecution in more detail to substantiate this bird's-eye view.

4.5 CATHOLIC ELITES AND ANTI-SEMITISM

In 1868, the biggest media outlet for Jews in the north of the Netherlands, *het Nieuw Israelitisch Weekblad*, observed the slow rise of anti-Semitism among some Catholics with which we started this chapter. Despite this rise, the Jewish weekly kept referring to Catholics as "brothers-in-arms" with whom they fought for equal religious rights (Ramakers 2006, p. 61). Indeed, important Catholic elites in the north, in part inspired by this shared fight for religious equality, stepped up to defend Jews throughout the twentieth century. On February 6, 1900, Piet Aalberse, who would later become one the most prominent leaders of the Roman Catholic party, rejected any form of economic and political anti-Semitism during a meeting of his party in Amsterdam: "Socialism is too complex of a problem to be explained as a Jewish issue ... Anti-Semitism is in itself an unintentional form of socialism" (Ramakers 2006, p. 61).

He continued his speech by arguing against the introduction of specific laws targeting Jewish practices. He pointed out that Catholics themselves had fought for equal rights, evoking a similarity frame. Rescinding these rights for Jews would be the beginning of the end: "*On commence par le Juif, on finit par le Jesuite*" (Ramakers 2006, p. 61). Together with fellow party leader Herman Schaepman and other Catholic politicians, Aalberse kept repeating his warnings against anti-Semitism throughout the early twentieth century, until conservative sentiments against Jews within the Catholic community disappeared (Poorthuis and Salemink 2006).

Similarity and pluralism frames trickled down to the Catholic mass media. The following editorial in *De Tijd* provides a good example of this: "Presenting Jews as enemies of the country. How long ago is it that anti-Catholic Holland, misled by similar propaganda, accepted the notion that a good Catholic could never be a good Dutch man?"[6] Instead of portraying minorities as enemies of the state, *De Tijd* followed its political leaders and argued in favor of mutual recognition of group rights: "Protestants, Israelites, Socialists are respected as long as they are respectful to others."[7]

The same similarity and pluralism frames also surfaced in response to Jewish persecutions in the Soviet Union and Nazi Germany. In 1938, *De Tijd* quotes Roman Catholic parliament member Laurentius Deckers who suggested that anti-Semitic persecution by the Nazis has the

---

[6] *Dagblad De Tijd 7/11/1937.*
[7] *Dagblad De Tijd 4/7/1931.*

special interest of Catholics as "they themselves know what it is like to be persecuted."[8] Again, claims by Catholics evoked their own history of persecution and the notion that they would be next in line if they were not to protest anti-Semitic legislation. This latter logic is nicely illustrated by the following 1933 editorial in *De Tijd*, which repudiates an endorsement of Jewish persecutions by the Nazis in a different Catholic media outlet: "If the Hitlerians seize power here as well, the Catholics, knowing what has happened in Munich, will regret participating in creating an anti-Jewish climate."[9] Elsewhere the same newspaper writes: "One of the things we need to do is pray for those who suffer from the persecutions. It is definitely not unthinkable that what is happening in neighboring Germany will also befall the Catholics."[10] In general, anti-Jewish violence in Germany was cited as an important reason to defend the Dutch model of pluralism, as this editorial in *De Tijd* from around the same period indicates: "Much like Catholics, Protestants, liberals socialists etcetera openly and with restraint tell each other the truth and live with each other in peace, that is how it should be with Jews as well. The way it is going right now is really dumb and embarrassing ... What is happening in Germany should be a warning that we should never let it come so far."[11]

Majority Catholics often emphasized differences between Jews and Christians when talking about religious persecutions abroad. Instead of unequivocally rejecting Nazi violence against Jews, editorials in the *Het Limburgs Dagblad*, repeatedly attacked socialists, liberals and others for expressing outrage about anti-Jewish legislation while not standing up for Roman Catholics undergoing a similar fate. In July 1933, the newspaper wrote: "When the Jews were persecuted in Germany, the whole world was outraged. But now. When it happens to Catholics? Silence. The international press is silent. Is it not sad? We Catholics can only rely on ourselves."[12] In 1936, *Het Limburgs Dagblad* went even further by stating that the brutal attacks on Catholics in Germany were much worse and more damaging to the German image than the relatively minor persecutions of Jews.[13] The Catholic newspaper further downplayed the

---

[8] *Dagblad De Tijd 3/12/1938.*
[9] *Dagblad De Tijd 14/6/1933.*
[10] *Dagblad De Tijd 14/11/1938.*
[11] *Dagblad De Tijd 31/8/1933.*
[12] *Dagblad Het Limburgs Dagblad 6/7/1933.*
[13] *Dagblad Het Limburgs Dagblad 17/6/1936.*

severity of anti-Jewish attacks in Germany, citing busy Jewish shops in Germany as evidence that Jews were not hurting at all (Cammaert 1994).

Although some majority Catholics recognized the importance of religious freedom, others struck a different tone.[14] Newspaper articles frequently drew an explicit link between the influx of Jews and moral decay (Cammaert 1994). Several Catholic elites in the south therefore insisted that Jews give up their distinct position completely and instead assimilated into southern culture. This sentiment expressed itself most clearly in claims about conversion. Catholic professors, priests and journalists alike contended that "Jews did not understand God's word"[15] and "had to be brought back from the synagogue to the mother church"[16] as the Roman Catholic Church was "the real completed Judaic church."[17] Meanwhile bishops organized prayers dedicated to conversion[18] and celebrated every notable conversion in public ceremonies.[19]

A strong Catholic response against domestic anti-Semitism also did not emerge in the south of the country.[20] Neither political nor clerical elites seemed to have taken an open stance against the rise of local anti-Jewish sentiments. As a result, numerous historians have observed that Catholic anti-Semitism became quite prevalent in the southern provinces before the German invasion (Vellenga 1975; Weustink 1985; Hilbrink 1989; Michman, Beem and Michman 1999; Blom and Cahen 2002).[21] Radical Catholic clerics such as Wouter Lutkie, a priest from the Catholic city of Den Bosch and admirer of Mussolini, espoused an intolerant and anti-pluralistic form of Catholicism in local newspapers and magazines, creating an infrastructure for anti-Semitic organizations to build on (Poorthuis and Salemink 2006). The political party Zwart Front, which

---

[14] Interestingly, the majority claim most clearly expressing this sentiment was only picked up by minority newspaper *De Tijd* (*Dagblad De Tijd 4/7/1931*).

[15] *Dagblad Het Limburgs Dagblad 23/12/1933.*

[16] *Dagblad Het Limburgs Dagblad 27/10/1932.*

[17] *Dagblad Het Limburgs Dagblad 1/10/1932.*

[18] *Dagblad Het Limburgs Dagblad 1/8/1938.*

[19] *Dagblad Het Limburgs Dagblad 24/9/1930.*

[20] Roman Catholic politicians started attacking the Dutch National Socialist Movement after 1935 when the latter emerged as a electoral threat to the Roman Catholic party RKSP. Pro-Semitism, however, did not seem to play a prominent role in these attacks (Vellenga 1975).

[21] Interestingly, in line with this pattern, although the Catholic episcopacy collectively protested anti-Jewish legislation before and during the war, the Catholic bishop of the completely Catholic region Noord-Brabant was also the most reluctant to protest (Stokman 1945).

found its strongest supporters in the Catholic cities of Nijmegen en Breda, is a case in point. Its leader Arnold Meijer, a former associate of Lutkie, claimed that Catholicism had always recognized the threat that Jews posed. Jews could never be part of the nation, played a monstrous role in the socialist movement and, according to Meijer, should be excluded from government jobs. He considered Zwart Front "a tool in the hands of god to save the people from their deepest anguish produced by Judaic cinema industry which threatened the family by propagating extramarital affairs" (Zondergeld 1986).[22] At the onset of the German occupation, National Socialist propagandists from Germany also argued that Roman Catholicism historically had a more exclusive and nationalist character in the southern provinces, something that could be exploited for inducing local Nazi support.[23]

4.6 PROTESTANT ELITES AND ANTI-SEMITISM

A considerable number of mainstream Protestants in the north were attracted to similar blends of exclusive nationalism and Christianity (Van Roon 1990), including some influential Dutch Reformed reverends (Tijssen 2009). Dutch Reformed theologian Wilhelm Theodor Boissevain is probably the most infamous representative of this group. An influential advisor to leaders of the Dutch Nationalist Socialist Party, Boissevain rejected pluralism and religious group rights, both of which he considered a threat to unity of the Christian nation. Instead he believed in a homogenous public community that found its origin in a shared faith, – "blood and soil" – and had to be protected from the materialist and bolshevik threats that the sectarian church of Israel posed (Tijssen 2009, p. 127).

Although most Protestants were not as extreme as Boissevain, who soon became known as the "Nazi reverend," mild forms of religious and political anti-Semitism definitely existed among the Dutch Reformed in the north. Several prominent members in the more conservative wing of the church considered Jews to be a communist force that was part of a separate nation (Bosma 2015). In a similar vein, Dutch Reformed magazines frequently depicted Jews as Christ killers or radical socialists

---

[22] Very similar blends of Catholicism and anti-Semitism were to be found in the Belgian Verdinaso movement, which had around 500 members in the southern parts of the Netherlands (Joosten 1964).

[23] *Archives Stokman collection, Katholiek Documentatie Centrum Nijmegen (Stokman 939).*

who threatened Christian values.[24] These sentiments also came to the surface during debates on anti-Jewish persecutions in Germany and the Soviet Union. Protestant frontmen in the Dutch parliament denounced the violence in general, but also argued that none of this would have happened if the Jews had just listened to God (Van Klinken 2001).[25] Others accused socialist politicians of smuggling in too many Jewish allies under the guise of humanitarian assistance,[26] considered Jews to be complacent and responsible for their own fate[27] and complained that refugees were taking over every piece of land and industry at the expense of Christian citizens (Bosma 2015).

It is striking and in support of the empathy mechanism that the first steps toward humanitarian help for Jews within the Protestant community came from minority congregations. Quakers, Arminians, Anabaptists, Evangelicals, mainstream Protestants in Catholic areas and, most importantly, Orthodox Protestants initiated humanitarian assistance movements for Jews and encouraged others within the mainstream Protestant community to do the same, either by pointing out how Nazi policies went against the pluralistic, tolerant and democratic tenets of Dutch society or by setting up inter-confessional networks (Van Roon 1990).[28] In line with this, Orthodox Protestants were also among the first to set up an organizational infrastructure to provide assistance to Jewish refugees in Catholic Maastricht, the capital of Limburg located near the German border (Cammaert 1994).[29]

The role of Orthodox Protestant communities is particularly noteworthy in light of the minority hypothesis. Historically, these more dogmatic groups had been the most hostile toward Jews. In the nineteenth century, founding father Abraham Kuyper recognized that aggressive forms of anti-Semitism were incompatible with Protestant morality, but also argued in favor of rescinding citizenship rights for Jews, fearing the church of Israel as a skillful adversary in a spiritual fight for the soul (Klinken 1996). Although Kuyper's ideas remained influential in the late 1930s they were countered by an alternative narrative. Influenced by

---

[24] *Tijdschrift De Klok 8/9/39. Tijdschrift De Klok 10/6/38.*

[25] *Dagblad De Tijd 3/4/1930.*

[26] *Dagblad De Tijd 3/10/1939.*

[27] *Tijdschrift De Klok 4/5/34.*

[28] It is telling that even the early pro-Jewish activists mentioned in commemoration books of the Dutch Reformed Church tend to be affiliated with minority congregations (Aukes 1956).

[29] *Dagblad De Tijd 23/12/1930.*

religious persecutions throughout Europe, Orthodox Protestant thinkers, often engaged in missionary activities, depicted Jews as pitied victims whose political, economic and cultural influence had been overestimated (Van Roon 1990). As a result, more Orthodox elites started recognizing similarities between their own fate and that of the persecuted Jews. Reverend Wisse of Arnhem for instance crowned the Netherlands the "Israel of the West," drawing a parallel between the Jewish struggle against Egypt and the Calvinist battle for freedom and democracy against the Catholic king of Spain (Bosma 2015, p. 88). More and more, the strong emphasis on the Old Testament that existed within Orthodox factions became appropriated for framing Jews and Orthodox as similar – after all, both communities were God's chosen people (Moore 2010). On a local level, ministers and reverends started highlighting the shared faith of Calvinists and Jews, as both had historically formed persecuted and isolated communities (Wijbenga 1995).

In line with the empathy mechanism, Protestant sentiments toward Jews reveal that minorities are more likely to identify and sympathize with persecuted outsiders as they recognize that what happens to the other can easily befall themselves. Moreover, the evolution of Jewish framing indicates that minority mechanisms are most likely to get activated when pluralism is under threat. It was when the Nazi's started attacking pluralism that enhanced perspective taking activated arousal and sympathy for Jews among fellow minorities.

4.7 RESISTANCE NEWSPAPERS

To assess whether prewar differences in minority empathy with Jews carried over into the first years of the occupation, I conduct a content analysis of Dutch resistance newspapers. Immediately after the German invasion, small groups of individuals started to produce clandestine periodicals in order to escape Nazi censorship. By secretly writing and distributing these magazines and newspapers, resistance workers hoped to boost morale, counterbalance German propaganda, provide information about military developments and eventually instigate revolt (Winkel and de Vries 1989).

Over 900 different outlets produced 284,593 different issues. Small embryonic networks, rooted in local religious or political associations, emerged to illegally write, print and disseminate all these newspapers among their neighbors. To a large extent, clandestine periodicals became the mouthpiece of the congregations and communities in which they were embedded, informing people in their immediate surroundings about specific frustrations with the Nazi regime (Winkel and de Vries 1989).

The Dutch Institute of War Documentation, in collaboration with the Royal Dutch Library, has systematically collected and digitalized copies of all resistance newspapers that survived the war.[30] For each of these newspapers, I coded whether the newspaper was published by a Catholic, Protestant or secular resistance group and in which part of the country it was distributed.[31] After establishing the religious denomination of a resistance newspaper, I deployed an automatic content analysis to identify the proportion of its issues that reported on Jewish persecution.[32] In order to ascertain whether attention to Jewish issues during World War II by resistance newspapers indeed reflected empathy, I coded all articles manually, marking all pro-Semitic statements.

Matching pro-Semitic claims with newspapers of different religions enables me to examine the differences in empathy between religious minority and majority newspapers. This resulted in a data base of 1,076 Dutch resistance newspapers. Whether newspapers paid attention to the fate of Jews gives a strong indication of its overall empathy. Figure 4.4 presents the percentage of resistance newspapers that covered Jewish persecutions per religious group. In line with the minority hypothesis, Catholic minority newspapers were more likely than their majority counterparts to pay attention to the misery of the Jews. While 82 percent of all Catholic minority newspapers reported on Jewish persecutions, the same was true for less than 60 percent of Catholic majority newspapers. The

---

[30] Already in 1943 did Nicolaas Posthumus start collecting illegal newspapers. After the war his work was continued by the previously mentioned Dutch Institute of War Documentation (NIOD), a research consortium he himself helped found. Through a radio campaign Dutch citizens were encouraged to submit copies of their newspapers to the NIOD. These newspapers can be accessed at www.delpher.nl/nl/kranten.

[31] This was done based on Winkel and de Vries (Winkel and de Vries 1989). Unfortunately, it was not possible to distinguish between mainstream Protestant and Orthodox Protestant resistance organizations. I was therefore forced to treat all Protestant newspapers as part of the mainstream church. This could result in an overestimation of Protestant attention to Jews, as Orthodox organizations, which formed minorities everywhere, are marked as majority Protestants. However, this bias makes finding a difference between minority and majority newspapers less likely, even if it actually exists. As the bias is stacked against finding support for the minority hypothesis, we can be more confident the empathy mechanism holds if we indeed find that minorities are more likely to pay attention to the Jewish plight.

[32] I deployed the same search string as used in this chapter to analyze prewar discourse: Joden* OR Joodsch* OR Jood* OR Israel*

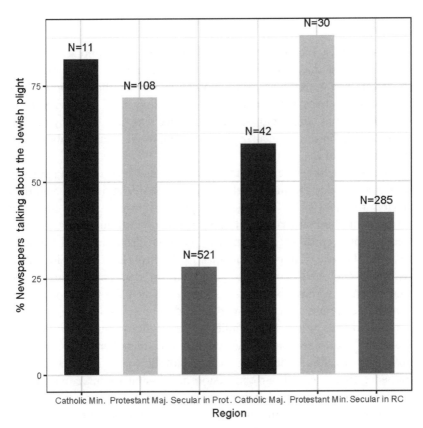

FIGURE 4.4 Percentage of resistance newspapers reporting on the Jewish plight by religion, 1940–1945.

story flips when we look at Protestant resistance newspapers. While 88 percent of all Protestant resistance newspapers payed attention to Jewish persecutions in Catholic areas, only 72 percent did so in parts of the country where Protestants formed a majority.[33]

In sum, the analysis of resistance newspapers reveals that minority congregations were more likely to produce clandestine newspapers that paid attention to the Jewish plight, indicating that the higher prewar levels of empathy embraced by minorities persisted during the German occupation.

[33] Unpaired t-tests of these differences suggest that these differences are significant with P-values < 0.0001.

4.8 CONCLUSION

In this chapter I compared attitudes toward Jews among Christian minorities and majorities in the Netherlands before the deportations started. In line with the minority hypothesis, we saw that Catholic elites in Protestant areas were more pro-Semitic than their counterparts in Catholic regions. Importantly, this difference was not driven by general regional differences, as secular claim making looked remarkably similar in both parts of the country.

The comparison reveals that attitudes toward Jews evolved similarly until the turn of the nineteenth century, when religious anti-Semitism started to fuse with economic and political forms of anti-Semitism throughout the Netherlands. The response of Catholic elites to these trends, however, differed enormously between Protestant and Catholic regions. Whereas Catholic minorities in the Protestant north identified with Jews and openly combatted anti-Semitism, their counterparts in the south seemed to have been less responsive. It was the local position of Christian communities that created these differences: Catholic minorities considered Jews to be religious allies in their fight for minority rights and the battle against secularism. Although pluralism and empathy were not absent from Catholic discourse in the Catholic south, they exerted less influence than ideas about conversion and assimilation. A remarkably similar patterns emerged for Protestants. A semi-automatic content analysis of clandestine resistance newspapers indicates that minority empathy persisted after the Wehrmacht invaded the country.

Now that we have established that minority elites in the Netherlands were indeed more pro-Semitic than leaders of majority groups, the question becomes whether they were also able to mobilize their followers to act upon these norms. The next chapter will use a unique geo-referenced database of Jewish victimization to investigate this.

5

Religious Minorities and Evasion in the Netherlands

5.1 INTRODUCTION

Let us start this chapter by briefly returning to the puzzle with which I started this research endeavor. I mentioned in the Introduction that in Almelo a Catholic rescue operation was able to shelter 42 percent of all Jews living around the Sint Gregorius church from the Nazis, while Catholic rescue attempts were thwarted early on in the neighboring Borne, five kilometers to the east. The central thesis of this book is that religious minorities are more likely to impede campaigns of mass violence.

Figure 5.1 reveals that the minority theory offers significant leverage in explaining the variation between Almelo and Borne. Because Almelo was located on the predominantly Protestant side of the religious fault line that cut through the Netherlands, Jews happened to live in proximity to a Catholic minority community that proved able to setup and sustain an underground movement coordinated by Chaplains Bodde and Middelkoop (Weustink 1985), and Catholic boy scout leaders.[1] Borne, however, was overwhelmingly Catholic. As a result, the leaders of nearby majority churches lacked either empathy or the isolated hubs of commitment required for prolonged clandestine resistance to the Nazis. Instead, a Dutch Reformed minister[2] and Mennonite community[3] living in other parts of town stepped up to provide assistance to threatened Jewish neighbors. In Almelo, on the other hand, it was majority Protestants

---

[1] *SVB-file 47, DOCDIRECT, Winschoten.*
[2] *SVB-file 51, DOCDIRECT, Winschoten.*
[3] *Yad Vashem file H. Dijkhuis in Michman et al.*

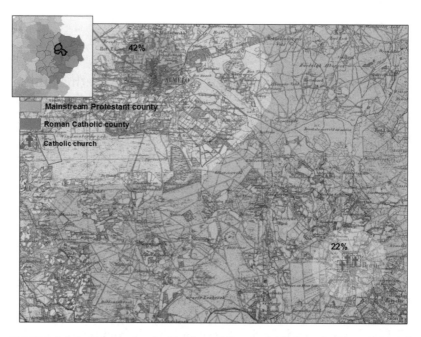

FIGURE 5.1 Jewish evasion in Almelo and Borne. A black-and-white version of this figure will appear in some formats. For the colour version, please refer to the plate section.

who were less successful in providing assistance to Jews. De Geus, a Protestant minister who had just moved to Almelo from the Catholic south, saw his early attempts to mobilize his parish end in arrests by the Sicherheitspolizei (Hovingh 2015).

Needless to say, we cannot extrapolate from one paired comparison. In this chapter, I therefore exploit a unique microlevel database of Jewish victimization to assess whether Jews living close to minority enclaves were more likely to evade deportation throughout the country. Instead of relying on one comparison between a small number of village churches, I will analyze thousands of them in one statistical analysis. By pairing German registrations of Jews with commemoration books and camp lists, I am able to map where Jews lived and whether they evaded deportation or not. This data is combined with geocoded information on Catholic and Protestant communities throughout the country. Auto-logistic models of 93 percent of all Dutch Jews show a strong and positive correlation between the presence of minority churches and evasion. Whereas proximity to Catholic Churches increased evasion by 60 percent in Protestant parts of the Netherlands, proximity to Protestant communities increased evasion by more than 20 percent in Catholic areas.

Using distance from Delft, the working terrain of the first vicar to the Catholic mission in the Protestant northern Netherlands, as an instrument for Catholicism enables me to isolate the effect of minority churches from preexisting levels of tolerance for subsets of cases. County-level fixed effects and spatial lags are deployed to reduce local-level omitted variable bias.

Although this data does not directly measure rescue operations, it has a big advantage over more commonly deployed postwar testimonies of rescuers and survivors in evaluating the minority argument. People are more likely to remember striking characteristics of others (Kahneman 2011). Followers of less common denominations will therefore be more memorable than those who belonged to dominant congregations. Consequently, minorities are probably overrepresented in postwar testimonies due to cognitive biases. Using actual survival data allows us to objectively assess whether minority mobilization played a role in protecting victims of the Holocaust.

The next section will discuss how the German registration lists are deployed to retrieve exact residential information for over 120,000 Jews. Following that, I will describe how information on registered Jews is paired with commemoration books to obtain individual-level data on evasion. Geocoded data on church communities is discussed in Section 5.3. Sections 5.4 and 5.5 detail the chosen statistical techniques. Baseline results are presented in Section 5.4, while the instrumental variable is analyzed in Section 5.5. In the conclusion, I briefly highlight the limitations of the chosen approach.

5.2 REGISTRATIONS

In order to systematically test the hypotheses outlined in Chapter 2, I have constructed an individual-level dataset of Jews based on German registration lists (Croes and Tammes 2004). At the end of 1941, the German authorities forced local governments to collect individual-level data on all Jews living in their counties. These lists recorded religion, address, birth date and country of birth for all Jews.

The SIPO-SD in collaboration with local governments created 496 lists, one for each county, on which they listed information of 140,000 Jews.[4] In July 1942, shortly before the deportations started, the

---

[4] Citizens were considered full Jews if at least three grand parents were members of the Jewish faith. Citizens with two Jewish grandparents were only considered Jewish if they themselves or their spouses were members of the Jewish faith.

registration lists were updated. This was done to obtain information on 9,000 Jews living in coastal regions, Noord-Holland and Utrecht that were recently evacuated to Amsterdam as part of German residential concentration efforts (Presser 1965). Copies of these lists are available at the NIOD, the Jewish History Museum, local archives, the Central Bureau for Genealogy and Yad Vashem. As fewer than 100 Jews refused to register (De Jong 1969–1991), I can be confident that registration lists provided a complete picture of the Jewish population right before the deportations.

I have been able to digitalize the information of 128,921 Jews living in 464 counties. It is important to emphasize that, in order to create this database, I have built on the efforts of other scholars. Croes, Tammes (Croes and Tammes 2004; Tammes 2011) and Van Rens (Van Rens 2013) together had already digitalized names and birth dates of 107,000 Jews living in 288 counties. Information of around 1,647 Jews from thirty-two counties is missing in the final dataset.

As we saw in Chapter 3, Dutch Jews lived throughout the country (see Figure 3.2) in regions of different religious composition due to their long history in the Netherlands, creating sufficient variation on the dependent variable. Since we are interested in how rescue organizations shaped survival chances, two groups of Jews are disregarded in the analysis because they were either never at risk of deportation or evaded deportation through legal means. First, I took out 1,647 Jews who died a natural death or committed suicide before July 1942. Data on cause of death is obtained from the Dutch Digital Monument, described later. Second, I identified Jews who were able to evade deportation legally by appealing their Jewish identity. This information was obtained from lists compiled by the Referat Innere Verwaltung that included all Jews who were exempted from deportation (De Jong 1969–1991).

A third group was taken out mostly for pragmatic reasons. For most counties, 1942 lists were available. For Amsterdam, however, this was not the case and I had to rely on a 1941 list instead. By taking this list, however, I automatically excluded information on Jews who were evacuated to Amsterdam from other parts of the country. Disregarding this group, however, also makes sense substantively. Since this group was technically already inside the bureaucratic system of the occupiers, the chances that its members would be able to make use of rescue networks in a region in which they had just arrived was pretty slim.[5]

---

[5] Additional analyses were done excluding Jews living in the Amsterdam area. I also estimated models including Jews who evaded legally or died a natural death. All results

The addresses recorded in the registration lists were used to retrieve fine-grained coordinates of residential location for all Jews in the dataset. As a first step, addresses were automatically geocoded using Google's Geocoding API. Addresses for which no precise coordinates were returned were then coded manually. This was done by consulting information compiled by the Jewish History Museum on address names that were changed after the war. For 3,578 Jews it was not possible to identify exact coordinates because address information was missing or only neighborhood codes were provided. As a result, the presented analysis was based on 122,694 Jews who lived in 439 counties. In an additional analysis I randomly assigned coordinates within counties for these 3,578 cases. Results were almost identical to the ones presented later.

5.3 COMMEMORATION BOOKS AND RETURN LISTS

In order to determine which of the registered Jews were able to evade deportation, I matched the digital registration lists against the Dutch Digital Monument (DDD) and lists of Jews returned from camps after the liberation. The DDD is an online portal maintained by the Jewish History Museum that commemorates all Jews who died during the war. It is constructed out of a wide array of sources: commemoration books, the Netherlands Red Cross, registers from transit camps Vught, Westerbork and Amersfoort, obituaries from Jewish weeklies and honor rolls of resistance fighters. Figure 5.4 shows an example of an online profile. As one can see, the DDD lists name, date of birth and place of death. Based on this information, I selected all Jews who died inside camps and marked them as deported. In addition, I matched the 122,214 names against lists of 5,400 Jews who were found in camps alive after the liberation. These people survived the war so were not recorded in the DDD, but did get deported so need to be coded as such.

All the files were linked using the following matching procedure. For each case I created three identification strings that, taken together, uniquely identified all Jews on the lists. The first two strings contained the first and last name while the third string contained the date of birth.[6]

---

were consistent with the ones presented later. However, in models without the Amsterdam area, the effect of Orthodox Protestant minorities became insignificant using some buffers. This is in line with historical evidence that highlights the importance of Orthodox rescue for the Amsterdam region (Flim 1998).

[6] For 43,788 cases collected by Tammes and Croes only the first two letters of first and last name were digitalized.

Simply matching all the files based on these strings would be a bad idea. Due to spelling errors, coding mistakes, formatting variation, and missing information this would result in an vast number of mismatches. Therefore, I made use of a two-stage matching procedure that combined statistical and manual techniques. For the first part I used a statistical matching procedure developed by Blasnik (2010). When pairing cases, this procedure calculates an overlap percentage for all pairs of observations. This percentage was used to identify potential matches that needed to be inspected manually. To do this, I first had to determine what overlap percentages indicate potential matches and which ones do not. I did this by coding 1,500 matches manually and comparing the number of manual matches per overlap score.

This procedure suggests that cases with an overlap score below sixty did not include any actual matches (see Figure 5.2). Based on this, I decided to manually inspect all pairs that had an overlap score above 60 percent. After matching all cases, the overall evasion rate was 28 percent; this is close to the overall estimate of 26 percent for the Netherlands provided by Hirschfeld (1991). To make sure that our matching procedure did not introduce any regional bias, I compared it with completely manually matched data for the 407 Jews living in the province of Limburg provided by historian Van Rens (2013). Overall, individual mistakes are rare. Of the 407 Jews, six were incorrectly identified as deported, and for two cases the opposite mistake was made. Mismatches were due to incomplete information because civil servants forgot to provide information on dates of birth. The correlation between county-level evasion

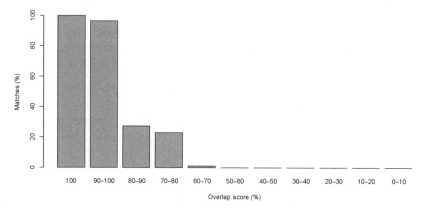

FIGURE 5.2 Percentage of matches per overlap score.

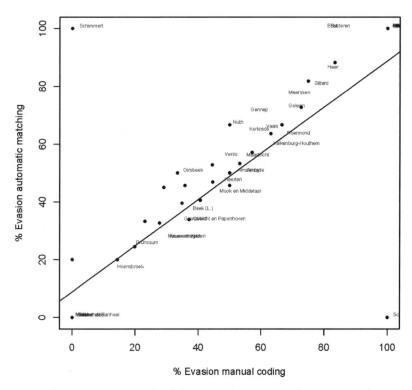

FIGURE 5.3 County-level deportation rates according to manual
and automatic matching.

rates, graphed in Figure 5.3, was high (r=0.95), indicating regional bias
is limited.

5.4 MEASURING MINORITY CHURCHES

To investigate whether a relationship between evasion and proximity to
minority churches exists, I pair this data with a geo-referenced database
of all Christian churches in 1942, the year the major deportations started.
Address information for churches is retrieved from the Dutch Inventory
for Church Buildings compiled by the late Sonneveld and maintained
by the Free Universty in Amsterdam (IKGN 2011). These two geo-
referenced databases are exploited to assess whether Jews living close to
minority churches were better able to evade deportation. The assumption
underlying this operationalization is that the extent to which networks of
religious groups intersect increases with geographic proximity. Research

has pointed out that prewar friendships, acquaintanceships and other face-to-face contacts were crucial to bring Jews into contact with rescue networks (Varese and Yaish 2000). In Heerlen, Reverend Pontier actually approached Jews in his neighborhood himself and encouraged them to go underground (Flim 1997). Others suggest that Jews often took the first step in contacting nearby rescuers (Varese and Yaish 2000). Regardless of who took the initiative, the bridges between rescuers and rescued often clustered in space. A coding of 2,798 postwar testimonies also suggested that 89 percent of all Jews who found shelter mentioned local social contacts. Sixty-three percent of 11,421 Jews for which information of hiding is available found shelter in the region where they were living legally in the first year of the war. Needless to say, a much larger percentage made use of local networks to illegally migrate within and between regions.

I assume that Jews live close to a minority group when a church in their immediate environment belongs to a minority congregation. To capture the spatial clustering of religious groups, I draw a circular buffer area around each Jewish individual. In Figure 5.4 this is illustrated for Protestant county Vriezenveen and Catholic county Tubbergen, which were just like Almelo and Borne, located alongside the frontline of Rome and Reformation. Within this buffer I count the number of churches for each denomination. Based on these counts I create two religious proximity measures: a) the proportion of Catholic (i.e., non-Protestant) churches to tap the relative strength of Catholic versus Protestant groups in the immediate environment and the proportion of church buildings that belong to Orthodox Protestant communities to assess the strength of other minority groups. The Catholic proximity measure is interacted with the overall proportion of all Christians in the region that belongs to the Roman Catholic Church and not to any of the Protestant churches. Region is defined as the county in which a Jew lives and all adjacent counties. This is done to do justice to the fact that churches falling within a buffer are sometimes located in a neighboring county.[7] Since all churches and Christians in the Netherlands are either Protestant or Catholic, the Catholic proximity measure is exactly the inverse of the Protestant proximity measure, and Catholic strength is exactly the inverse of Protestant strength. Hence, if the minority theory holds, one would expect Catholic proximity

---

[7] In a supplemental analysis I also interacted the Catholic proximity measure with the proportion of the population that belongs to the Catholic Church and the proportion of the population that belongs to any of the Protestant churches. Results are very similar, but asymmetric due to the presence of seculars and Jews.

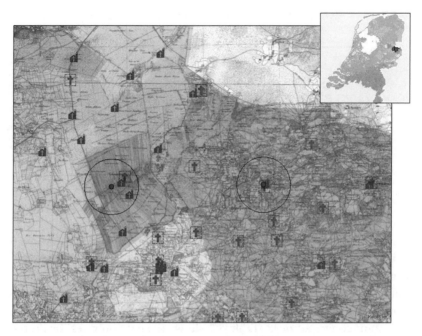

FIGURE 5.4 Example buffer: Vriezenveen and Tubbergen. A black-and-white version of this figure will appear in some formats. For the colour version, please refer to the plate section.

(non-Protestant proximity) to have a positive effect on evasion in Protestant parts of the country and a negative effect in regions dominated by Catholics. In addition, one would expect a direct and positive correlation between the presence of Orthodox Protestant churches and survival regardless of context since they form minorities everywhere. Data on religious membership is obtained from the 1930 census (CBS 1931).

Since the threshold for what constitutes proximity is not obvious, I conduct different analyses in which I vary the radius of the buffer from 10 minutes (1 km) to 30 minutes (3 km) walking distance. This lower threshold is chosen because the number of Jews not living close to a single Christian church increases enormously when we use a one kilometer radius (3,064 versus 877 for a 1.25 km threshold).[8] If we assume that social networks decline with distance, we would expect the effect of Catholic proximity on evasion to become weaker with distance.

---

[8] When the catchment area of the buffer does not include any churches, the measure gets the same value as when using a two kilometer buffer.

TABLE 5.1 *Evasion rates in minority and majority*
neighborhoods (2-km buffer)

	County	
Neighborhood	Catholic	Protestant
Catholic	29%	42%
Protestant	42%	25%

Catholic counties > 50% population Catholic.
Catholic neighborhoods > 60% church buildings Catholic.
Protestant neighborhoods < 40% church buildings Catholic.

5.5 COMPARING EVASION

As a first cut at the data, I divided the Netherlands in majority Protestant and majority Catholic counties. Within these counties, I then marked neighborhoods as Catholic if more than 60 percent of all the church buildings belonged to Catholic parishes and marked neighborhoods as Protestant if more than 60 percent of all church buildings belonged to Protestant congregations.[9] Table 5.1 shows the evasion rates for Protestant and Catholic neighborhoods in both parts of the Netherlands. As we can see, 42 percent of Jews living in minority neighborhoods were able to evade deportation, while around 25 percent evaded deportation in majority neighborhoods.

This descriptive analysis indeed suggests that Jews living near minority communities had more opportunities to escape Nazi roundups. However, it would be naive to interpret this as conclusive evidence for the minority thesis. Investigating the effect of minority churches on evasion requires evaluation of a counterfactual claim: would the possibility to evade have been lower if no minority church was present? In observational settings these types of claims are hard to assess because regions are likely to vary along multiple other dimensions related to both evasion and the clustering of religious minorities. In order to reduce this problem as much as possible, I will rely on logistic regressions with a) county-level FEs, b) geocoded controls and c) exogenous variation in Catholicism to assess the robustness of the overall results.

First, scholars have pointed out that county characteristics resulted in the geographical clusters of evasion (Croes and Tammes 2004). To make sure that this is not driving the results, FEs for counties are included in

---

[9] For these calculations, I made use of the two-kilometer buffers.

the analysis. This means that survival chances of Jews living in the same county and not Jews living in completely different part of the Netherlands are being compared. The fine-grained nature of this comparison makes it less likely that unobserved variables are driving the results.

In addition, I include three sets of control variables. First, I include counts of the number of Jews and churches in the corresponding buffers to make sure I am not comparing regions that are completely different in terms of ethnic composition and demography. The second set deals with regional differences in repressive capacity. It is plausible that remote areas in which divergent congregations flourished were harder to reach for the repressive apparatus of the Nazis. I deal with this by controlling for the distance to the nearest SIPO-SD office and city center. The third set of controls tap social integration. Previous research suggests that social integration affected evasion both positively and negatively (Moore 2010; Finkel 2017). It is also likely that integration was impacted by the religious environment as we would expect divergent groups to be more inward looking and less interested in outsiders. Four measures of social integration are included in the analysis: whether a Jew 1) lived near a synagogue (using varying circular buffers), 2) converted to Christianity, 3) had Dutch citizenship and 4) was married to a gentile. Finally, I also exploit exogenous variation in Catholicism due to missionary activities in the seventeenth century. The logic underlying this procedure will be discussed in more detail in Section 5.7.

For the main analysis, I distinguish five different types of counties: counties that are dominated by Catholics (>80% Catholic), majority Catholic (between 80% and 60% Catholic), religiously mixed (between 40% and 60% Catholic), majority Protestant (between 80% and 60% Protestant) and dominated by Protestants (>80% Protestants).

For each of these regions I then determined the effect of increasing Catholic proximity from its minimum to its maximum value while controlling for between-county heterogeneity and the geocoded measures described earlier. If the minority thesis is correct, we would expect proximity to Catholic Churches to have a positive effect on evasion in the first two regions, no effect on evasion in the religiously mixed region and negative effects on evasion in the last two regions.[10]

The regions correspond with the geographic areas for which more detailed case studies will be presented in the next two chapters. While the

---

[10] This is the case because in these latter two regions Jews would want to live close to Protestant churches.

Noord-Brabant and Limburg are dominantly Catholic, the northeast of Twente is majority Catholic, the southwest of Twente is majority Protestant and Groningen and Friesland are dominated by Protestantism. As a result, the different effects for each region can be explicitly linked to the qualitative material to be found later in the book.

Results of logistic regression analysis with county-level FEs, controls and clustered standard errors are visualized in Figures 5.5–5.7.[11] The first two figures plot the effect of moving the Catholic proximity measure from its minimum to its maximum value for varying levels of Roman Catholic strength in the region. Figure 5.5 shows that Catholic Church proximity increases evasion by almost 60 percent in largely Protestant counties when using a two-kilometer buffer. In Protestant Holland, Jews living in Protestant neighborhoods would have a 20 percent chance to evade deportation, while their counterparts living in a Catholic neighborhood would have a 78 percent chance to survive the war. We will read in Sections 7.4 and 7.5 that in these minority neighborhoods rescue networks led by chaplains such as Gerard Jansen in Sneek or Catholic

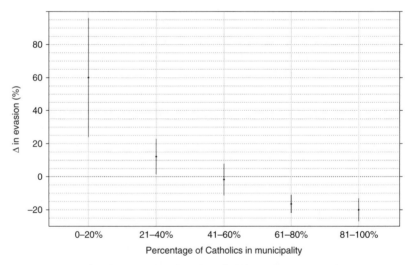

FIGURE 5.5 The change in predicted probability of evasion with 90 percent confidence intervals as Catholic proximity moves from its minimum to its maximum value conditional on Catholic strength in region using 2-km buffer. Point estimates are represented by points with 90 percent confidence intervals.

[11] Due to the inclusion of the county-level FEs, Jews living in counties without internal variation in evasion are disregarded from the analysis.

association leaders such as Scholte in the city of Groningen provided Jews with the opportunity to go underground. In majority neighborhoods, on the other hand, elites mobilized their communities with less vigor and were more likely to get exposed once they did.

Catholic proximity increased evasion by almost 15 percent in counties where between 60 and 80 percent of the population was Protestant. Whereas Jews living in the vicinity of Protestant communities had a 23 percent evasion chance, Jews in nearby Catholic communities were able to avoid deportation 35 percent of the time. The Protestant half of Twente, which will be introduced in more detail in the next chapter, provides numerous examples of Catholic rescue networks that provided humanitarian assistance to Jews in this part of the country; examples include the parishes of Catholic chaplains Bodde, Middelkoop, Hesselink, Tijhuis, Van Der Brink and Aalders, who all produced protection networks for Jews.

Catholic proximity has no effect on evasion in religiously mixed regions. In these regions, neither Protestant nor Catholic communities formed local minorities. Both groups, therefore, had the same motivation and capacity to mobilize against the Nazis.

Catholic proximity reduced evasion by almost 20 percent in counties that were predominantly Catholic. In these counties, evasion rates were significantly higher for Jews living in Protestant neighborhoods. Hence, Catholic networks formed shells of protection around Jews in Protestant parts of the country; Protestant networks had the same effect in Catholic regions. The rescue networks built by Protestant leaders Pontier, Staal and Van Wijhe, discussed in more detail the next two chapters, were the driving force behind evasion in the Catholic south.

Figure 5.6 reveals that these minority effects are not driven by the threshold of the radius used to calculate proportions. Regardless of whether we count churches within a 2.25, 2, 1.75, 1.5 or 1.25 kilometer radius, Catholic proximity protects Jews in Protestant regions, while the inverse is true in Catholic regions. The overall minority effects, however, decreases with the size of the buffers and disappears when we move beyond the 2.5-kilometer radius. This makes sense, given that the overlap between space and social networks declines with distance.

Figure 5.7 indicates that the presence of Orthodox Protestant churches increased evasion rates. This suggests that proximity to Orthodox Protestant churches made it easier for Jews to find shelter. When using a 1.25-kilometer radius to calculate proximity, the presence of Orthodox communities increases evasion by more than 30 percent. For a Jew,

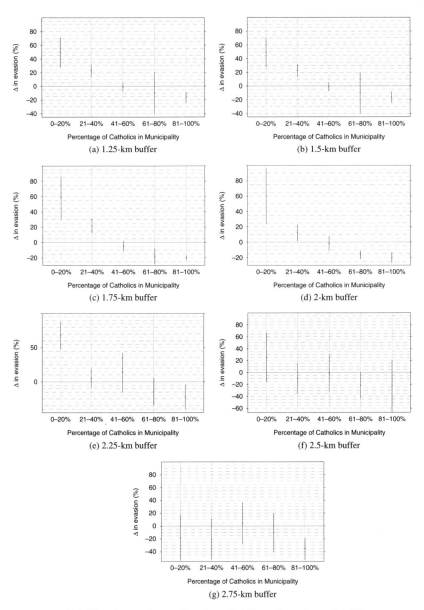

FIGURE 5.6 The change in predicted probability of evasion with 90 percent confidence intervals as Catholic proximity moves from its minimum to its maximum value conditional on Catholic strength in region using different buffers. Point estimates are represented by points with 90 percent confidence intervals.

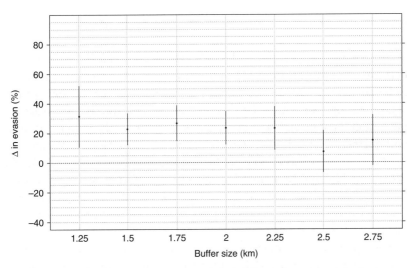

FIGURE 5.7 The change in predicted probability of evasion as Orthodox Protestant proximity moves from its minimum to its maximum value. Point estimates are represented by points with 90 percent confidence intervals.

moving within the same county from a majority neighborhood to an Orthodox Protestant neighborhood would have increased the chance of evasion from 29 to 59 percent. As we will see in the next two chapters, it was in these Orthodox neighborhoods that minority leaders such as Overduin, Hamming, Coelingh, Hamming and Flim motivated their followers to shelter Jews when the Nazi security police started the roundups. Similar to what we saw in Figure 5.6, the effect declines with distance and disappears once we move beyond the 2.5-kilometer radius.

5.6 INSTRUMENTAL VARIABLE

A major methodological concern stems from migration patterns. As neither Jews nor minority churches were randomly distributed over counties, it is possible that factors determining where they ended up also affected deportation. There may be reason to believe that this is indeed the case. Both Jews and other religious minorities might have decided to move to places that were more pluralistic or tolerant overall (Knippenberg 1992). This is a factor that is hard to capture empirically, but does potentially influence the willingness of the local population to provide shelter. In order to solve this problem I employ a two-stage procedure using distance to missionary hotbed Delft as an instrument for Catholic

Church strength in the Protestant northern Netherlands. This procedure will be described in more detail later.

To rule out worries about tolerance being a confounder, I use a particular aspect of the diffusion of Catholic minority enclaves that is unlikely to be correlated with local tolerance. As mentioned earlier, some of the denominational variation in the Netherlands can be traced back to acts of individual missionaries. The existence of Catholic enclaves in the Protestant northern Netherlands is largely due to one man: Sasbout Vosmeer.[12] In 1602, Vosmeer was appointed the first Vicar to the Catholic mission in Protestant Holland by Pope Clemens VIII. Right after his appointment, he had to move back in with his parents who lived in strictly Protestant Delft because the Reformation had destroyed most Catholic resources in the north (Rogier 1964).

Historians of Catholicism refer to the Counter-Reformation as a wildfire, spreading from Delft outward to other parts of the northern Netherlands. Whomever was closest to Vosmeer's "fire" was most likely to return to the Roman Catholic Church. Rogier even goes as far as to say that the religious map of the northern Netherlands would have looked fundamentally different if Vosmeer's parents had decided to move to Dordrecht or Utrecht (Rogier 1964). Given the absence of strong Catholic networks in this region, Vosmeer had to travel by night dressed up as a landworker and relying on personal networks to win back the hearts and minds of the Hollanders. Vosmeer initially met with limited success, but over time his efforts began to payoff as he built enclaves of Catholics in the region (Rogier 1964). Due to the arduous nature of sixteenth-century travel, his successes undoubtedly declined with distance.

I assume that the concentric spread of Catholicism around Delft has created a lasting imprint on religious deviance in the northern Netherlands that is unrelated to latent tolerance toward minority groups. In the first-stage regression, I deploy an OLS model to predict a Jew's proximity to Catholic churches in the northern Netherlands with a variable that measures the distance to Delft in kilometers. The measure is divided by 1,000 to reduce the number of digits. Again, standard errors are clustered on a county level. As is evident from the large F-Statistics distance in Models 1 and 2 in Table 5.2, the distance to Delft is a strong

---

[12] The province of North Holland, however, forms an exception. Because its bishop stayed in place during the religious wars of the sixteenth century, the influence of missionary activities on local-level Catholicism in this province was reduced. In the analysis, I therefore exclude the province of North Holland (see Chapter 10).

TABLE 5.2 *The effect of religious minorities on evasion: Results based on the distance to Delft*

	1st stage: OLS		2nd stage: Probit	
	(1)	(2)	(3)	(4)
	Catholic proximity		Evasion	
Distance to Delft (km)/1,000	−0.753***	−0.742***	−2.249***	
	(0.197)	(0.155)	(0.875)	
Instrument				2.721***
				(1.069)
Number of Jews/1,000		0.001	−0.127**	−0.115***
		(0.009)	(0.027)	(0.028)
Number of churches/1,000		0.118	−4.300**	−4.173*
		(1.468)	(3.875)	(5.296)
Constant	0.412***	0.424***	−0.157	−1.253***
	(0.022)	(0.037)	(0.116)	(0.321)
Controls	N	N	N	N
County FEs	N	N	N	N
Buffer	1.25 km	1.25 km	1.25 km	1.25 km
Counties	279	279	279	279
Jews	37,970	37,970	37,970	37,970
F-Statistic first stage	14.59	22.84		

Models 1–2: entries are unstandardized regression coefficients.
Models 3–4: entries are Probit regression coefficients.
County clustered standard errors are in parentheses.
*$p<0.05$; **$p<0.01$; ***$p<0.001$.

instrument for the share of Catholic churches, regardless of whether we control for the number of churches, Jews and spatial autocorrelation. The reduced form analysis, presented in model 3, shows a negative relationship between evasion and the distance to Delft. Model 4 presents the second stage of a two-stage probit model. This second stage uses only the Catholic proximity that is due to the distance from Delft (instrument) to predict individual-level evasion. The effect of Catholicism on evasion in the Protestant northern Netherlands is robust in the instrumental variable specification. Increasing the instrument from its minimum to its maximum value increases evasion by 18 percent.

I corroborated the assumption that the distance to Delft is unrelated to overall tolerance by regressing it against the presence of other religious minorities and other proxies for local-level tolerance. As we can see in Table 5.3 the instrument is not significantly related to the presence of any

TABLE 5.3 *Validity of the distance to Delft as an instrument (1)*

	OLS			
	(5) Ref. Orthodox	(6) Chr. Ref. Orthodox	(7) % Jews	(8) Catholics in the south
Distance to Delft (km)/1,000	−3.743	4.028	0.030	0.408
	(12.030)	(12.082)	(0.022)	(0.815)
Constant	−20.713***	20.993***	0.012***	0.816***
	(0.697)	(0.703)	(0.003)	(0.032)
Autocovariate	N	N	N	N
Controls	N	N	N	N
County FEs	N	N	N	N
Buffer	1.25 km	1.25 km	1.25 km	1.25 km
Counties	279	279	279	71
Jews	37,970	37,970	37,970	2,290
R^2	0.001	0.001	0.003	0.030

Entries are unstandardized regression coefficients.
County clustered standard errors are in parentheses.
*$p<0.05$; **$p<0.01$; ***$p<0.001$.

of the Orthodox Protestant churches or Jews in the region, membership among citizens and police officers of the anti-Semitic National Socialist Movement in the Netherlands (NSB), the percentage of the population that volunteered to arrest Jews or the percentage of the population that spied for the Nazis. Taken together, this suggests that the distance to Delft indeed affected the diffusion of Catholicism in ways unrelated to tolerance for minority groups. To assess whether the distance to Delft might affect other socioeconomic characteristics of regions related to Catholicism, I regress the measure against unemployment levels, population and the percentage of people working in trade, industry and agriculture in the relevant counties. Data was obtained from the 1930 census (CBS 1931).

Tables 5.4 and 5.5 show that no considerable relationships exist. Finally, I also conducted a placebo test, testing whether the distance to Delft affected the Catholic Church share in the nearby south where missionary effects should not be visible given the overall dominance of the Roman Catholic Church. As model 8 suggests, the distance to Delft did not influence the proximity to Catholic Churches for Jews living in this predominantly Catholic region, providing further evidence for the notion that it captures the imprint of missionary activities unrelated to other factors.

TABLE 5.4 *Validity of the distance to Delft as an instrument (2)*

	OLS			
	(9) % NSB	(10) % NSB Police	(11) % Voluntary Police	(12) % Spies
Distance to Delft (km)/1,000	0.053	0.019	0.188	−0.001
	(0.034)	(0.019)	(0.126)	(0.001)
Constant	0.023***	0.013***	0.064**	0.000*
	(0.005)	(0.002)	(0.022)	(0.000)
Counties	640	640	640	640
R^2	0.003	0.004	0.002	0.000

Entries are unstandardized regression coefficients.
Robust standard errors are in parentheses.
*p<0.05; **p<0.01; ***p<0.001.

TABLE 5.5 *Validity of the distance to Delft as an instrument (3)*

	OLS				
	(13) % Trade	(14) % Industry	(15) % Unemploy	(16) % Agriculture	(17) Population
Distance to Delft (km)/1,000	6.529	0.954	6.751	−5.276	−47321.700
	(6.807)	(10.085)	(4.734)	(14.950)	(34708.3100)
Constant	6.807***	26.499***	9.498***	52.959***	13655.480**
	(0.702)	(1.223)	(0.572)	(1.705)	(4779.878)
Counties	640	640	640	640	640
R^2	0.002	0.000	0.003	0.000	0.005

Entries are unstandardized regression coefficients.
Robust standard errors are in parentheses.
*p<0.05; **p<0.01; ***p<0.001.

5.7 CONCLUSION

The analysis presented in this chapter deployed extremely fine-grained data to assess how proximity to specific church communities affected the opportunities for Jews to evade. In line with the minority hypothesis, Jews in Catholic parts of the Netherlands were more likely to escape deportation when they lived close to Protestant churches and vice versa. In addition, proximity to Orthodox minority enclaves also increased evasion.

Although this analysis shows that spatial patterns of evasion are in accordance with our theoretical model, it does not tell us whether actual rescue missions by minority Christians were driving this result. Therefore, I will complement this analysis with focused comparative case studies in Twente, a region in the east of the Netherlands that spans the Catholic–Protestant fault line and cuts the country in half. Based on these case studies, I hope to identify whether minority enclaves, regardless of congregation, were indeed more likely to setup clandestine operations and how they did so.

5.A APPENDIX

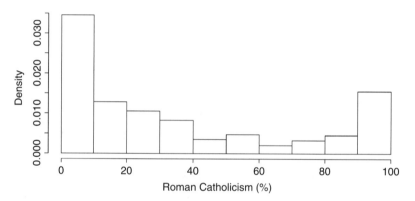

FIGURE 5.A1 Catholic strength of Dutch counties in which Jews were living in 1942.

TABLE 5.A1 *Descriptive statistics*

Variable	N	Mean	SD	Min	Max
Evasion	122694	0.28	0.449	0	1
Catholic proximity (1.25 km)	122694	0.414	0.156	0	1
Catholic proximity (1.5 km)	122694	0.413	0.145	0	1
Catholic proximity (1.75 km)	122694	0.413	0.137	0	1
Catholic proximity (2 km)	122694	0.417	0.13	0	1
Catholic strength	122694	.369	0.121	0	.999
Orthodox proximity (1.25 km)	122694	0.31	0.137	0	1
Orthodox proximity (1.5 km)	122694	0.31	0.12	0	1

TABLE 5.A1 *(continued)*

Variable	N	Mean	SD	Min	Max
Orthodox proximity (1.75 km)	122694	0.303	0.107	0	1
Orthodox proximity (2 km)	122694	0.29	0.094	0	1
Number of Jews (1.25 km)	122694	14.884	13.825	0	41.204
Number of Jews (1.5 km)	122694	19.072	17.394	0	50.611
Number of Jews (1.75 km)	122694	23.171	20.58	0	60.461
Number of Jews (2 km)	122694	27.075	23.328	0	64.673
Number of churches/ 1,000 (1.25 km)	122694	0.034	.017	0	0.071
Number of churches/ 1,000 (1.5 km)	122694	0.028	.014	0	0.064
Number of churches/ 1,000 (1.75 km)	122694	0.021	.011	0	0.056
Number of churches/ 1,000 (2 km)	122694	0.016	0.008	0	0.046
Autocovariate	122694	0.278	0.084	0	1

TABLE 5.A2 *Regression of Jewish evasion with county FEs (1.25–2-km buffers)*

	LOGIT			
	(18)	(19)	(20)	(21)
		Evasion		
Catholic proximity in 0–20% Catholic municipalities	1.730***	2.102***	2.409***	2.426**
	(0.449)	(0.483)	(0.608)	(0.804)
Catholic proximity in 21–40% Catholic municipalities	−0.789*	−0.994**	−1.369*	−1.816*
	(0.380)	(0.419)	(0.602)	(0.905)
Catholic proximity in 41–60% Catholic municipalities	−1.619***	−2.178***	−2.715***	−2.528***
	(0.461)	(0.471)	(0.672)	(0.791)
Catholic proximity in 61–80% Catholic municipalities	−2.485***	−2.843	−4.933***	−3.742***
	(1.027)	(1.771)	(2.437)	(0.666)
Catholic proximity in 81–100% Catholic municipalities	−3.358***	−3.721***	−6.641**	−4.370***
	(0.789)	(0.975)	(0.975)	(1.146)

(continued)

TABLE 5.A2 *(continued)*

	LOGIT			
	(18)	(19)	(20)	(21)
		Evasion		
Orthodox proximity	1.157***	1.349***	1.177***	1.163**
	(0.325)	(0.366)	(0.336)	(0.440)
Number of Jews/ 1,000	−0.025***	−0.017***	−0.011**	−0.007*
	(0.005)	(0.004)	(0.004)	(0.004)
Number of churches/ 1,000	−28.612***	−22.566***	−19.586***	−17.416***
	(2.508)	(1.058)	(1.092)	(1.167)
Constant	−0.416	−0.209	0.020	0.134
	(0.762)	(0.726)	(0.736)	(0.725)
Controls	Y	Y	Y	Y
County FEs	Y	Y	Y	Y
Buffer	1.25 km	1.5 km	1.75 km	2 km
Counties	439	439	439	439
Jews	122,694	122,694	122,694	122,694
Log-likelihood	−70,072.942	−70,092.196	−70,194.982	−70,248.593

Entries are unstandardized regression coefficients.
County clustered standard errors are in parentheses.
*p<0.05; **p<0.01; ***p<0.001.

TABLE 5.A3 *Regression of Jewish evasion with county FEs (1.25–2-km buffers)*

	LOGIT		
	(22)	(23)	(24)
		Evasion	
Catholic proximity in 0–20% Catholic municipalities	2.706*	1.049	−0.913
	(1.172)	(0.976)	(1.266)
Catholic proximity in 21–40% Catholic municipalities	−2.462*	−1.560	−0.153
	(1.325)	(1.237)	(1.479)
Catholic proximity in 41–60% Catholic municipalities	−2.046*	−1.108	1.096
	(1.141)	(1.162)	(1.442)

TABLE 5.A3 *(continued)*

	LOGIT		
	(22)	(23) Evasion	(24)
Catholic proximity in 61–80% Catholic municipalities	−3.690**	−6.878**	−8.505
	(1.418)	(2.854)	(5.965)
Catholic proximity in 81–100% Catholic municipalities	−4.732*	−2.523	−2.286
	(2.525)	(2.786)	(4.676)
Orthodox proximity	1.571**	0.369	0.752
	(0.621)	(0.433)	(0.526)
Number of Jews/1,000	−0.007*	−0.005	−0.004
	(0.004)	(0.005)	(0.005)
Number of churches/1,000	−0.015***	−0.015***	−0.014***
	(0.002)	(0.003)	(0.004)
Constant	−0.185	0.399	0.410
	(0.643)	(0.714)	(0.710)
Controls	Y	Y	Y
County FEs	Y	Y	Y
Buffer	2.25 km	2.5 km	2.75 km
Counties	439	439	439
Jews	122,694	122,694	122,694
Log-likelihood	−70,072.942	−70,092.196	−70,194.982

Entries are unstandardized regression coefficients.
County clustered standard errors are in parentheses.
*$p<0.05$; **$p<0.01$; ***$p<0.001$.

6

Religious Minorities and Clandestine Collective
Action in Twente

6.1 INTRODUCTION

How did individual Christians respond to the Jewish persecutions? If
nascent resistance fighters were indeed facing a clandestine collective
action dilemma, we would expect that a lot of people willing to rescue
refrained from doing so out of fear. Indeed, diaries from non-rescuers in
Twente, the eastern region in the Netherlands that this chapter focuses
on, seem to paint this picture. Partly under the influence of their religious
leaders, who repeatedly protested the Nazis, the overall attitude of Christians in Twente was pro-Jewish and anti-German. Sjouke Wynia from
Denekamp remembered his father being furious when their Jewish neighbors had to leave their house (Demant 2015, p. 139). Willem Dingelheim,
also from Denekamp wrote in his diary that "everyone was heartbroken"
because of the "undefinable suffering of the Jews." Several high school
headmasters in the Twente area were seen crying when explaining to their
pupils that their Jewish classmates and teacher were no longer allowed
to attend their institution. The diary written by the head of the Jewish
Council of Enschede confirms that the general population resented the
deportations (Demant 2015, p. 139).

Postwar interviews with both Jews and gentiles in Twente indicate that
sympathy translated into small-scale help for Jews before the roundups
started. When Jews were no longer allowed to buy groceries in regular
stores, a shop owner in Haaksbergen provided food to former Jewish customers for free under the counter. In Enschede, gentiles secretly bought
groceries for Jews living on their street (Demant 2015, p. 134). Other

neighbors helped to soften financial strain by lending money or providing employment (Geritz-Koster 1999). It has even been argued that in Enschede Jews and gentiles grew closer to each other than ever before during the early years of the war (Demant 2015). On occasion, gentiles even displayed public support for their persecuted neighbors. In Almelo as well as Enschede, groups of gentiles actively protested the introduction of the Jewish star by wearing one themselves. This open form of resistance, however, was short lived and ended when the police started arresting participants (Demant 2015).

These relatively low-risk activities notwithstanding, large-scale clandestine protection of Jews was rare. Risk perceptions formed an important impediment to this form of resistance. After observing Jewish mothers asking gentiles to save their children, a bystander wrote in her diary: "who has the courage to do that? It is not allowed. You will undergo the same fate." The clandestine nature of the operation was deemed particularly challenging: "How on earth could you hide five grown ups, three children ... " a woman wrote after hearing about the arrest of a Jewish family that had gone into hiding to avoid deportation (Van Der Boom 2012, p. 244). Although outraged by what happened to the Jews, gentiles also recognized that protecting Jews was difficult and risky. When responding to the question of whether he ever considered sheltering Jews, Benno van Delden of Enschede said: "No never ... the SS, the camps, firing squads, torture and all that misery. You had to be very strong to shelter someone" (Demant 2015, p. 141).

Fear and uncertainty resulted in an overall feeling of helplessness. Mees, for instance, characterized the first roundups as "systematic elimination against which we could not do anything." Trying to capture the overall mental state of bystanders, a female witness to an early roundup wrote: "Everyone was deeply moved. Outraged out of pure powerlessness" (Van Der Boom 2012, p. 244).

The risks involved made it hard for people to imagine any form of organized solidarity with Jews, as revealed in the following statement by a non-rescuer: "I am willing to go to jail for my convictions. It would have an enormous impact if everyone was willing to do this, but this is not the case ... It is hard to know what to do" (Van Der Boom 2012, p. 244). Another diary reveals that this prospect of punishment created passivity among Dutch citizens: "We poor Christians could not do anything but follow Luke 22:53. Follow from afar that is our fate and cross. Let's hope our sympathy can revitalize Jews" (Van Der Boom 2012, p. 244).[1]

After studying testimonies of successful protection networks, it is not hard to understand where feelings of powerlessness among gentiles came from. Successful rescue organizations had to supply Jews with fake identifications papers, rationing cards, produce, clothes, information about upcoming roundups, medical care, funeral services,[2] marriage counseling,[3] psychological treatment,[4] safe houses, ability to travel, communication lines[5] and, most importantly, numerous hiding places, as few rescuers were able to provide shelter for a long period of time. Even though most Christians were outraged by anti-Jewish legislation, they recognized that they could not simply engage in clandestine collective action because it was too dangerous. Yet, as I will show in this chapter, being embedded in a minority congregation increased the impact an outraged citizen could have on evasion by reducing both the actual and perceived danger.

The previous chapter showed that geographical patterns of evasion are in line with the minority hypothesis. Whereas Jewish proximity to Catholic churches increased evasion rates in Protestant parts of the Netherlands, being close to Protestant churches had the same effect in Catholic parts of the country. While the analysis showed a statistical association between the presence of minority enclaves and evasion at a fine-grained level, it also deployed administrative data from when the killings were unfolding, preventing the retrospective biases that are introduced by analyzing commonly used postwar testimonies. Relying on statistical evasion data alone, however, also comes at a cost; it cannot tell us whether clandestine mobilization of minority communities drove the differential survival of Jews, nor can it explain whether and how minorities were able to overcome the clandestine collective action dilemma that the aforementioned stories reveal.

---

[1] It is, of course, possible that gentiles were trying to find easy excuses to legitimate their passive behavior. However, testimonies from Twente Jews seem to suggest that the feelings of powerlessness were justifiable. During postwar interviews with social scientist Demant in the early 2000s, several of them asked themselves what they would they have done as gentiles and concluded that passivity was a normal response in times of hardship and threat (Demant 2015, p. 183).

[2] *SVB-file 23, DOCDIRECT, Winschoten.*

[3] *SVB-file 8, DOCDIRECT, Winschoten.*

[4] *Yad Vashem file L. Gerritsen in Michman et al.*

[5] *Dagboek Douwes, NIOD 244 1065, Amsterdam.*

In this chapter, therefore, I explicitly focus on religious rescue activities to assess whether minorities were indeed better able to setup clandestine missions to protect threatened neighbors. Because a complete analysis of all rescue networks in the Low Countries would pose serious challenges for data collection and measurement quality as well as inflate unobservable omitted variable bias, I deploy a highly structured comparison of rescue activities in one region, which overcomes aforementioned problems. The narrower geographical scope of this study allows for more detailed data collection as well as superior measurement and, hence, enables me to better assess the role played by minority congregations in rescuing victims of mass persecution.

For this purpose, I examine the region of Twente, the home of Almelo and Borne with which this book began. Importantly, Twente is an economically and socially integrated region located across the Catholic–Protestant fault line that divided Western Europe. As a result, important economic and social factors can be kept constant when comparing Protestant and Catholic groups in minority and majority contexts. The extraordinary availability of unused archival sources presented by the Holocaust in Twente enables me to study clandestine collective action in an extremely detailed fashion.

For the Twente region, I was able to retrieve two unique collections of postwar testimonies. The first collection consists of research done in light of an honors pension program and contains information about people who either themselves have protected Jews or lost family members who did so. The second body of documents is collected in light of postwar trials of collaborators and provides information about the detection of Jews in hiding. In combination with existing work on the mentality of non-rescuers (Hilbrink 1989; Van Der Boom 2012; Demant 2015), these sources provide an unusual opportunity to trace the evolution of successful and unsuccessful clandestine rescue operations.

In the following section, I introduce the region of Twente and describe the developments that led to its religious split. I then describe the archival materials that allow me interrogate the roots of clandestine collective action. The analysis is presented in subsequent sections and proceeds in eight steps: I first give a bird's-eye view of all religious rescue operations in Twente, before describing some emblematic cases of successful and unsuccessful mobilization in more detail. The discussion of these cases is organized according to three mechanisms that link minority isolation to clandestine collective action: 1) assurance, 2) selective survival and 3) organizers' selectivity. I then use data from Twente to emphasize four important themes. The first highlights how rescue operations inherited prewar religious segregation and points out how religious mixing undermined the minority advantage by reducing isolation. Second, I use the qualitative data to show how, despite existing religious segregation, Jews and gentiles came into contact. Third, I talk about the unanticipated but important ability of minority groups to exploit cross-regional linkages they had developed before the war, enabling these groups to funnel Jews from one locality to another. Finally, I also use the detailed data from Twente to compare rescue operations for Jews with other types of clandestine resistance in the region. If empathy with persecuted outsiders plays a role in producing minority resistance to genocide, we would expect the minority advantage to be stronger for the former than the latter.

6.2 TWENTE

During the war between Calvinist insurgents and the Catholic king of Spain detailed in Chapter 3, Twente lay in the middle of the battlefield and, as a result, ended up spanning the major religious fault line that divided Western Europe, in general, and the Netherlands, in particular. The establishment of Twente as a unified political entity dates back to 804 when the Netherlands became part of the Holy Roman Empire. With an eye on existing tribal boundaries, Charles the Great turned the region into a separate shire that, later, became part of the Episcopal principality of Utrecht. Under the rule of the bishop, the region turned completely Catholic and stayed this way after the Burgundian and Habsburg emperors took over in the fourteenth century.

This changed when a coalition of Dutch merchants and Calvinists staged a revolt against the Catholic king of Spain. The local elite in Twente reluctantly joined the Dutch revolt in order to maintain local privileges. In 1597, the whole of Twente became part of the Dutch republic after an intense military battle. However, peace did not last long as a new wave of violence in 1605 led the region, which had been unified for more than 600 years, to split. Whereas the northwest remained Dutch, the southeast came under Spanish rule for a little more then twenty years, after which General Casimir reunited both parts within the Dutch Republic (Klokhuis 1982).

This short-term political split had a long-term impact on the religious composition of the Twente region because both the Reformation and Counter-Reformation were raging. While the northwest became dominated by Protestants, the southeast remained a Catholic stronghold. Minority church communities were able to maintain themselves on both sides of the divide. In the Catholic south, Protestants were able to penetrate with help from the federal government, while, in the Protestant north, Catholic enclaves survived with help from co-religionists living in nearby Germany. Under German influence, the region also became a hotbed of Orthodox Protestant movements that left the mainstream church out of dissatisfaction with modernist tendencies throughout the nineteenth and twentieth centuries (Demant 2015).

The political geography of three centuries was still visible at the onset of the Holocaust. The maps in Figures 6.1 and 6.2 show the distribution of Catholicism, Protestantism and Orthodoxy in Twente in the 1940s.[6] As one can see, Catholics were still dominant in the southeast, Protestants dominated the northwest, and minority enclaves of Protestants and

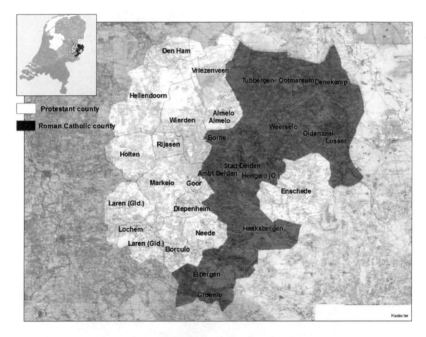

FIGURE 6.1 Twente, 1940.

[6] Data on religious composition comes from the Central Bureau for Statistics (CBS 1931). Information on churches is obtained from the Dutch inventory for Church buildings compiled by Sonneveld and maintained by the Free University in Amsterdam (IKGN 2011).

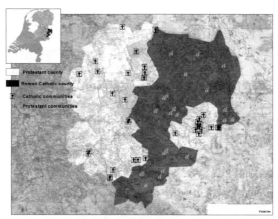

(a) Catholic and Protestant minorities

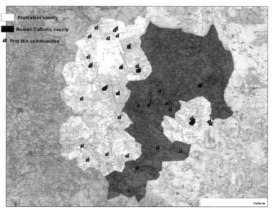

(b) Minority Protestants

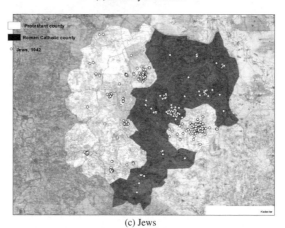

(c) Jews

FIGURE 6.2 Religious minorities in Twente, 1942.

Catholics existed on either side of the religious fault line (the green and red churches). The middle map in Figure 6.2 reveals that both Catholic and Protestant parts of Twente were home to numerous smaller Orthodox Protestant communities. The lower third of Figure 6.2 shows that in 1942, right before the deportations started, almost 3,000 Jews were living across Twente. As Jews resided in both Catholic and Protestant parts of Twente, it becomes possible to compare rescue in the Protestant and Catholic parts of the region.[7]

A second factor that makes Twente so unique is that, with the exception of the twenty years of the Counter-Reformation, it has always been a unified administrative territory. Religious differences notwithstanding, the region integrated economically and politically under Dutch rule. Because it was relatively isolated from the rest of the country, the region independently developed a textile industry by relying on an extensive cottage industry (Willink 2010). In 1830, the Dutch government designated Twente to become the integrated textile center of the country, further reinforcing the region's unity (Klokhuis 1982).

This level of economic integration guaranteed that, the major religious divergence aside, the region's economic and political homogeneity was sustained. This enables us to keep other factors that could potentially explain minority mobilization constant. Figure 6.3 compares newly

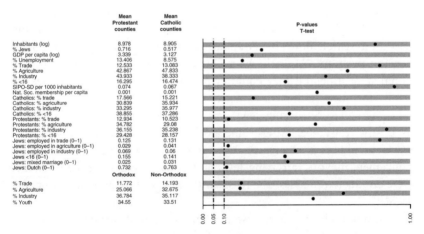

FIGURE 6.3 Comparison of Catholic and Protestant counties in Twente, 1942/1947.

[7] Geocoded data on Jews is missing for the town of Groenlo.

digitalized census data for different religious groups living in Protestant and Catholic parts of Twente in 1947 (the year closest to World War II for which subgroup-level data is available), and Jewish census data from early 1942 (before the deportations started). It presents difference in means test and accompanying p-values for Jews, Protestants, Orthodox Protestants and Catholics living in Catholic and Protestant counties for a range of socioeconomic variables. The similar means in Protestant and Catholic counties indicate that Jews, Protestants and Catholics residing in the northwest of Twente were indeed roughly comparable to their counterparts in the southeast in terms of age, economic activity and levels of integration.[8]

6.3 DATA

Studying clandestine behavior is hard. In addition to the unique comparative advantages, studying Twente offers a rich body of archival material with which to compare between 1) clandestine collective action and non-mobilization and 2) successful and failed clandestine networks. This allows us to assess overall differences in the mobilization capacity of minority and majority groups.

Hilbrink provides a comprehensive list of all recognized resistance fighters in the region (Hilbrink 1989). Based on this list, it is possible to access a unique and underutilized collection of postwar testimonies that sheds light on successful resistance to genocide. The collection consists of research done by Foundation 40/45 in light of an honorary pension program. After the war, Dutch citizens could request an additional state stipend if they could prove that they or deceased immediate family members had extra expenses or suffered injury because of resistance activities. Sheltering Jews was one of the activities that qualified as costly resistance. After someone had filed a request, *Foundation 40/45* would start an investigation. Interviews with neighbors, reliable policemen, mayors, surviving Jews and other members of the resistance were conducted to assess the trustworthiness of the claimant (Cammaert 1994).

Testimonies from other resistance fighters proved particularly useful in reconstructing the social structure of clandestine organization as almost all interviews started with a brief description of how the testifier and the

---

[8] The high P-values confirm this as well (in all cases p>0.1). However, given the relatively small sample sizes, the P-values should be taken with skepticism.

claimant had come into contact with each other. The files are stored by the Social Insurance Bank and can be consulted in Winschoten, a city in the eastern Netherlands. In total, I consulted 207 files, which provided information on fifty-three rescue networks active in twenty-one of all twenty-six counties. In total, eight of these twenty-one counties were Catholic. Religious organization plays an important role in forty-two out of the fifty-three identified networks. Because these files are based on testimonies of survivors, they mostly provide information on successful networks.[9]

To allow for a comparison of successful and unsuccessful mobilization, I combine the files from the Social Insurance Bank with those of postwar trials of collaborators who were active in Twente. Denouncing and arresting innocent Jews is, of course, unconstitutional and was heavily persecuted after the war. They were also crimes that were relatively easy to prove as the Nazis kept records of how they used Dutch collaborators. As a result, trials often provide information on Jews that were arrested in hiding, enabling us to get information on failed resistance. The trial documents also provide information on how the Nazis tried to detect associates of captured individuals, giving some insight into how and why some networks failed. Trial documents are stored in the National Archives in The Hague.

In order to compare successful mobilization with non-mobilization, I complement the two bodies of testimonies with diaries and existing interviews of people who decided not to save Jews (Hilbrink 1989; Van Der Boom 2012; Demant 2015). These accounts might give insight into obstacles to mobilization, which this book hypothesizes will be easier to overcome for minorities. Postwar testimonies are probably biased by the testifier's desire to justify his or her own behavior. However, this bias should not be different for minority and majority rescuers. As a result, the conclusions drawn from comparisons between the two should still be valid. Moreover, scholars have demonstrated that accounts of the Holocaust are stable and consistent over time, in particular, when they concern factual information about collaborators and arrests (Greenspan 2001).

---

[9] I redid all the analyses relying only on testimonies provided by surviving Jews to make sure that the data generation process was not driven by stronger minority networks. I also redid all the analysis relying only on testimonies from rescuers to make sure that selective memory of divergent traits by outsiders was driving the results. In both cases, outcomes were in line with the ones presented later.

6.4 THE MINORITY ADVANTAGE

The central hypothesis of this book is that minority groups are better able to overcome the clandestine collective action dilemma outlined in the previous section. To assess this systematically, I have coded all rescue groups active in Twente that could be found in the files of Foundation 40/45. I marked all groups that sheltered at least one Jew who survived World War II as successful and groups that mobilized but were not able to successfully shelter a single Jew as unsuccessful. I code a network as religious if it was setup by a religious leader such as a reverend, priest, chaplain, religious school teacher or politician active in a religious party. Based on the denomination of the religious leaders active in the organization, I determined the denominational leaning of the organization. If the minority hypothesis holds, we would expect Protestant networks to be most successful in the Catholic southeast, Catholic networks to be most successful in the Protestant northwest and Orthodox Protestant groups to be successful throughout Twente.

Successful networks are depicted in Figure 6.4 and are largely in line with the minority hypothesis. All but two of the eight Protestant rescue organizations were active in areas dominated by Catholics. When we look at Catholic networks we see a similar picture with only two of the fifteen successful movements operating in Catholic territory. Orthodox Protestant protection of Jews emerged in both Catholic and mainstream Protestant areas. This is in line with our theory as the Orthodox formed minority communities everywhere.[10]

Figure 6.4c displays the five unsuccessful networks that could be found in the files. As we can see, all of these networks are connected to majority congregations.[11] Overall, this spatial pattern suggests that minority networks were better able to produce and sustain successful rescue operations, while attempts of majority groups were more likely to fail. In the next subsections, I describe the core processes that led to the emergence of this pattern.

---

[10] The four majority networks emerged in tiny villages or were inspired by interregional movement entrepreneurs, suggesting that geographical isolation and external efforts can compensate for a lack of minority secrecy. See Chapter 8 for more details.

[11] Because of the lenient criteria for success (one Jewish survivor) only five networks failed according to my coding. Relaxing these criteria is hard to do with the present data. However, the case studies mentioned later reveal that selective retention played an important role in producing resistance within isolated hubs of commitment.

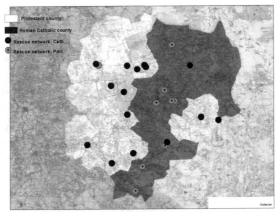

(a) Roman Catholic and Protestant networks

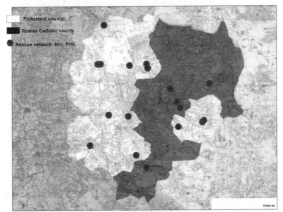

(b) Orthodox Protestant networks

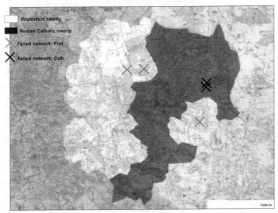

(c) Failed networks

FIGURE 6.4 Rescue networks in Twente.

6.5 ASSURANCE

Why were minorities better at producing clandestine collective action? In a postwar interview, Catholic Chaplain Visser, who was active in the predominantly Protestant town of Wierden, explicitly talks about the importance of minority isolation in assuring him that mobilization was possible. Acting out of sympathy for those in need, he knew that he could always rely on specific local Catholic farmers for help in providing food and shelter. They, in turn, blindly trusted their Catholic front man and were suspicious of everyone outside of their pillar. Catholic farmers in the area even went to the chaplain and local Catholic headmaster for medical advice because they refused to listen to the local doctor who happened to be a Protestant.[12]

Exploiting the commitment of his followers, Visser purposively created an isolated organization to reduce exposure. He built his organization around people he could trust and ignored contacts outside of his own congregation: "I always wanted to stay independent. Nobody outside my parish knew what I was doing ... My own people knew but they kept quiet" (Hilbrink 1989).

In Protestant Enschede, Chaplain Van Der Brink tells a similar story of how minority isolation enabled clandestine mobilization by assuring both secrecy and commitment. Already, before the war, Van Der Brink's church had successfully summoned Catholics to leave the Dutch Nazi party. When the deportations started, he convinced Catholic police officers to refuse cooperation. Inspired by his brother, who provided him with illegal newspapers, fake identity papers and food vouchers, he setup an underground network with the help of parish members and police patrolmen. He was able to find several shelters for Jews among members of his community after temporarily hiding them in presbyteries. Catholic boy scouts were used as couriers, while funding for his organization was obtained from businessmen who were part of his parish. When roundups were coming up, a local police officer would post a warning note on the doors of Catholic Churches (Bekkenkamp 2000). All contacts ran via the presbyteries to maintain the exclusive Catholic character of the operation. Similar to what we saw in Wierden, the chaplain of Enschede never forayed outside his parish in order to reduce exposure. "Within your own

---

[12] It is striking that religious substance in and of itself was not the driving force of group commitment. One Catholic from Wierden remarks that their chaplains: "do not talk that much about religion. Real Catholics do not really do that" (Hilbrink 1989).

parish you knew who to approach for help. Those people will not let you down."[13]

A similar movement, driven by minority assurance, emerged in Catholic Hengelo, indicating that this process was not unique to minority Catholics. While raised an atheist, Schipper converted to Protestantism to marry his wife. Like most converts, he was extremely committed to his church and played a leading role in local Protestant community life. He was a council member of the Protestant political party (AR), sent his kids to a Protestant school, joined the Orthodox men's association and served as a deacon. Because of his central position within the church, Schipper realized that people could be trusted and that mobilization was possible. The importance of the church as a guaranteed safe space is illustrated by this statement of his daughter: "If you would go to church on Sunday you would see numerous Orthodox families together with their Jewish children."[14] Orthodox Protestants were not the only resistance organizers in this Catholic stronghold that demonstrate the importance of minority *assurance*. Mainstream Protestant Sikko Vis created a rescue network out of the Association for Christian Education, which he chaired. People on the board of this organization were all extremely influential members in their churches and, according to Vis, could exploit commitment among followers to provide shelter.[15]

Minority mobilization did not always stop at county borders. According to Haaksbergen's Grunningman, a prudent leader of the Roman Catholic boy scout association in Twente, his rescue efforts did not rely heavily on coordination: "I did not think it was good to just gather people and set up a resistance organizations. For me it should be based on intuition." However, his more "intuitive" approach in combination with his interregional boy scout network, led him in the end to embed most of his operation in a minority congregation. After failing to find good helpers in the predominantly Catholic towns of Hengelo, Haaksbergen and Oldenzaal and refusing to work with mainstream Protestant leaders, he was finally successful in placing Jews with a local pastor and Catholic gamekeeper in dominantly Protestant Neede.[16] Grunningman's story illustrates how some religious leaders with interregional ties

---

[13] *Interview kapelaan Van Der Brink, NIOD, Amsterdam.*

[14] *Archive Flim NIOD 471 13 B, Amsterdam.*

[15] *Archive Flim NIOD 771 12D, Amsterdam. Yad Vashem file S. Vis in Michman et al.*

[16] *Interview Grunningman. Archive NIOD 251a-117, Amsterdam.*

purposively picked pockets of reliable contacts from a wider range of communities while shunning religious leaders of different denominations. Grunningman, however, did not pick them because they were minority communities, but because these congregations seemed more likely to provide the required networks of trust and commitment, or, in other words, because they *assured* the organizer that mobilization was possible.

6.6 SELECTIVE SURVIVAL

Compared to their counterparts in minority enclaves, majority leaders were less successful in creating and sustaining clandestine organizations. Their attempts to setup coordinated resistance along lines of trust were often disrupted because of early denunciations by uncommitted parish members. As a result, retention of their rescue organizations was less likely (Aldrich 1999). This reinforced the minority advantage in clandestine collective action.

The previous section introduced us to Chaplain Van Der Brink who exploited minority commitment in Protestant Enschede. If we compare the successful minority operations of Van Der Brink with rescue attempts by majority Protestants in the same city, it becomes clear that maintaining a cloak of secrecy was hard for those who were not embedded in a committed and isolated minority community. Via a good friend working at the police, a mainstream Protestant in Enschede identified as L., received four Jewish refugees in his home. Soon after their arrival, however, they were forced to leave. An anonymous note signed by "a good neighbor" was delivered to the house: "Get rid of your guests as soon as possible. People are looking at you."[17] Apparently, L. was not able to keep sensitive information out of the hands of uncommitted outsiders.

Contrary to Van Der Brink and in a similar vein as mainstream Protestant L., Dutch majority Reverends Van Gelder from Steenwijk, Van Staaij from Wierden, Le Roy from Almelo and De Geus from Almelo were all arrested early on while mobilizing their congregations because their activities became exposed by disloyal adherents (Hovingh 2015). The case of De Geus particularly illustrates the dangers that a religious leader faced when moving from a minority to a majority community, revealing that the selective survival mechanism was more important than individual organizing skills. Before coming to Almelo, De Geus was at the helm

---

[17] *SVB-file 23, DOCDIRECT, Winschoten.*

of a small Dutch Reformed congregation in the Catholic town of Beuningen, near Nijmegen. Within this enclave he forcefully and freely preached against the Nazis without any repercussions. Despite numerous warnings from within his congregation, he continued his anti-Nazi tirades when he was transferred to Protestant Almelo in 1940. "If Church and Christ no longer tell the truth no one will" was his response when his closest followers tried to caution him (Touw 1946, p. 620). In line with the fears of congregation members, De Geus was apprehended by the SIPO-SD when they found out he had distributed a pro-Jewish texts among his followers in January 1942 (Touw 1946).

This story of De Geus also demonstrates the further reverberations that selective survival could have for patterns of religious resistance. Right before his arrest, the reverend was approached by a small group of Protestant rescuers who required assistance with sheltering Jews. As soon as they learned about De Geus's fate, the rescuers had to shift gears and approached an Orthodox minister to set up a clandestine operation. This minister was able to create an efficient underground movement by exploiting the loyalty of his followers. He was able to mobilize several parish members, including a baker,[18] textile manufacturer[19] and police officer,[20] who together were able to provide food and clothes as well as implement an efficient warning system.

The story of Pastor Stokman from Oldenzaal reveals that *selective retention* also operated in the Catholic southeast. Before the German invasion, Stokman worked with Catholic mayor Bloemen to help Jewish refugees from Germany. He called upon his followers to open their houses for those fleeing anti-Semitic legislation and convinced both the local Franciscan monastery and the parish house to setup emergency kitchens. Numerous followers answered his requests. A Roman Catholic cinema owner even made one of his theater rooms available as a shelter.

Of course, Stokman had to abandon his open help to Jewish refugees when the Germans took over the country. Instead, he shifted his focus to a more covert operation. He tried to mobilize people he knew from the Catholic labor union to help Jews and distribute anti-Nazi pamphlets. Unfortunately, he failed miserably as his activities became known to the Nazis within weeks. One of his followers had leaked information. Already in 1940, two years before the major deportations started,

---

[18] *SVB-file 28, DOCDIRECT, Winschoten.*
[19] *SVB-file 20, DOCDIRECT, Winschoten.*
[20] *SVB-file 17, DOCDIRECT, Winschoten.*

he had to flee Oldenzaal. His partner, Mayor Bloemen, was imprisoned. Despite the revealed preference for resistance, no Catholic rescue network filled the void left by Stokman's departure (Weustink 1985). Creating a clandestine organization in Oldenzaal, however, did not turn out to be impossible, as a small pocket of Orthodox Protestants, activated by clergymen, deacons, school teachers and prominent politicians, did engage in the clandestine rescue of Jews. Within this Orthodox enclave, further recruitment took place along denominational lines as it provided a basis for trust. Church choirs, parish meetings, religious soccer teams and councils of aldermen formed the infrastructure for the illegal organization. The church always played a central role, as money for the movements was collected during Sunday services and meetings were held in church buildings and rectories.[21] Hence, in Oldenzaal, both majority and minority Christians tried to mobilize, but only the latter survived the challenges of clandestine collective action.

6.7 ORGANIZERS' SELECTIVITY

Close inspection of rescue operations in the town of Z. suggest that a minority shell also made it easier for religious leaders to recognize and recruit committed members. The Roukema family was part of a tightly knit Orthodox minority enclave of *Vrijgemaakten*, within which there "were no social boundaries." Although they were not particularly interested in politics, family members listened to the sermons of the militant Reverend Klaas Schilder, who called on true believers to step up against anti-Jewish policies during the early years of the war. The oldest son, Gijs, was motivated by Schilder's words: "he encouraged us to stop talking and resist forcefully. Out of the emergency shelter, into your uniform."

The leadership of the Vrijgemaakten church was soon made aware of Gijs's attitudes toward the Nazis. A local pastor happened to be in the Roukema residence when Gijs openly expressed how excited he was about the foresight of resistance. Not much later, another reverend visited the family. He heard about Gijs's defiance toward the occupiers and knew the family because Roukema senior had been his teacher in high school. The pastor approached Gijs to become his assistant in an illegal rescue organization, an organization that came to help hundreds of Jews.

A couple of blocks from where the Roukemas lived, Spanhaak also got inspired by one of his religious foremen: Horreeus de Haas. In debates with National Socialist leader Anton Mussert, De Haas attacked

---

[21] *SVB-file 33, DOCDIRECT, Winschoten.*

the anti-Semitic foundations of the Dutch Nazi party. When he lost his job, Spanhaak was committed to do something about German policies. However, as a mainstream Protestant, he was unaware of the activities deployed in the nearby minority enclave of the Vrijgemaakten church until much later. Although willing to participate, he always remained "an outsider" to the better organized clandestine resistance networks of the small Orthodox community a few blocks away and, as a result, was never able to fully engage in organized resistance (Hilbrink 1998).

As the comparison between Roukema and Spanhaak illustrates, being a member of a minority congregation conditioned the impact that a motivated resistance fighter could have on the fate of Jews, because nascent rescuers were dependent on leadership and organization to make a difference. Compared to their majority counterparts, minority leaders had the advantage of organizers' selectivity, that is, they were more likely to recognize committed recruits and incorporate them in rescue operations (Marwell and Oliver 1993).

Intelligence created by the distinct setup of minority networks also played a role among mainstream Protestants in Catholic Groenlo, where Reverend Haspels placed Jews with those members of the Protestant youth organization whom he knew would fulfill their Christian duty of neighborly love. Men who served on the board of the Protestant Church brought Jews to their temporary hideouts. At least eighty Jews were able to find shelter in this minority community of around 500 individuals (Touw 1946).

The reverse also happened. Sometimes, minority leaders could exploit their local intelligence to determine who was not suited for clandestine work. In Goor, for instance, church chaplains refused to incorporate one of their followers into their rescue operations. As it turns out, this was a wise idea. The devoted Catholic was somewhat delusional, thinking he could single-handedly win the war by encircling city hall.[22]

Not being embedded in a community of dedicated fellows not only hampered secrecy, it also made it hard to to solve complex problems such as finding enough financial resources. The nervous diary entry of Jewish Theresa Wertheim, who decided to go underground in Enschede but was not helped by a minority congregation, is emblematic: "When does the misery finally stop? Two or three months at most and our money will be gone ... We are starting to get worried. Soon we will run out of money. Then what will happen?"[23]

---

[22] *SVB-file 40, DOCDIRECT, Winschoten.*
[23] *Diary Theresa Wertheim, www.joodscheraadenschede.nl.*

Minorities, on the other hand, were able to find financial resources because leaders had enough intelligence to selectively recruit actors with a wide range of skill sets who were willing to support their cause. When discussing the rescue activities of Catholic Chaplain Van Der Brink we already saw that minority leaders were able to mobilize funds from rich and committed parish members to overcome the problems that Theresa Wertheim was facing. Sometimes, however, the coordination of different skillsets was so strong that it solved financial problems simply by turning a rescue operation into little autarkic firms for which Jewish fugitives provided labor. In Nijverdal, an Orthodox reverend brought together an owner of a fabric store, a baker and a group of farmers, some of whom already knew each other from the Orthodox school, church or singing association.[24] The baker provided food for Jews, who in turn made bags out of straw provided by the farmers. The straw bags were then sold by the shopkeeper who used the money to pay for food. As a result, ninety Jews could be helped without any outside money.[25]

This reveals that minority networks in which close social relationships abound not only embed rescue organizers in hubs of commitment, but also create an inventory of different skills and resources available within the confines of trusted enclaves. The enclosed networks of minorities, in this way, cut across individuals with different skillsets, allowing for coordinated solutions to complex problems while minimizing risks of defection (Burt 2009).

6.8 SEGREGATION AND MIXING

One striking feature of both Catholic and Protestant rescue operations was that they tended to be completely segregated by religion. Despite cooperation among religious leaders at the national level, local clandestine networks simply reproduced the structure of Dutch society. As prewar religious networks were completely separated at a local level, recruitment of helpers was in some cases almost automatically contained within one congregation. A baker's son from Nijverdal who mobilized rescuers explains this general pattern: "We were Orthodox, hence so were our friends and customers. So these were the people where you brought [Jewish] children ... This way I placed ten Jews."[26]

---

[24] *Archive Flim NIOD 471 13 D, Amsterdam.*
[25] *SVB-file 8, DOCDIRECT, Winschoten.*
[26] *Interview Flim, Archive Flim NIOD 471 13C.*

Mutual distrust and ignorance of other different religious groups reinforced network segregation. Protestants either did not know or refused to accept that Catholics were effective organizers of rescue operations. Despite the fact that Catholic Chaplain Van Der Brink from Enschede, mentioned earlier, was able to run a rescue operation that sheltered almost 500 individuals, some Protestants still considered him reckless, incompetent and unorganized. The leader of a Protestant group in Hengelo even claimed that Catholics in general were nothing more than passive bystanders who were either cowardly or pro-German.[27] No one, however, was as extreme as Orthodox leader Johannes ter Horst, who repeatedly expressed his contempt for people from different backgrounds. He went so far as to say that he would shoot members of another denomination if he ran into them during a secret operation (Hilbrink 1989, p. 78).

Stereotypes also permeated Catholic society. Members of Catholic networks in Twente used the pejorative term "a Reverend's clique" to allude to what they saw as the passiveness and insolence of Orthodox Protestants. Mutual disrespect was equally widespread. On the rare occasion that actors from different denominations did come together, Catholics voiced annoyance with the fact that Protestants always had to start every act of communication with prayer (Hilbrink 1989).

Inherited mistrust could even trump proven dedication to the illegal cause. In Catholic Borne, a member of the majority church volunteered to join a Protestant resistance organization after helping one of its leaders escape a German security official. Despite the risks that the boy had taken to save the life of one of its core members, the organization refused his further services because he was considered "too loose" by the Protestant community. This reputation, it should be noted, was partly created by his mother, who spread salacious rumors about him to sabotage his recent relationship with a Protestant girl. As a good Catholic, she could not approve of this interreligious relationship.[28]

Actors aiming to bridge religious divides were seen as intruders by other resistance fighters. In Almelo, a social democrat decided to join an Orthodox group in 1943. Despite the fact that he had already proven to be a dedicated resistance worker on his own, he could not make it past the status of outsider. Other Orthodox Protestants found it difficult to cooperate with him and looked at him with contempt. On more than one

---

[27] *SVB-file 22, DOCDIRECT, Winschoten. Archive NIOD, 251a 61.*
[28] *SVB-file 52, DOCDIRECT, Winschoten.*

occasion they tried to get rid of him by providing misinformation about future meetings and activities. A year after he joined the organization, he was arrested.[29]

As came up in the stories of Chaplains Van Der Brink and Visser, religious leaders often actively guarded the boundaries of their groups. In the same vein, Leendert Overduin, reverend of the tiny "Reformed Church in Restored Dependency" in Enschede, also made sure that his networks did not interfere more than strictly necessary with the activities of other groups. Overduin was infuriated when he found out that one of the families in his network had recently started to house an illegal worker, who was on a mission to kill a local collaborator on behalf of a different resistance network. He did everything in his power to prevent the murder from happening and had the resistance member removed from the household (Weustink 1985).

Overduin had repeated arguments with a secular rescuer, Tusveld, about who should take care of specific Jews. Overduin did not trust Tusveld, and both men refused to cooperate with each other despite the fact that they were sheltering members of the same family (Bekkenkamp 2000).[30] Overduin's closest accomplice commented that "you got reprimanded"[31] by Overduin for engaging in other resistance activities and networks.[32]

In one extreme case, arguments over segregation even created a rupture within one organization. In Catholic Oldenzaal, a Protestant rescue mission led by political party leaders Van Der V. and P. operated at the margins because it could not recruit widely. Van Der V. tried to circumvent this problem by coopting the help of a few Catholics from outside his trusted circle. P. was outraged when he found out about this and immediately decided to separate himself from the already minuscule organization. After the war, it was discovered that P. was on to something as the two Catholic recruits were actually traitors.[33]

---

[29] *SVB-file 41, DOCDIRECT, Winschoten.*

[30] *SVB-file 28, DOCDIRECT, Winschoten. SVB-file 13, DOCDIRECT, Winschoten.*

[31] *SVB-file 14, DOCDIRECT, Winschoten.*

[32] The fact that Overduin tried to keep his organization isolated from outside influences is also revealed by the postwar story of Gonny Mensink. She was an important Catholic member of the resistance working at city hall who, by accident, took Overduin for a traitor. Mensink had never heard of Overduin resistance work because she mostly interacted with members of the Roman Catholic community of Enschede (Bekkenkamp 2000).

[33] *SVB-file 50, DOCDIRECT, Winschoten. SVB-file 33, DOCDIRECT, Winschoten.*

Several other cases reveal that minority leaders had good reason to be concerned about religious mixing, as it often undermined their clandestine mobilization advantage by increasing exposure. When information left the confines of the minority enclave, coordination problems emerged, and denunciation became more likely. The story of Catholic boy scout leader Van Hessen and his friend Jan Buiter in Protestant Almelo, is insightful. Although the network emerged within the confines of a Catholic minority community, it suddenly expanded outward. This turned out to have dramatic consequences for the movement. For Van Hessen, secrecy was of the utmost importance. He even refused to tell his own brother the exact details of his activities. After a while, however, Buiter became less careful and started to recruit outside of his friend's safe network, feeling that the Catholic enclave was too small for his ambitions. The resulting inclusion of people from different backgrounds caused internal conflict about which strategy to pursue and, eventually, became Buiter's downfall, at least according to Van Hessen: "In the beginning, he [Buiter] relied heavily on my contacts to build up a resistance network. Soon, however he seemed to know more people than I did. He even forged a link between our group and the LO [Protestant]. Soon after, the network was betrayed and infiltrated by a V-Man [Nazi-spy]."[34] Together with Orthodox Protestant organizers Breteler and Van Heek, several members of the movement, including Buiter, were arrested. Before the arrest, several people had already warned Buiter that the movement was becoming too visible (Hilbrink 1989).

After this period of German repression and backlash, Van Hessen moved back to a more segregated setup, which in his own view was safer: "we decided to go fully underground again. Shield the organization from the outside world to make it harder to penetrate by outsiders. Create a more camouflaged and fragmented organization."[35]

The story of Buiter and Van Hessen is emblematic of numerous cases where religious boundary crossing resulted in operational failure of whole rescue missions. Mixing, however, could also affect the success rate within the same rescue operation. In Catholic Borne, an anonymous Protestant minister encouraged at least two families within his parish to shelter Jews.[36] Whereas the first worked in isolation and was able to keep Jews underground despite several searches,[37] the latter failed to

---

[34] *SVB-file 47, DOCDIRECT, Winschoten.*
[35] *SVB-file 47, DOCDIRECT, Winschoten.*
[36] *SVB-file 51, DOCDIRECT, Winschoten.*
[37] *SVB-file 30, DOCDIRECT, Winschoten.*

do so. The head of the second household was arrested during a meeting with socialist and Catholic resistance workers. The meeting was setup to resolve disagreements about the distribution of food coupons between different factions within the network.[38] All but one of the attendees was arrested (Hilbrink 1989).

All of these examples reveal how selective retention amplifies the overall segregation of clandestine organizations. Expansion of recruitment outside the confines of existing groups was appealing to some as it could enlarge an organization's impact and scope. Unfortunately, networks that scaled outward often created internal differences in ideology, strategy or style. This triggered innate strife and, in turn, increased the demand for coordination and reduced the likelihood that a rescue organization could keep intelligence out of the hands of stronger opponents.

6.9 HOW DO JEWS ENTER MINORITY NETWORKS?

Given these high levels of religious segregation, one wonders how Jews and nascent Christian rescuers came into contact. Based on postwar testimonies, it is possible to identify three common pathways through which this happened. First, religious leaders sometimes made the first step and contacted Jews in their neighborhood to offer their help or motivated their parish members to do so (Weustink 1985).[39] This is what the aforementioned Leendert Overduin did. Shocked by the early roundup of Jews in September 1941, he started convincing Jews to go underground.[40] The first Jews he helped lived on his street and were brought in by his parish member, Arend Holl, who lived nearby (Bekkenkamp 2000). The chaplain of Glanerbrug also took the first step in forging a link between Jews and parish members (Weustink 1985). Catholic Grunningman told Jews in his neighborhood: "If you want to leave, just tell me."[41] Reverend Dijkhuis from Borne asked Jewish refugees whom she housed before the war to come live with her in her Mennonite retreat after the German invasion.[42]

Second, Jews sometimes themselves took the initiative to ask local clergy for help. This often happened on a collective basis via Jewish

---

[38] *SVB-file 51, DOCDIRECT, Winschoten.*

[39] *Yad Vashem file B. Oskam, in Michman et al. Interview Grunningman. Archive NIOD 251a-117, Amsterdam. Yad Vashem file H. Dijkhuis in Michman et al.*

[40] *Yad Vashem file B. Oskam, in Michman et al.*

[41] *Interview Grunningman. Archive NIOD 251a-117, Amsterdam.*

[42] *Yad Vashem file H. Dijkhuis in Michman et al.*

councils or rabbis. As early as September 1941, the local Jewish council of Enschede contacted local clergy to find addresses for twenty-one Jews (Bekkenkamp 2000). The third and most frequent bridge between Christian communities and Jews was formed through a process of scale shift (McAdam, Tarrow and Tilly 2001). Initially, Jews were often helped by neighbors (Bekkenkamp 2000),[43] colleagues,[44] family physicians,[45] neighborhood patrolmen,[46] business relationships,[47] former customers or nearby friends (Rossum 2011).[48] After a while, these localized early helpers realized that, despite their best intentions, they could not manage to keep Jews sheltered for prolonged periods of time without outside help. The extent to which one could find help within local communities then determined whether one could continue rescue activities. Looking for help within one's own faith-based community was a self-evident next step because people found it hard to believe that someone in their own church would let them down. In general, religious leaders were the default contacts for their parishioners in times of need. People who had problems housing Jews were simply recommended by their friends "to go to the pastor" (Hilbrink 1998, p. 134).

Throughout the country, individual rescuers were forced to consult religious leaders or religious resistance groups when confronted with Jewish demands for more moving space,[49] additional requests for protection (Noltus 1983), food shortages,[50] increased risk of exposure,[51] imminent house searches,[52] financial problems,[53] health issues,[54] military destruction[55] and leaked information.[56] In some cases, unorganized

---

[43] *SVB-file 34, DOCDIRECT, Winschoten.*
[44] *Yad Vashem file J. Hofstra in Michman et al. Yad Vashem file M. Coelingh in Michman et al.*
[45] *Yad Vashem file T. Velsing in Michman et al.*
[46] *SVB-file 23, DOCDIRECT, Winschoten.*
[47] *SVB-file 9, DOCDIRECT, Winschoten. SVB-file 36, DOCDIRECT, Winschoten. Yad Vashem file F. Pakker in Michman et al.*
[48] *Yad Vashem file G. Olink in Michman et al. Yad Vashem file D. Somsen in Michman et al.*
[49] Hovingh (2015).
[50] *Yad Vashem file A. Ten Tije in Michman et al.*
[51] *SVB-file 55, DOCDIRECT, Winschoten.*
[52] *SVB-file 34, DOCDIRECT, Winschoten.*
[53] *SVB-file 42, DOCDIRECT, Winschoten.*
[54] *Yad Vashem file L. Gerritsen in Michman et al.*
[55] *Yad Vashem file N. Talsma in Michman et al.*
[56] *Yad Vashem A. Hijmans in Michman et al.*

helpers also asked their religious leaders for advice, spiritual guidance[57] or even approval before they would take in a Jew.[58] As a result, isolated attempts often coalesced into religious rescue networks once collective action problems surfaced, shifting the scale of collective action from the household to the community level.

6.10 INTERREGIONAL TIES

Apart from confirming the importance of isolation and commitment, the case studies also reveal a third mechanism that links minority status to successful rescue: the ability to setup interregional ties to move Jews from one locality to another. Although reliance on help elsewhere entailed risks, it also facilitated clandestinity. Sometimes Jews were both well known and unpopular in their neighborhoods. In these cases, it would be easy for Nazis to detect Jews if they stayed near their original home. This made relocation important for retaining secrecy.[59]

Due to a lack of critical mass within their own locality, minority groups were often forced to cooperate with like-minded groups across local borders to keep their religious activities running. During the war, such ties with religious fellows in different localities could now be exploited to funnel Jews from one county to another. For instance, when the deportations intensified, Overduin's small parish in Enschede reached the limits of its carrying capacity. To expand his network, he exploited his contacts with Protestant leaders in other parts of the country. He placed Jews with religious leaders in the east (Nijmegen, Harderwijk), west (Hilversum), south (Limburg) and even the far north (Hovingh 2015).[60] Instead of only leading his parish, he now became a middleman located between different religious minority leaders who were at the helm of their own rescue congregations. For safety reasons, however, he never interfered in local relationships between these minority leaders and their followers and only communicated with religious leaders.[61] The same is true for Catholics, as the previously mentioned boy scout networks of Buiter and Grunningman often forged links between localities. In a similar vein, Catholic Chaplain Van Der Brink from Enschede placed Jews

---

[57] *Yad Vashem file Scheffer in Michman et al.*
[58] *Yad Vashem file J. Musch in Michman et al.*
[59] *Yad Vashem file G. Haveman in Michman et al.*
[60] *Yad Vashem file C. Moulijn in Michman et al.*
[61] *SVB-file 51, DOCDIRECT, Winschoten.*

with congregants living on farms in villages twenty kilometers outside of the city.[62]

This role of interregional networks, however, was most pronounced among Orthodox Protestants. Although most Orthodox rescue operation emerged in local isolation, ties between reverends did facilitate some interregional cooperation on an ad hoc basis. When the baker's son Flim contacted the Orthodox Protestant Reverend Hamming in Nijverdal to place eighty Jews, the latter realized that it would be impossible to do so in his small parish. Hamming wrote a letter of introduction to his colleagues Vogelaar and Teeuwen in the neighboring towns of Lemele and Heerde, explaining the situation. Together, the three parishes were able to find the required addresses to keep the group of Jews hidden throughout the war.[63]

The enhanced ability of minority groups to setup strong interregional networks, dovetails nicely with the (rather famous) argument that small religious groups formed a crucial role in the creation of long-distance capitalism (Weber 1985; Greif 2006). According to Greif, Jewish traders in the eleventh century formed the backbone of premodern trade relations between different regions within the Muslim Mediterranean. Because Jews formed isolated pockets throughout the region, they were able to constitute an interregional coalition within which partners could credibly communicate expected obligations of implicit trade contracts. As a result, traders could enforce agreements by tarnishing community reputations in cases of negligence.

Weber made a related, but distinct, observation about Protestants sects in the United States. He was surprised by the fact that businessmen who were trying to establish themselves in a new locality were always asked about their religious background. He later found out that religious denomination acted as an important marker of trust and credibility. According to the German sociologist, members of small congregations were more likely to find trade partners who trusted them as "Whereever he goes the member finds a small congregation of fellow believers which receives him as a brother upon recommendation from his previous congregation ... an advantage shared by all diaspora religions, such as Judaism" (Weber [1968] 1978).

The parallel with rescue networks is clear. In both cases, members of minority communities could find reliable partners in different regions

---

[62] *Interview kapelaan Van Der Brink, NIOD, Amsterdam.*
[63] *Yad Vashem file R. Hamming in Michman et al.*

who could help funnel either highly valued goods or people. The notion that minorities were so successful in staging resistance of the Holocaust because they formed interregional networks connecting dense tight-knit pockets of committed members also resonates with the literature on violent mobilization. When writing about powerful insurgencies in southeast Asia, Staniland argues that violence against states can be sustained longest when it is embedded in localized hubs of commitment that are connected by strong supra-local ties between communities (Staniland 2014).

6.11 EMPATHY AND THE PROTECTION OF GENTILES

One way to assess whether empathy and pluralistic norms played a role in activating resistance to genocide is to compare rescue operations for excluded Jews with resistance operations that represented the interests of in-group members. Both types of rescue organizations heavily rely on clandestinity to survive. However, only the former type of rescue mission would be strengthened by empathy with outsiders, as protecting members of one's own ethnic or religious group does not require this moral impetus.

If, on top of clandestine capacity, empathy for marginalized groups was driving minority mobilization against genocide, we would expect religious minority congregations to be more strongly overrepresented among rescue operations for Jews than among rescue operations for fellow gentiles. If clandestine capacity alone was driving the minority advantage, we would not expect to see a difference in minority overrepresentation between the two types of clandestine resistance.

As was mentioned in Chapter 3, deportations were extended to include gentiles in late 1943, although students and the unemployed were persecuted throughout the war. I have culled the postwar testimonies for Twente described earlier to retrieve information on faith-based resistance organizations that protected coreligionists. They are mapped in Figures 6.5 and 6.6. For the reader's convenience, I have also reprinted religious rescue networks for Jews. It is immediately clear that rescue operations for gentiles were more widespread than rescue operations for Jews.

When comparing the religious representation on these maps, it becomes clear that, although religious minority groups are overrepresented, they played a less prominent role for resistance groups that sheltered coreligionists. In Twente, slightly more than 50 percent or

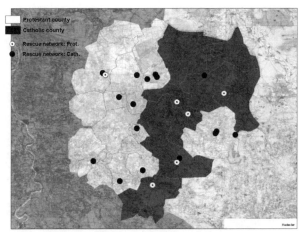

(a) Protestant and Catholic networks rescuing Jews

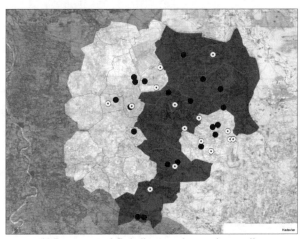

(b) Protestant and Catholic networks rescuing gentiles

FIGURE 6.5 Protestant and Catholic networks in Twente.

twenty-one out of forty-one of all resistance groups for gentiles were embedded in minority congregations, while more than 90 percent of all missions rescuing Jews emerged out of minority enclaves. It is important to highlight that fourteen networks saved both Jews and gentiles, resulting in a total of only six minority operations that were set up for gentiles only. Often, rescue networks for gentiles build on clandestine operations that had emerged in response to the Holocaust. Taken together, this suggests that on top of the clandestine capacity of minority congregations, minority empathy with marginalized outsiders functioned

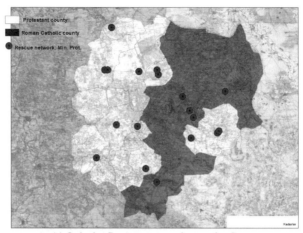

(a) Orthodox Protestant networks rescuing Jews

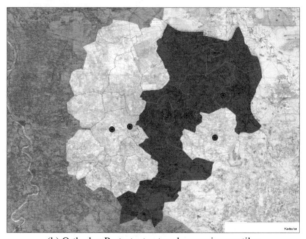

(b) Orthodox Protestant networks rescuing gentiles

FIGURE 6.6 Orthodox Protestant networks in Twente.

as an additional mechanism linking minority status to rescue operations for victims of mass persecution.

6.12 CONCLUSION

In support of the minority thesis, the narrowly confined comparison of rescue operations in Catholic and Protestant Twente reveals that a) religious minority leaders were able to exploit the mobilizing capacity of committed members to overcome the clandestine collective action dilemma; b) majority leaders that tried to do this were more likely to get denounced early on; c) religious mixing undermined the minority advantage by undercutting isolation; and d) as a result of this, insulated pockets of Protestants were more successful in protecting Jews in areas dominated by Catholics, while the same was true for Catholic enclaves in Protestant regions.

In addition to providing support for the minority hypothesis, the case study also helps us link deeply structural factors to actual outcomes by suggesting three feedback mechanisms that translate the (somewhat) abstract minority advantage into actual higher levels of clandestine mobilization. Group commitment assures members that mobilization is possible (Elster 1979), helps leaders to recruit the right operatives (Marwell and Oliver 1993) and improves the selective survival of groups by reducing infiltration from outsiders (Aldrich 1999). Whereas the first two hinge on the recognition of opportunities by forward-looking actors, the latter, selective survival, is more evolutionary in logic.

Interestingly, the structured comparison also highlights an unanticipated advantage that minorities had when setting up rescue operations. Dovetailing with existing work that centers on the important role that small religious groups play in creating and sustaining long-distance economic collaboration (Weber 1985; Greif 2006), postwar testimonies show that minority congregations were better at fostering interregional ties that helped Jews escape to other parts of the country. A comparison between clandestine rescue operations for Jews and fellow Christians showed that the minority advantage was much stronger for the former than the latter. This provides suggestive evidence for the fact that, on top of enhanced capacity, empathy with outsiders plays an important role in producing minority resistance to genocide.

In this chapter I assessed the minority hypothesis with high-quality data while keeping a large number of potential confounding variables constant. The downside of a narrowly confined comparison is that it limits the external validity of the study. How do we know that the findings are not unique to the small geographical region under study? The case studies give some reason to believe that this is indeed the case. When talking about the Roman Catholic network setup by Grunningman, we saw that a minority rescue operation emerged because he had more success in creating clandestine organizations in minority areas than in majority areas. This process of course only operates in regions with a diverse religious landscape where organizers can move back and forth between majority and minority congregations of the same religious color. Therefore, the apparent minority effect that we observe in Twente could be unique to border regions or regions that are religiously diverse. To see whether this is the case or not, I conduct shadow case studies of rescue networks in two homogeneously Protestant and two homogeneously Catholic provinces as well as a quantitative analysis of rescuers throughout the Netherlands in the next chapter. If the minority pattern is also visible in these analyses, we can be more certain that we are capturing a general process.

6.A APPENDIX

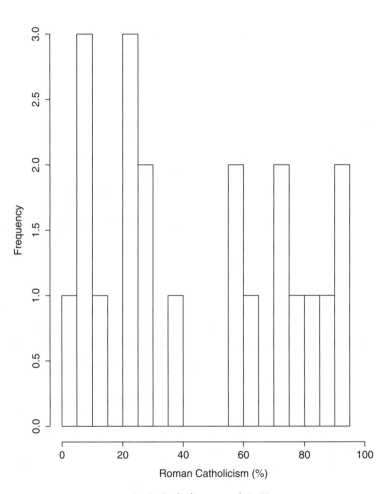

FIGURE 6.A1 Catholic strength in Twente.

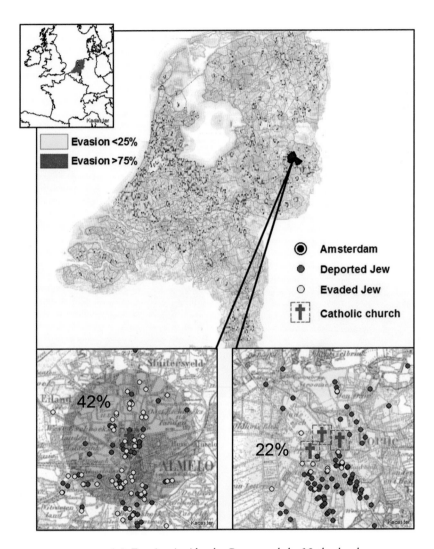

Evasion <25%

Evasion >75%

Amsterdam

Deported Jew

Evaded Jew

Catholic church

42%

22%

FIGURE 1.1 Evasion in Almelo, Borne and the Netherlands.

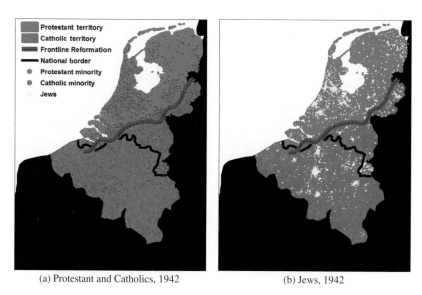

(a) Protestant and Catholics, 1942 (b) Jews, 1942

FIGURE 1.2 Religious minorities in the Netherlands and Belgium.

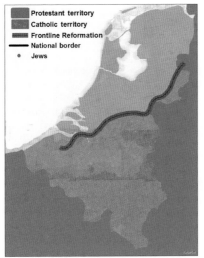

(a) Frontline insurgency 1579

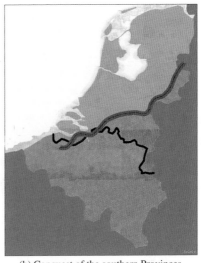

(b) Conquest of the southern Provinces and national split, 1648

(c) Religion in the Low Countries before outbreak of World War II

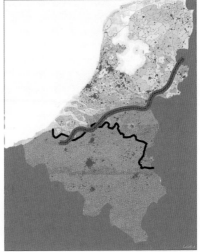

(d) Jews in the Low Countries, 1942

FIGURE 3.1 Evolution of religion in the Low Countries, 1579–1945.

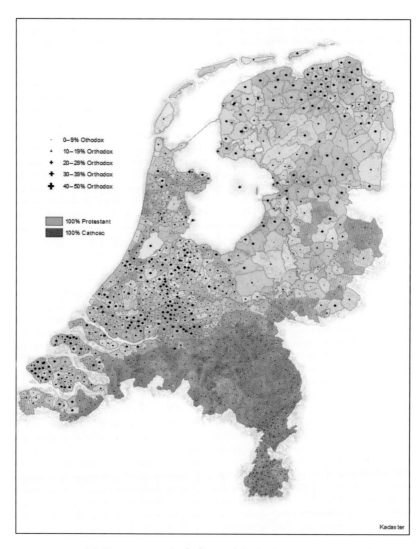

FIGURE 3.2 Protestants, Catholics and Orthodox Protestants in the
Netherlands, 1930 (CBS 1931).

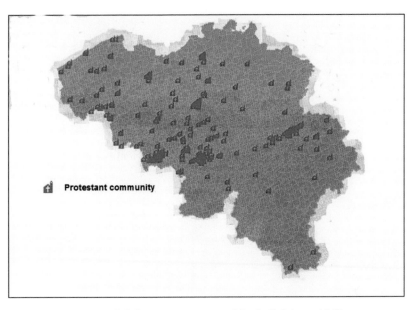

FIGURE 3.3 Protestant communities in Belgium, 1950
(Katholiek jaarboek van Belgie 1950).

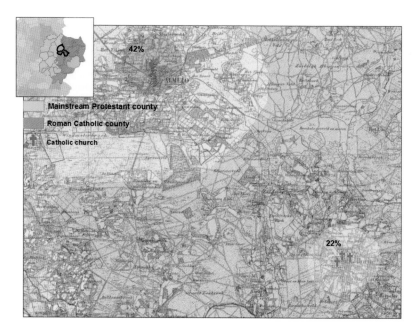

FIGURE 5.1 Jewish evasion in Almelo and Borne.

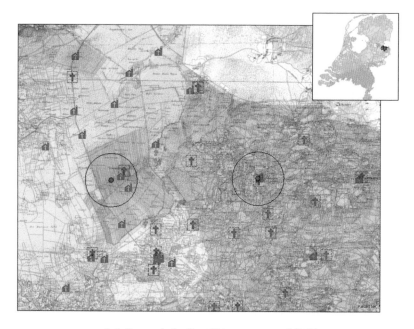

FIGURE 5.4 Example buffer: Vriezenveen and Tubbergen.

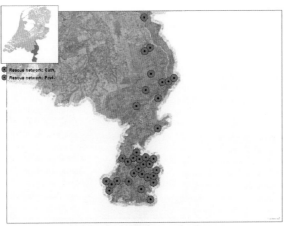
(a) Minority networks rescuing Jews

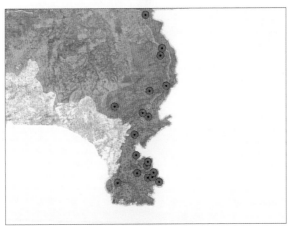
(b) Majority networks rescuing Jews

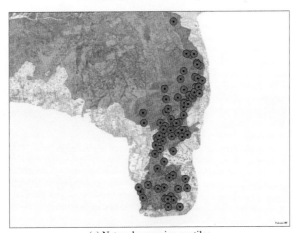
(c) Networks rescuing gentiles

FIGURE 7.1 Resistance networks in Limburg.

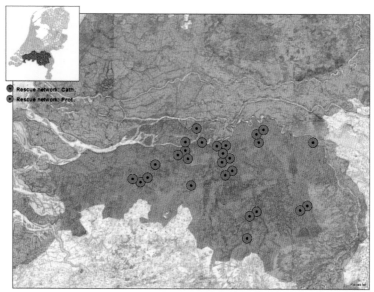

(a) Minority networks

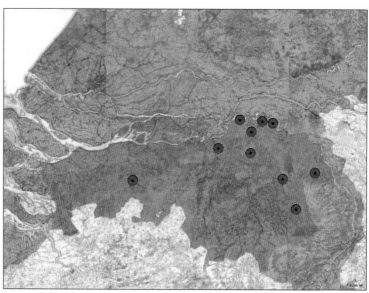

(b) Majority networks

FIGURE 7.2 Rescue networks in Brabant.

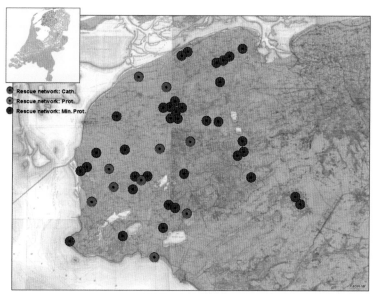

(a) Minority networks

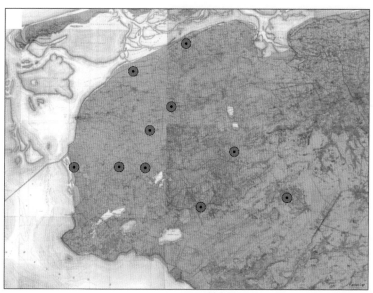

(b) Majority networks

FIGURE 7.3 Rescue networks in Friesland.

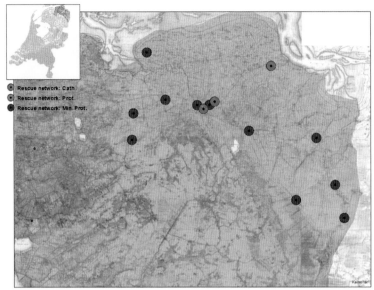

(a) Minority networks

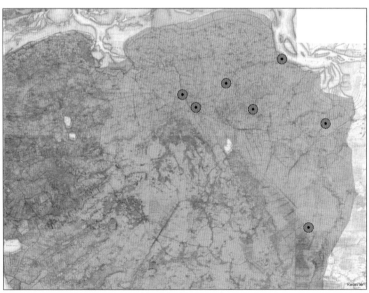

(b) Majority networks

FIGURE 7.4 Rescue networks in Groningen.

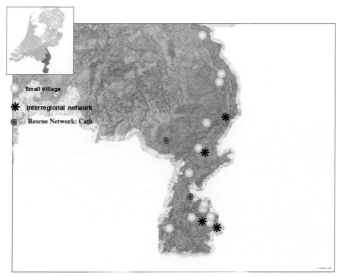

(a) Zuid-Limburg

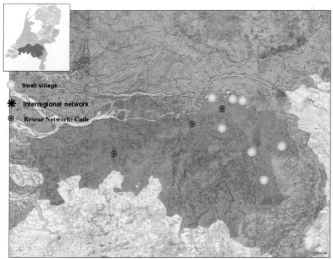

(b) Noord-Brabant

FIGURE 8.2 Majority networks in southern provinces.

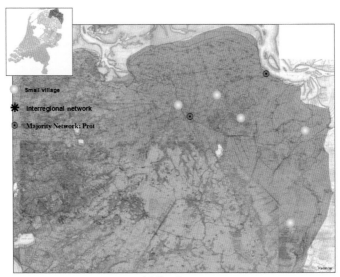

(a) Groningen

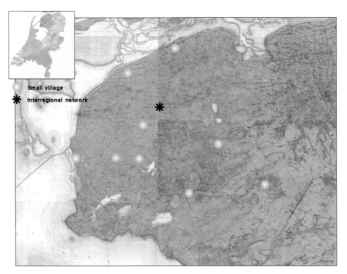

(b) Friesland

FIGURE 8.3 Majority networks in northern provinces.

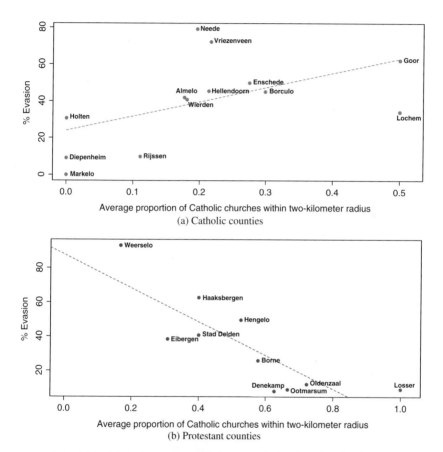

FIGURE 8.4 Evasion and proximity to Catholic churches in Twente
(counties Jews>10).

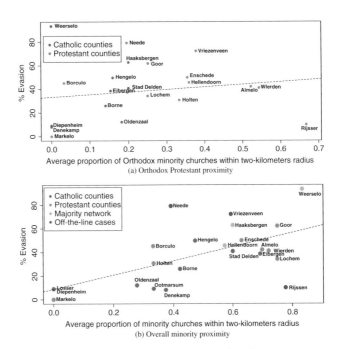

FIGURE 8.5 Evasion and proximity to minority churches in Twente (counties Jews>10).

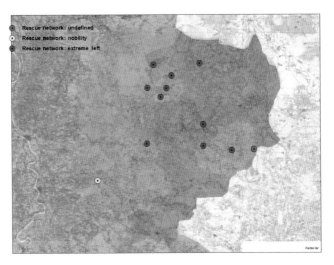

FIGURE 8.6 Secular rescue networks in Twente.

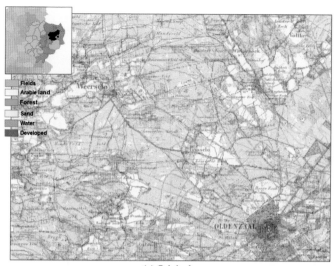

(a) Original

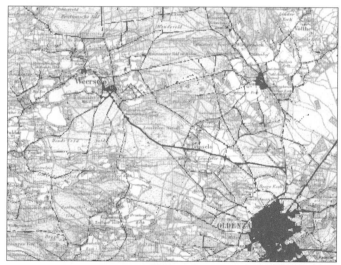

(b) Created

FIGURE 8.7 Example land-use data: Weerselo and Oldenzaal, 1960.

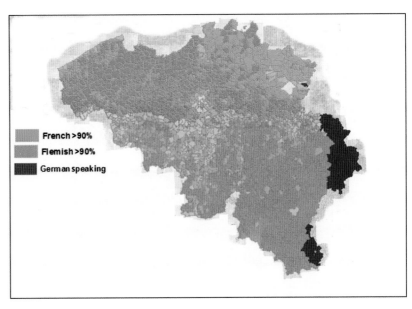

FIGURE 10.4 Geographical distribution of the French and Flemish in Belgium, 1930 (Vanhaute and Vrielinck 2013).

7

Religious Minorities and Rescue beyond Twente

7.1 INTRODUCTION

During the winter of 1942, Gerald Pontier, a Protestant minister in the Catholic town of Heerlen, Limburg, was approached by two fellow Protestants from Amsterdam who were carrying a recommendation letter from his big-city colleague, Orthodox Reverend Sikkel, whom he greatly admired (Hovingh 2015). The men were trying to find shelter for the Jewish Braun family. Pontier was able to step up and provided the two Amsterdammers with a list of reliable Protestant families whom they could contact for help (Flim 1997). After Heerlen, the two Protestants went on to Catholic Venlo,[1] Sittard,[2] Geleen,[3] Treebeek,[4] Hengelo and Rossum[5] to setup new rescue "districts" with the help of Protestant clerics or congregants who Pontier knew from before the war.[6]

The two men had, without much success, used the same recommendation letter to try to find shelter for Jews in the Protestant provinces Groningen and Holland.[7] Despite the abundance of Protestant congregations, no help could be found. Everywhere they went they got the same message: "We sympathize with the Jews but we have no room to place

---

[1] SVB-file 25, DOCDIRECT, Winschoten. SVB-file 32, DOCDIRECT, Winschoten.
[2] SVB-file 39, DOCDIRECT, Winschoten.
[3] Yad Vashem file J. Tabak in Michman et al.
[4] Yad Vashem file D. Spoelstra in Michman et al.
[5] Archive Flim NIOD 471 13 B, Amsterdam.
[6] Archive Flim NIOD 471 13 B, Amsterdam.
[7] SVB-file 49, DOCDIRECT, Winschoten.

them."[8] After several failed attempts, the men did find a religious leader in the Protestant north who was willing to help out. The leader, however, was not, as one would expect, a fellow Protestant; rather, Chaplain Jansen helmed a minority enclave of Catholics in Sneek. Inspired by their successful cooperation with Jansen, the same students tried to involve chaplains in more Catholic regions of the country, without much success. Here they instead had to confine their shelters to the Protestant addresses provided by Protestant reverend Pontier.[9]

The previous chapter presented evidence that minority mobilization indeed drove the differential evasion of Jews in the Netherlands. It also established that minority mobilization was less important for other types of clandestine resistance, indicating that minority empathy operated in conjunction with minority capacity to produce networks of assistance for threatened outsiders. The analysis, however, was based on a small-scale comparison in an area of limited geographical scope.

To make sure that the specific dynamics of the Twente region are not driving the findings, this chapter presents shadow case studies for two completely Protestant provinces in the north and two completely Catholic provinces in the south in addition to a statistical analysis of Christian rescue throughout the Netherlands. I focus on four religiously homogenous regions of the country to establish that the minority hypothesis is not specific to areas close to the religious fault line. Data for the four shadow cases are again obtained from the earlier discussed *Foundation 40/45*. Based on a name list of 1,013 religious rescues compiled by Yad Vashem (Michman et al. 2004), I was able to track down dossiers of 500 rescuers who requested an additional stipend from the state and were living outside of Twente. These files are complemented with existing literature to fill contextual gaps.

The lists provided by Yad Vashem are also utilized for the statistical analysis. Yad Vashem's files provide information on the locations where religious rescuers were active during the war and whether they were arrested or not. This information is deployed to statistically analyze whether minority groups were indeed more likely to mobilize and less likely to get arrested once they did. In addition, I compare the secretive mobilization on behalf of Jews with other types of clandestine resistance to assess the overall importance of empathy in producing resistance to genocide. Although the data for the shadow cases is less refined and less complete than that presented in the previous chapter, it does indicate that

---

[8] *SVB-file 14, DOCDIRECT, Winschoten.*
[9] *Archive Flim NIOD 471 11 B, Amsterdam.*

the lessons drawn from the Twente case travel well beyond its borders. As the story at the start of this chapter reveals, even the success of one and the same rescue organization throughout the country depended on whether it approached isolated minority enclaves.

7.2 CATHOLIC ZUID-LIMBURG

Located near the border with Belgium is the Catholic province of Limburg. One of the main forces underlying the rescue activities in the provincial capital Maastricht was Van A., a member of a tiny Protestant parish in this Catholic bulwark. As a tax officer, he had substantial contact with local Jewish business men, whom he began helping when the deportations started. Together with his fellow parish members, including an alderman who owned a grocery store and could provide food, a local police officer who warned about upcoming raids and a photographer who forged identity papers, Van A. represents yet another enclave that encompassed and mobilized a wide range of different skill sets (Bronzwaer 2010).

Religious bonds of trust within his minority enclave enabled Van A. to funnel Jews to several small Protestant communities throughout the southern part of the province, which were connected because they all attended the same central church in the city.[10] Here we see how interregional networks emerge because minority groups lacked critical mass and were forced to form congregations with coreligionists outside their own village.

This was not the only rescue operation produced by the Protestants in Maastricht. Courrech Staal was an alderman of the Dutch Reformed community. One late evening in 1942 he rang the bell at the home of the Jewish Salmangs, who lived right across the street. After a brief chat, Staal proposed to shelter the two Salmang children, Eva and Otto, an offer that in Eva Salmang's words, "saved my live."[11] Largely thanks to these two operations, over 49 percent of all Jews living in the vicinity of Protestant churches survived the war in and around Maastricht, the largest number in the whole province.

As in Twente, the contrast with Catholic majority rescue operations in Maastricht is stark. Inspired by the pro-Semitic protests of the

---

[10] *SVB-file 6, DOCDIRECT, Winschoten. SVB-file 24, DOCDIRECT, Winschoten. SVB-file 53, DOCDIRECT, Winschoten.*

[11] *Yad Vashem file C. Staal in Michman et al.*

Episcopate, a local trader and an almoner who knew each other from the Catholic youth movement started providing Jews with illegal paperwork. Their efforts were short lived as both men were arrested in early 1943. A postwar testimony from the owner of the nearby grocery store reveals why: "He told everyone in my store that he was anti-German and that he possessed illegal military coordinates on a map. He trusted everyone. This became his downfall."[12] In much the same way, a Catholic chaplain in the Amby neighborhood of Maastricht who sheltered Jews was betrayed by one of his own parish members.[13]

The seemingly higher risks involved in majority rescue often inhibited mobilization altogether. With few exceptions (see the next chapter), Catholic clergy were extremely reluctant to help in the southern city of Roermond, about thirty kilometers to the north of Maastricht, as they considered resistance "reckless" and feared infiltration. Even the extremely well-organized labor unions could not be exploited to setup clandestine operations.[14] Tragically, the chaplains that did participate in rescue operations were forced to flee the country[15] or ended up in internment camps.[16] It bears mentioning that I have not discovered any evidence of Protestant networks in this area.[17]

Protestants did, however, play a key role in initiating pro-Jewish resistance in neighboring Heerlen. The main organizer here was Reverend Gerard Pontier, who we met at the beginning of this chapter. He approached the Jewish Silber family, which was living nearby, saying: "if you ever need help, come to us" (Flim 1997). After encouraging Jews living in his neighborhood to go underground, he organized his isolated parish into a tight-knit community that insulated Jews from outside infiltration (Van Rens 2013). Because of this religious deviance, Catholic neighbors accused Pontier's followers of being Nazis and shied away from contact. This enhanced their already existing isolation and prevented people from finding out about their clandestine operations.[18] The

---

[12] *SVB-file 12, DOCDIRECT, Winschoten.*

[13] *SVB-file 54, DOCDIRECT, Winschoten.*

[14] *Archive NIOD, 251a 119.*

[15] *Archive NIOD, 251a 119.*

[16] *SVB-file 46, DOCDIRECT, Winschoten.*

[17] There is some evidence that a Protestant safe house was located in Roermond, but I have not been able to find any information about any rescue network associated with it (Cammaert 1994).

[18] *SVB-file 7, DOCDIRECT, Winschoten. Yad Vashem file H. Bockma in Michman et al. Archive Flim NIOD 471 13 B, Amsterdam.*

overall process is probably best symbolized by how Jewish children were transported from one safe house to another within Heerlen; because some of these children had "Semitic looks," they could not simply walk openly in public. Instead, a group of Protestant children gathered, formed a line and played a game of leapfrog, limiting exposure of facial characteristics by forming a human caterpillar.[19] Quite literally, Protestants in Heerlen placed a protective shell around Jews. As a result, 53 percent of all Jews living in and around Pontier's parish survived the war.

The importance of Protestant isolation for sustaining secrecy becomes apparent when we compare Pontier's network with Catholic rescue missions that also emerged in and around Heerlen. The Catholic Hustinx family, for instance, started sheltering Louis Mossel in August 1943, treating him like a member of the family. However, they were not able to keep his stay a secret. In the fall of the same year, Louis had to leave the Hustinx household because neighbors, who were members of the local Nazi party, threatened to betray them. Discouraged by the situation, Louis left for a new shelter.[20] The outcome could have been worse as other Catholic families in Heerlen sheltering Jews were actually exposed and arrested due to personally motived denunciations,[21] German intelligence work,[22] community gossiping,[23] infiltration[24] or betrayal from nearby collaborators.[25] A local chaplain in Heerlen was even arrested after delivering an anti-German sermon.[26]

Similar to what we saw in Twente, Pontier's network operated independently of Catholic resistance groups. After the war, Protestant resistance operatives in Heerlen were unable to testify about the illegal activities of Catholic counterparts, as they alway operated separately. Catholics were seen as acting and dressing strangely, going to ungodly bars and believing that Mary was a saint, and hence they could not be trusted.[27] When asked to name Protestant rescuers, however, the same people provided pages of notes.[28]

[19] *SVB-file 39, DOCDIRECT, Winschoten.*

[20] *Yad Vashem file G. Hustinx in Michman et al.*

[21] *SVB-file 5, DOCDIRECT, Winschoten.*

[22] *SVB-file 19, DOCDIRECT, Winschoten.*

[23] *SVB-file 29, DOCDIRECT, Winschoten.*

[24] *SVB-file 2, DOCDIRECT, Winschoten.*

[25] *SVB-file 4, DOCDIRECT, Winschoten.*

[26] *SVB-file 35, DOCDIRECT, Winschoten.*

[27] *SVB-file 29, DOCDIRECT, Winschoten. Archive Flim NIOD 471 13 B, Amsterdam.*

[28] *Yad Vashem file H. Bockma in Michman et al.*

In part, mutual unawareness can be explained by the fact that in times of uncertainty, people are more hesitant to trust strangers and, thus, they only recruit along existing lines of trust.[29] It seems equally important that rescue coordinators in Heerlen, much like Leendert Overduin in Twente, aggressively kept their operation separate from resistance movements surrounding them.[30] When one of Pontier's contact men found out that the operation's helpers had forged a link with a Catholic organization that helped downed allied pilots, he scolded the operative and destroyed the tie immediately.[31] It is quite plausible that this move benefited the operation, as the Catholic pilot organization was infiltrated in the summer of 1943, bringing down several clandestine missions in the region, including one in Maastricht that focused on protecting Jews (Cammaert 1994).

The most compelling evidence that minority isolation played a crucial role in sustaining protection reveals itself in the summer of 1944, when waves of repression, initiated by the SIPO-SD and bounty hunters, dismantled numerous Catholic majority rescue networks in Venray, Oirlo, Broekhuizervorst and Castenray. With few exceptions, Protestant operations remain intact. This development did not go unnoticed by interregional rescue workers, who started to worry about the safety of Catholic networks in the south and instead attempted to focus more on their Protestant counterparts (Cammaert 1994).

Interestingly, Catholics from Limburg were able to mobilize only if they moved to a Protestant environment. The Holocaust put an enormous administrative pressure on the bureaucracy of Amsterdam. Because of this increased workload, the city had to hire civil servants from other parts of the country. Two of these new workers came from Limburg. While rescue in their hometowns was largely a Protestant phenomenon, the new recruits were able to exploit their newly acquired minority position to set up an illegal warning system for Jews. As for the functioning of this warning system, one of them later said: "In a hostile environment where you could not know who was good or bad, trust was crucial. A little too much babbling could be fatal. We, however, were both from Limburg and knew each other's culture. Because of this we were able

---

[29] *SVB-file 43, DOCDIRECT, Winschoten.*

[30] Only reluctantly were some Catholics allowed into the operation. Here strong interreligious friendship ties formed the bridge (Cammaert 1994).

[31] *Yad Vashem file J. Musch in Michman et al. SVB-file 49, DOCDIRECT, Winschoten.*

to develop a meticulous approach. It was important that we stayed independent of our other colleagues."[32]

A bird's-eye view of the whole province in Figure 7.1 confirms the importance of minority rescue. Although less than 4 percent of the population of Limburg was Protestant, thirty-three out of all fifty-one networks emerged within the confines of a Protestant congregation.

In the last part of the previous chapter, I showed that minority mobilization was more important for resistance to genocide than for other types of clandestine mobilization, revealing that the former is jointly produced by minority capacity and empathy. I will now conduct a similar analysis for the province of Limburg to see whether the same is true outside of Twente. Cammaert (1994) utilized the files of the Foundation 40/45 to provide a comprehensive overview of resistance networks for gentiles for this southern part of the country. The networks that Cammaert found are depicted in the lower third of Figure 7.1. Again, we see that rescue for fellow Christians was more prevalent than rescue for Jews. More importantly, the minority contrast is even more striking than what we saw for Twente. Only one of the eighty networks for gentiles active in Limburg was rooted in a minority congregation. Recall that thirty-three out of all fifty-one networks helping Jews emerged within the confines of a religiously deviant congregation.

All in all, the comparison between Jewish rescue networks and resistance networks for gentiles reveals that the minority advantage was more prominent for the former than the latter. Hence, minority congregations were more strongly overrepresented among Jewish rescue networks than among resistance groups that helped gentiles. Since both types of networks were strongly dependent on clandestinity to survive, this suggests that mobilization against the Holocaust was relatively stronger among minority enclaves because they were both more able and more willing to protect victims of purification campaigns.

7.3 CATHOLIC NOORD-BRABANT

The minority advantage for clandestine resistance to genocide seemed even more pronounced in the Catholic province of Noord-Brabant. Provincial resistance organizer Piet de Goede declared after the war that during his reign Catholics were too late in developing a resistance

---

[32] *SVB-file 1, DOCDIRECT, Winschoten.*

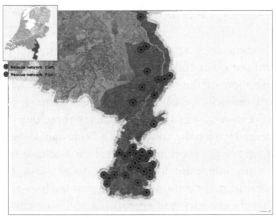

(a) Minority networks rescuing Jews

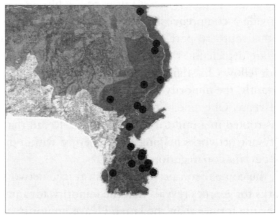

(b) Majority networks rescuing Jews

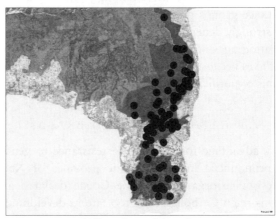

(c) Networks rescuing gentiles

FIGURE 7.1 Resistance networks in Limburg. A black-and-white version of this figure will appear in some formats. For the colour version, please refer to the plate section.

mentality and hardly ever sheltered Jews: "I could never count on my Catholic friends if people needed to go underground. And then I went to Onno and we placed people in no time among Protestants. Protestants also provided funding ... We tried to get money from Catholic clerics but failed."[33] As a result, Protestant reverends were frontrunners in setting up rescue operations in numerous Brabant counties. This can be seen in Figure 7.2, which reveals that twenty-eight out of thirty-eight rescue networks (74 percent) are embedded in Protestant minority enclaves. This is a striking proportion, given that only 9 percent of the population was Protestant.

Minority rescue in the village of Vught demonstrates the importance of interregional ties. Because of the limited number of Protestants in Brabant, Dutch Reformed minister Van Wijhe served as a reverend in three localities: Boxtel, Esch and Vught. This enabled him to funnel Jews from one place to another in times of need (Flim 1997). When Jews hidden in his vacation home were detected by collaborating police forces,[34] he and several Jews were able to escape and go underground elsewhere (Hovingh 2015). One of his operatives, Curate Van Der Veen, was arrested. However, Van Der Veen was so dedicated to his leader and community that he refused to give anyone up (Hovingh 2015). Hence, Van Der Veer's commitment literally prevented the expected suboptimal outcome in this prisoner's dilemma. As a result, forty percent of all Jews living around the Protestant church in Vught evaded deportation.

The case of Oss, located twenty kilometers to the east of Vught, likewise demonstrates the importance of religious segregation. In this medium-sized industrial city, Jan Faber helped Jews find shelter. Faber was a mainstream Protestant who relied heavily on the networks of his father, a reverend with good contacts in local Christian communities in and around Oss. In collaboration with Reverend Veldman, he was able to find shelter for several Jews. Underlining the importance of segregation, postwar testimonies reveal that the Catholic community was unaware of his underground activities. Van Hoeckel, a local chaplain who was considered an expert witness on resistance, knew nothing of the work Faber did for local Jews. A former colleague who belonged to the Catholic Church stated that "We had know idea whether we could trust this man, so we decided to ignore him."[35] In line with the minority argument, this

---

[33] Although De Goede might have been biased because of his own religious background, some Catholics actually confirm his observation (*Archive NIOD, 251a 119*).

[34] *Archive Flim NIOD 471 13 D, Amsterdam.*

[35] *SVB-file 10, DOCDIRECT, Winschoten.*

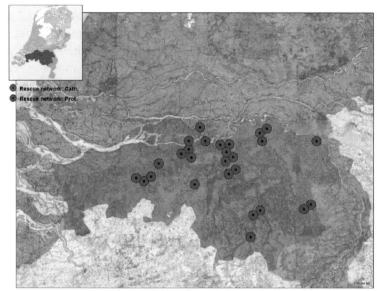

(a) Minority networks

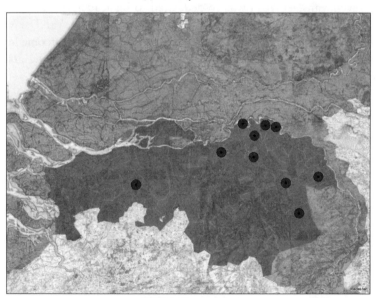

(b) Majority networks

FIGURE 7.2 Rescue networks in Brabant. A black-and-white version of this figure will appear in some formats. For the colour version, please refer to the plate section.

separation proved beneficial for Faber as the resistance networks initiated by Catholic clerics and labor unions were uprooted near the end of the war.[36]

According to Protestants in Brabant, segregation was largely due to the fact that Catholics did not want to act as a unified group and protect Jews as everything in their view had to be "Brabants and Catholic, Brabant Nostra!" Others say that Protestants were simply not willing to include Catholics in their pro-Jewish rescue networks.[37] Regardless of who was at fault, it is indeed striking that even near the end of the war, when most rescue organizations were integrated into unified movements, this split between Protestants and Catholics persisted, with the Protestant wing focused on helping Jews and the Catholic wing focused on helping Catholics (Riessen, van Aerde and Algra 1951).

7.4 PROTESTANT FRIESLAND

That a minority position bolstered Catholics in Protestant parts of the country as well is nicely illustrated by rescue operations setup by Chaplain Gerard Janssen in the Friesian town of Sneek. In addition to twenty-five local Jews, Janssen also saved the lives of large number of Jews from western cities who arrived with the help of student networks (Michman, Beem and Michman 1999). Via a police officer, the chaplain was contacted by a local rabbi who needed help to keep his community out of the hands of the Nazis. Janssen understood the social relations within his parish and thus had no problem identifying reliable addresses to house Jews. He was assured that resistance was possible. In addition, he made it possible for Jews to stay in the local Roman Catholic hospital and attend the Roman Catholic school (Bazuin 2008). Statements of a Protestant vicar in predominantly Protestant Sneek underline the impact that Janssen had. In her postwar testimony, the vicar, who herself had a hard time mobilizing followers (Bazuin 2008), could not hide how amazed she was that her Roman Catholic counterpart was able to shelter significantly more Jews despite the fact that the Catholic community was three times smaller than hers (Flim 1997). Janssen himself was aware that the small size of his community made for its greater strength. Writing about some of his most dedicated helpers, he observed after the war:

---

[36] *Purification police file 3, National Archives, Den Haag. Purification police file 6, National Archives, Den Haag.*
[37] *Archive NIOD, 251a 119.*

"I already knew them for a long time as members of my parish. Sneek's community was so small. This way it was easy to find out that they were good patriots."[38] In other words, in creating clandestine operations, he could rely on organizers' selectivity. As a result of Janssen's network, 55 percent of the Jews living around his church were able to evade capture, making it the safest place in the whole province.

Janssen was not the only minority leader in Sneek who rescued Jews. Baptist Reverend Willem Mesdag led a congregation of 530 people. Before the war he coordinated a religiously inspired group that provided humanitarian assistance to Jewish refugees. In collaboration with a local resistance movement, he contacted Jews living around his church and encouraged them to go underground (Bazuin 2008).[39] Although Mesdag was extremely popular among his followers and assured that most of them would blindly obey him, he was also aware that members of the Baptist consistory were probably not willing to take any risks. Consequently, he mobilized his followers without informing any of the elders (Hovingh 2015). Hence, he deployed organizers' selectivity and knew who not to approach to ensure his rescue operation's success.

His house became a hub for regional rescue activities, and Jews were even sheltered inside the Baptist church (Flim 1997). Mesdag's networks also extended outside Sneek. The experienced reverend acted as a mentor for his junior colleagues in the region, and throughout the war he could use his contacts with young Baptist ministers to place Jews all over the province of Friesland (Bazuin 2008; Hovingh 2015). In the provincial capital of Leeuwarden, he involved his colleague Van der Wissel, the pastor of 1,450 Baptists, who mobilized several followers (Wijbenga 1995).[40] In a similar vein, his Catholic counterpart, Chaplain Janssen, brought Jews to Catholic minority enclaves in Bolsward, Blauwhuis and Oosterwierum, about a thirty-minute bike ride from Sneek (Flim 1997). In Oosterwierum, Jews even served as acolytes to make sure they would not be exposed to German soldiers attending mass (Bazuin 2008).

When discussing rescue operations in Sneek, the Orthodox Protestant community cannot be left unmentioned. When the local police commander received a telegram on March 9, 1943, announcing that all Jews were to be put on transport at 9:30 that same evening, he immediately informed the Orthodox Protestant resistance group Lever. After getting

[38] *SVB-file 37, DOCDIRECT, Winschoten.*
[39] There is also some evidence that a local rabbi was among his friends.
[40] Among them the famous resistance worker Krijn van der Helm.

the news, two of its members began offering their help to Jews they meet on the streets. At 9.00, thirty minutes before the actual deportations started, leaders of the same group began house visits to neighboring Jews to warn them of their upcoming fate and provided them with underground addresses (Bazuin 2008).

When a large number of Jews had to leave their shelter in the aftermath of a railroad strike in on September 17, 1944, it was again the Lever group that stepped up and funneled Jews to new addresses. The Frisian rescuer Turksma, who converted from the more liberal Dutch Reformed to the Orthodox Church right before the war, provides us with one reason why his new community was so powerful. Although initially skeptical about its dogmatic views, he was drawn into the Orthodox Church because its followers were so committed to the group and were like "real friends" to each other (Wijbenga 1995).

While group commitment led Orthodox Protestants, Catholics and Baptists to form the backbone of clandestine protection, the impact of the dominant Dutch Reformed clerics on rescue in Sneek was relatively limited. Mainstream Protestants in Sneek responded to the Holocaust in three ways. First, Reverend Schut, who became mayor of Sneek in 1941 with the Dutch National Socialist Party, simply endorsed the persecution of Jews because in his view: "God created the world but the Jews had to ruin it." Second, as mentioned earlier, some reverends tried to mobilize but could not find the similar support among their followers. A third group of mainstream Protestant reverends did actually mobilize against the Nazis but were denounced by their followers (Hovingh 2015).[41] As Figure 7.3 demonstrates, the town of Sneek was indicative of rescue patterns throughout the whole province of Friesland. Of the fifty-nine active religious rescue organizations, 80 percent was embedded within minority congregations.[42]

7.5 PROTESTANT GRONINGEN

Rescue stories from the northern province of Groningen further confirm that the minority advantage was often conditional on maintaining segregation. This is illustrated by the demise of a nascent network that emerged in the tight-knit Catholic parish of the city of Groningen (the

---

[41] Mesdag also got arrested during the last day of the war. However, this was not because of pro-Jewish mobilization but because he was found with illegal pamphlets.

[42] Twenty-nine percent of the population belonged to a minority congregation.

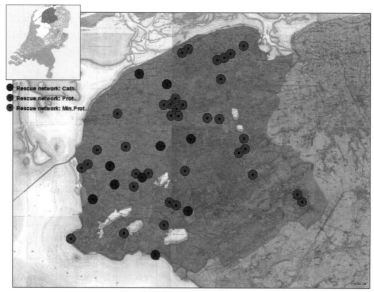

(a) Minority networks

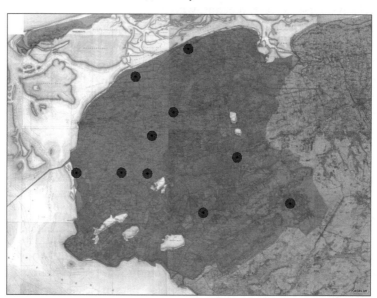

(b) Majority networks

FIGURE 7.3 Rescue networks in Friesland. A black-and-white version of this figure will appear in some formats. For the colour version, please refer to the plate section.

provincial capital that bears the same name). One of its members was Scholte, the cashier of the local food distribution office. Via his work, Scholte had access to food coupons, and with the help of Jagt and Naber, both of whom he knew from the Catholic Saint-Christophel Association for small businessmen, he was able to exploit this position to provide shelter for Jews.

Jagt managed a restaurant almost exclusively frequented by fellow Catholics, which served as safe meeting place, and Naber provided the organization with iron and tools via the hardware store that he owned. Although the majority of Catholic resistance fighters in Groningen shunned secular and Protestant resistance movements, Scholte established ties with Group De Groot, a communist underground organization, after working in isolation for a few months. Despite repeated calls by fellow Catholics to end cross-pillar collaboration, Scholte refused to give up these contacts, wanting to provide food to whomever needed help regardless of religious background. In the end, it was these ties outside of his own community that lead to the disruption of their resistance work. In January 1945, the leader of the De Groot group, Boekhoven, was arrested, and his whole personal administration, containing information on Scholte and his men, fell into the hands of the Sicherheitsdienst. Scholte was detained ten days after Boekhoven's arrest (Hamans 2008).

A very similar story reveals itself when one looks at Orthodox Protestants rescuers active in the village of Nieuw Vennep. A deputy minister of the Orthodox Protestant church in this region forged linkages between local traders and farmers that were crucial for setting up a sheltering infrastructure as the latter often had the space and resources to keep Jews underground for a prolonged period of time. In the village itself, two pockets of protection emerged separated by a series of houses owned by members of the National Socialist Party who, at any cost, had to be prevented from finding out (Braun 2016). A short distance from the village lived Hannes Bogaard, who saved approximately 100 Jews and was known as "the bush monkey," because he always "hung in there." The whole Orthodox Protestant community seemed to know what the bush monkey was up to; among the Orthodox Protestants, who harbored mixed feelings about his rescue activities, his farm was known as "the concentration camp," because it housed so many Jews. The church for him, however, always felt like a safe haven: "I trust all Orthodox people," he often said (Bank 1985). Less romantic testimonies reveal that Orthodox Protestant believers in the village were uncomfortable with what he was doing, but could not bring themselves to denounce someone they considered one of their own (Bank 1985). While Hannes often turned to fellow church members to collect money or to place Jews when his own house became too crowded, the Orthodox Protestant grocery and bakery provided Bogaard with food for "his guests." Equally important were the warnings he got from a local police officer when the Nazi security forces were actively looking for Jews in the area. Unfortunately, Hannes was arrested by the Nazis a few days after he mistook members of the Dutch Reformed (non-Orthodox) church for coreligionists and told them about his activities (Ommeren and Scherphuis 1985). Once again, we see that leaving denominational confines was fatal.

Despite such infiltrations due to religious mixing, minorities in Groningen still had an advantage in setting up clandestine operations. In Groningen city, at least three Orthodox Protestant congregations set up rescue missions (Hovingh 2015). Reverend Van Smeden, leader of the Christian Reformed congregation in the northern part of the city, went so far as to shelter Jews inside the main church building before moving them to committed members of his parish (Capellen and Oolders-Jurjens 2008). More than 30 percent of Jews living around Van Smeden's church were able to evade deportation. This is considerably higher than the city average of 18 percent and the provincial average of 22 percent. If we look at the province as a whole in Figure 7.4, we see that a majority of all rescue operations (fourteen out of twenty-two networks) was driven by small minority parishes.

7.6 QUANTITATIVE ANALYSIS

These shadow cases suggest that the lessons learned from Twente travel to both homogeneously Protestant and homogeneously Catholic provinces. The analysis, however, focuses on whole networks. This could potentially introduce a minority bias, as minority groups, because of their interregional ties, produced more scattered networks that are mistakingly coded as smaller and separate rescue operations due to missing network information. To test more systematically whether minority congregations indeed involved more people throughout the whole country, I also quantified the number of rescuers in the already mentioned files from Yad Vashem (Michman et al. 2004).

As a first cut at the data, I divided the Netherlands into municipalities where Protestantism was strongest and municipalities where Catholicism was strongest. Then I counted the number of Dutch Reformed rescuers in the latter half and the number of Catholic rescuers in the former half

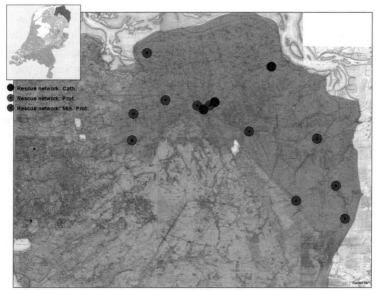

(a) Minority networks

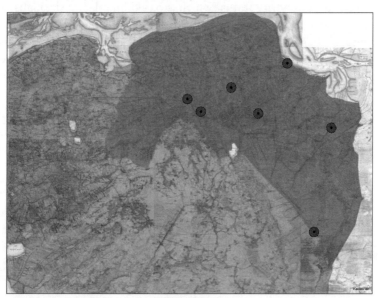

(b) Majority networks

FIGURE 7.4 Rescue networks in Groningen. A black-and-white version of this figure will appear in some formats. For the colour version, please refer to the plate section.

in addition to the number of rescuers belonging to Orthodox Protestant denominations. This sum was then divided by the total number of rescuers for whom the religion was known. The results are presented in Figure 7.5. According to this coding scheme, 32 percent of the population would belong to a minority religion. Overall, postwar testimonies seem to confirm that minority groups were more likely to rescue Jews. Of all the rescuers commemorated by Yad Vashem (Michman et al. 2004), 62 percent belonged to a minority church. The data have serious limitations, as Yad Vashem only recognizes altruistic rescue and ignores rescue provided out of financial or personal motives. Therefore, I conducted a similar analysis using survey data collected among Jewish survivors (Evers-Emden and Flim 1996). A similar picture emerges. Of the 226 rescuers for whom the religion was known, 61 percent adhered to a minority religion. As we can see, the percentage of minority rescuers are very close in both datasets, giving us some confidence that the measurement of minority overrepresentation is valid.

It is of course possible that geographical difference and other omitted variables might be driving this result. In particular, it is plausible that instead of minority status (which is based on relative size), absolute group size is causing mobilization. Smaller groups have a mobilization advantage because they are easier to monitor (Olson 1965). Therefore, I also analyzed the Yad Vashem data in a multivariate framework keeping geographical factors and absolute size constant.[43] I matched

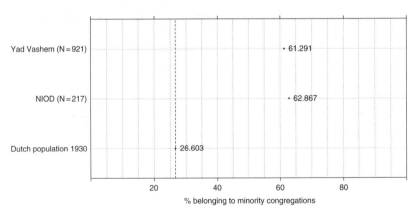

FIGURE 7.5 Minority rescue according to postwar testimonies.

[43] I prefer to use the Yad Vashem files over the survey data as the former has a broader coverage providing more opportunities to keep geographical factors constant. Analysis based on the survey data are consistent with the results presented later.

Yad Vashem's recognized rescuers to all Catholic, mainstream Protestant and Orthodox Protestant communities that existed in the Netherlands in 1930 (CBS 1931). This results in a database of 2,883 religious communities nested in 1,027 counties for which Yad Vashem has data on rescuers. If the minority hypothesis holds, we would expect Catholic communities to be more likely to produce rescuers in Protestant parts of the country, Protestant communities to produce more rescuers in Catholic parts of the country and Orthodox communities to be more likely to rescue everywhere. To capture this minority effect, I interact whether a community is Catholic with the percentage of Catholics in a municipality. The logic behind this is that Catholics should be more likely to rescue in areas where relatively few Catholics live, but less likely to rescue in areas where Catholicism is widespread (and Protestantism is not) because they are no longer a minority. I control for logged group size to disentangle the minority effect from small-group effects. Results of the analyses with municipality clustered standard errors are presented in Figures 7.6 and 7.7.

In line with the minority hypothesis, the effect of Catholicism on rescue is conditional on the overall strength of Catholicism in the region regardless of what outcome variable is chosen. As we can see in Figure 7.6b, Catholics are more than 50 percent more likely to produce networks of assistance to Jews in Protestant areas, while the same is true for Protestants in Catholic areas. Also in line with the minority hypothesis, Figure 7.7 reveals that Orthodox groups, who were the smallest congregation everywhere, are about 12 percent more likely to stage rescue operations than majority congregations. The results are robust to the inclusion of county-level fixed effect, suggesting that the minority effects are not driven by local-level omitted variable bias.

In the case study of Twente, we saw that minority networks were also less likely to be exposed and uprooted. Based on Yad Vashem's files, it is possible to retrieve whether rescuers were arrested, which can be used as a proxy for exposure. Again, the effect of Catholicism on getting arrested is conditional on the overall religious environment. As we can see in Figure 7.6d, Catholics engaged in rescue operations in Protestant parts of the Netherlands were more than 20 percent less likely to get arrested than their Protestant counterparts. This effect flips in areas dominated by Catholics, where mainstream Protestant clerics were almost 10 percent less likely to get arrested. Figure 7.7 shows that Orthodox Protestant clerics are about 8 percent less likely to get arrested overall. The effects become more pronounced when municipality level fixed effects

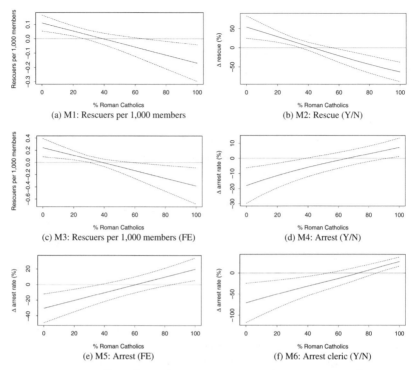

(a) M1: Rescuers per 1,000 members

(b) M2: Rescue (Y/N)

(c) M3: Rescuers per 1,000 members (FE)

(d) M4: Arrest (Y/N)

(e) M5: Arrest (FE)

(f) M6: Arrest cleric (Y/N)

FIGURE 7.6 Effect of a Catholic community with 90 percent confidence
intervals conditional on the Catholic strength in the
region.

are included, suggesting that the minority arguments is not likely to be
confounded by local geographical factors.

The Yad Vashem files are based on testimonies of Jewish survivors
and are therefore more likely to capture successful mobilization while
missing large numbers of exposed networks. This truncates the sample and could potentially bias the results. Because retrieving religious
information from all arrested rescuers in the country is probably impossible, I decided to focus on a important subset of rescuers for which
denominational information is easy to obtain: clerics. The earlier case
study revealed that clerics played a prominent role in almost all rescue
operations. It is therefore reasonable to assume that arrests of clerics
provide some insight into the overall exposure rate of religious groups. I
have constructed a database of 405 clerics from 200 municipalities who
engaged in rescue operations throughout the country by combining information on successful attempts culled from the already used Yad Vashem
files (Michman et al. 2004) with unsuccessful attempts obtained from

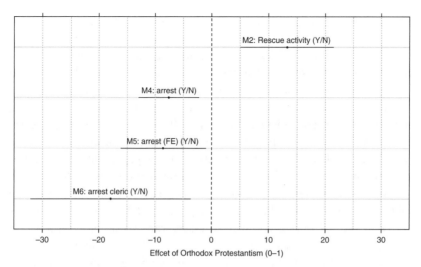

FIGURE 7.7 The effect of Orthodox Protestantism on occurrence of rescue
activities and arrests with 90 percent confidence intervals.

religious commemoration books (Hamans 2008; Hovingh 2015). This
allows me to compare arrests rates between minority and majority clerics.
Figure 7.6f visualizes the results.

In line with what we saw for rescuers culled from the Yad Vashem's
files only, Roman Catholic clerics active in Protestant areas were more
than 60 percent less likely to be apprehended by security forces, while
Protestants were 26 percent less likely to be exposed in Catholic areas.
Orthodox Protestants were 17 percent less likely to be arrested throughout the country. Focusing on clerics reduces the number of observations
and variation within municipalities. This makes it impossible to include
fine-grained fixed effects. Nevertheless, taken together, these analyses
provide compelling support for the minority hypothesis by suggesting
that in the Protestant parts of the Netherlands Catholics were more
likely to produce successful rescue operations that were less likely to be
exposed, while the same is true for Protestant communities in Catholic
parts of the country.

7.7 QUANTITATIVE ANALYSIS: FIGHTING SQUADS

In both Twente and Limburg, the importance of minority mobilization
was stronger for Jewish rescue operations than for other types of clandestine resistance. This suggests that empathy with outsiders asserts an
independent influence on the production of resistance to genocide. Commemoration books of the resistance organization the Fighting Squad

(KP) enables me to investigate whether this striking pattern holds for the whole of the Netherlands. The KP was an armed organization that engaged in violent attacks on distribution centers in order to obtain food coupons for sheltered gentiles who tried to escape the extended labor deployment. The KP saw its primary task as helping to protect fellow Christians from deportation. As a result, networks protecting Jews often operated independently of it (Riessen, van Aerde and Algra 1951). Although it is impossible to assess this for each individual member, it seems safe to assume that most of them engaged only in resistance activities benefiting coreligionists and refrained from helping Jews.

Based on commemoration books, I have retrieved information on the religious background and area of operation of 1,609 resistance members active in the KP during the war (Riessen, van Aerde and Algra 1951; Hilbrink 2015). Just as I did for rescuers of Jews commemorated by Yad Vashem, I match the information on individual resistance workers to all Catholic, mainstream Protestant and Orthodox Protestant communities that existed in the Netherlands in 1930 (CBS 1931). This results in a database of 2,886 religious communities nested in 1,027 counties for which we know how many KP members were active according to commemoration lists. To assess whether minorities were more likely to engage in resistance, I interact whether a community is Catholic with the percentage of Catholics in a county. Results of the analyses with county clustered standard errors and fixed effects are presented in Figures 7.8 and 7.9.

The commemoration books only provide information on resistance workers that perished during the war. In the earlier analysis, we saw that religious minorities are not only better able at mobilizing clandestine networks, they are also less likely get uprooted because of group isolation. It is therefore possible that the absence of a minority effect in the previous analysis is driven by the fact that I only looked at relatively unsuccessful resistance members who did not survive the war.

To circumvent this problem, I have also analyzed KP mobilization in the province of Noord-Holland, for which complete membership lists were reconstructed after the war.[44] The lists provide information on 108 additional resistance workers who fought for gentiles and survived the war. We find no minority effect on KP membership when analyzing community-level mobilization in Noord-Holland with complete

---

[44] *Archive LOKP NIOD 853, Amsterdam.*

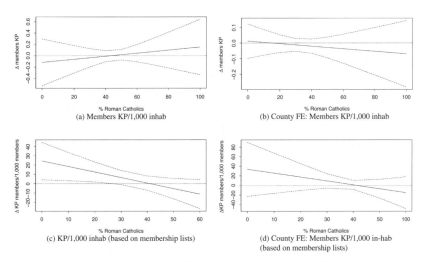

FIGURE 7.8 Effect of the Catholic community on membership in resistance organization conditional on the Catholic strength in the region. Point estimates are represented as points with 90 percent confidence intervals.

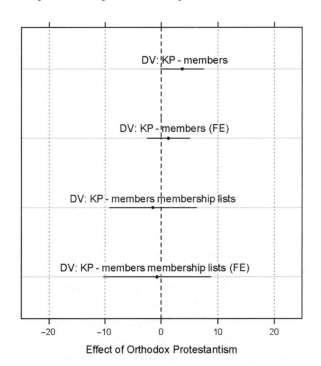

FIGURE 7.9 Effect of the Orthodox Protestant community on the membership of KP with 90 percent confidence intervals.

membership data (see Figures 7.8c and 7.8d). Hence, even if we use membership lists, general resistance networks did not seem to benefit as much from the minority advantage as did rescue networks for Jews. This confirms what we saw for Twente and Limburg: although a minority position bolstered rescue operations for Jews, this was less the case for rescue operations for coreligionists. Again, this suggests that on top of network insulation, empathy with other members of a shared minority religion activated minority mobilization against the Holocaust.

7.8 CONCLUSION

When the deportations started, Jews were encouraged by or relied on local contacts to go underground. Despite overall sympathy with Jews, people willing and able to help were rare given the high risks involved in initiating clandestine rescue activities. Sustaining clandestine missions was even harder, as it entailed solving complex problems that were too much work for one individual or household alone; at the same time, the required cooperation automatically increased exposure. As a result, the lives of Jews and their helpers sooner or later became dependent on whether local communities could secretly coordinate collective rescue attempts. The ability to do so was shaped by group commitment.

The case studies presented in this chapter reveal that this high premium on commitment restricted recruitment of rescuers because it was easier to generate group commitment between similar actors who had already engaged in frequent interaction before the war. Recruitment into illicit collective action, therefore, often proceeded via existing ties of trust, typically resting on kinship ties or other strong bonds. As a result, clandestine collective rescue during the Holocaust often inherited group structures that had been formed in uneventful times. The pillarized structure of Dutch group relationships, therefore, created the confines within which clandestine mobilization emerged.

Compared to dominant groups, minority enclaves within this pillarized system had a natural advantage in producing and sustaining clandestine networks because they were anchored in isolated hubs of commitment that provided relatively safe places for illicit mobilization. This, in turn, created an opportunity to overcome the dual challenge of high-risk collective action and secrecy. In addition, minority enclaves were more likely to have formed ties with minority communities elsewhere before the war, allowing them to build critical mass for their activities. These ties could be exploited in war time to illegally funnel Jews from one place to another.

As a result, Jews were more likely to survive when their individual networks overlapped with those of isolated minority groups. Neighborhood ties with enclave members were more likely to coalesce into sustainable assistance because the minority position of enclaves: 1) increased the number of potential recruits with specific skillsets that could be trusted because members were more committed to group and leadership; 2) assured organizers and followers alike that rescue operations were feasible; 3) improved the ability of organizers to recognize and select skilled recruits; and 4) decreased the spread of information to uncommitted outsiders, which in turn 5) enhanced the overall survival rate of minority missions and the Jews they encompassed.

7.A APPENDIX

TABLE 7.A1 *Religious communities and the rescue of Jews, 1940–1945*

	OLS	Logit	OLS
	(1) % Rescue	(2) Rescue (Y/N)	(3) % Rescue
Catholic community	0.011***	0.507***	0.024***
	(0.003)	(0.128)	(0.008)
Catholic strength	0.023**	0.718***	
	(0.009)	(0.181)	
Catholic community*Catholic strength	−0.028**	−1.162***	−0.063**
	(0.010)	(0.320)	(0.022)
Orthodox Community	0.013***	0.122***	0.009**
	(0.003)	(0.035)	(0.003)
Constant	0.004*	0.230***	−0.001***
	(0.002)	(0.045)	(0.000)
County FE	N	N	Y
Size control	Y	Y	Y
Observations	2, 883	2, 883	2, 883
Counties	1, 027	1, 027	1, 027
Log-likelihood	4, 191.963	−1, 972.327	4, 544.075

Models 1 and 3: Entries are regression coefficients.
Model 2: Entries are logistic regression coefficients.
County clustered standard errors are in parentheses.
*$p<0.05$; **$p<0.01$; ***$p<0.001$.

TABLE 7.A2 *Arrests of rescuers: Laymen (M4–5) and clerics (M6),* 1940–1945

	Logit	OLS	Logit
	(4) Arrest (Y/N)	(5) Arrest (Y/N)	(6) Arrest (Y/N)
Catholic community	−1.782** (0.658)	−0.304** (0.127)	−4.179** (1.742)
Catholic strength	−1.228* (0.569)		−0.909 (0.581)
Catholic community*Catholic strength	2.703*** (0.856)	0.503** (0.174)	5.699** (2.002)
Orthodox community	−0.748** (0.308)	−0.086* (0.052)	−0.873* (0.431)
Constant	−1.246*** (0.339)	0.302** (0.126)	−0.463* (0.202)
County FE	N	Y	N
Size control	Y	Y	Y
Observations	985	985	405
Counties	205	205	200
Log-likelihood	−345.211	−54.763	−240.162

Models 1 and 3: Entries are logistic regression coefficients.
Model 2: Entries are regression coefficients.
County clustered standard errors are in parentheses.
$*p<0.05$; $**p<0.01$; $***p<0.001$.

TABLE 7.A3 *Religious communities and membership of the KP, 1940–1945*

	OLS	OLS	OLS	OLS
	(7) Members KP/1,000 inhab	(8) Members KP/1,000 inhab	(9) Members KP/1,000 inhab	(10) Members KP/1,000 inhab
Protestant minority community	0.037 (0.019)	0.013 (0.019)	−0.013 (0.041)	−0.017 (0.047)
Catholic community	0.008 (0.024)	0.013 (0.056)	0.033 (0.098)	−0.116 (0.210)
Catholic strength	0.027 (0.070)		0.064 (0.277)	

TABLE 7.A3 *(continued)*

	OLS	OLS	OLS	OLS
	(7) Members KP/1,000 inhab	(8) Members KP/1,000 inhab	(9) Members KP/1,000 inhab	(10) Members KP/1,000 inhab
Catholic community* Catholic strength	−0.078	−0.082	−0.079	0.269
	(0.072)	(0.159)	(0.208)	(0.451)
Constant	0.064***	0.003	0.078	0.000
	(0.020)	(0.008)	(0.112)	(0.001)
County FE	N	N	Y	Y
Observations	2, 886	2, 886	2, 886	2, 886
Counties	1, 027	1, 027	1, 027	1, 027
Log-likelihood	−441.993	−4, 228.096	−111.928	−24.739

Entries are unstandardized regression coefficients.
County clustered standard errors are in parentheses.
*p<0.05; **p<0.01; ***p<0.001.

PART III

EXCEPTIONS AND SCOPE CONDITIONS

8

Off-the-Line Cases

8.1 INTRODUCTION

Armed with a gun in her purse, Aleida Smits, a devout Catholic, brought Jewish friends and neighbors to safe places (Geritz-Koster 1999). She received help from her pastor who "was willing to hide Jews underneath the alter if necessary," a Catholic head of police who "knew better where Jews were sheltered than anyone else"[1] and a Catholic doctor who let Jews stay in the local hospital. Smits's network was not, as we would expect, one rooted in a Catholic minority enclave surrounded by Protestants. On the contrary, she operated in Haaksbergen (Figure 6.1), an almost completely Catholic village.

Although the overall patterns presented in the last chapters largely confirm the minority hypothesis, we also observed that minority protection was not the only factor that enabled clandestine resistance to the Holocaust. What other types of networks played a role? And where did majority-grown networks come from? I address these questions in this chapter.

In the first section, I return to Twente and analyze the roots of the four majority rescue operations active in the area. These four case studies suggest that two factors can compensate for a lack of minority commitment: activation by interregional entrepreneurs and local isolation. In the same section, I also trace whether these factors can account for the emergence of majority rescue in the two homogeneously Protestant and Catholic provinces that were be analyzed in Sections 7.2–7.5. In short, the data

---

[1] *Purification police file 2, National Archive, Den Haag.*

suggest that majority groups were able to sustain clandestine collective action if they were rooted in small, insulated enclaves and/or were part of interregional networks; in other words, if their social structure resembled that of minority groups.

In the following two sections, I explore off-the-line cases in Twente, that is, cases with low evasion rates where proximity to minority churches was high and vice versa. Qualitative evidence from these cases suggests that evasion in religious majority regions was high if other types of minority communities, such as radical socialists and communists, stepped in and produced rescue organizations. Conversely, evasion in the vicinity of religious minority enclaves was low when police collaboration with the Nazis was high, due to mistrust among officers. These findings suggest that the minority argument can potentially be extended to non-religious groups, but is conditional on support from local police forces.

Section 8.3 tries to integrate the insights obtained from studying off-the-line and majority cases into a quantitative analysis. Based on the geocoded data presented in Chapter 6, a spatial regression analysis of Jewish evasion indicates that geographical isolation, interregional ties and the strength of left-wing minorities were indeed significantly, albeit weakly, correlated with evasion. No association between evasion and collaboration within the police apparatus could be established, although this is most likely due to the crude nature of available measures.

8.2 MAJORITY RESCUE IN TWENTE AND BEYOND

Looking at Figure 8.1, we see that, in total, four rescue operations in Twente go against what the minority hypothesis would predict: two Protestant networks in Nijverdal located near the western border of Twente and two Catholic organizations in the eastern towns of Haaksbergen, with which we started this chapter, and Weerselo rescued Jews.

Beginning with the last case, a Catholic chaplain was able to setup a rescue operation with a local police patrol, a dedicated member of his parish in predominantly Catholic Weerselo (Hilbrink 1989). How was this majority congregation able to mobilize its members while preventing exposure? The key to its success seems to be that the chaplain was able to place Jews with Catholic farmers who lived far removed from the main roads of town in houses that could only be reached by dirt tracks.[2] It is

---

[2] *SVB-file 3, DOCDIRECT, Winschoten.*

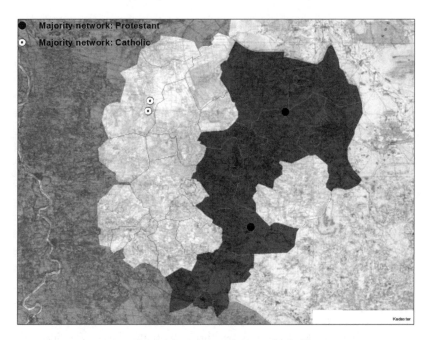

FIGURE 8.1 Majority rescue networks in Twente.

plausible that this geographic isolation compensated for the lack of social isolation and prevented denunciation.

The fact that staying away from pavement was crucial for Jewish survival in Weerselo is illustrated by the fate of the Zilversmids, a Jewish family that did not survive the war. At the beginning of the war, they were able to find shelter with the Junnick family, but this address was compromised when strangers saw members of the Zilversmid family cross a thoroughfare near the end of the war. A member of the Dutch Nazi party got hold of this information and reported them, after which the whole Ziversmid family was killed in a nearby bunker (Weustink 1985).[3]

A strong sense of community spirit present in the town of Haaksbergen might explain the ability of this majority group to protect its persecuted neighbors. Haaksbergen was a small church village with few cars. As a result, most people walked to their work, fostering the feeling

---

[3] The absence of geographical isolation also forced majority rescuers to forbear rescue. In Almelo, mainstream Protestants refused to hide people because their house was located too close to the road. Although this could have been a cheap excuse, it bears mentioning that a nearby fellow Protestant who temporarily housed a Jewish family did indeed get arrested (Cornelissen 2006).

that, religious fault lines notwithstanding, everyone knew each other personally (Geritz-Koster 1999). Jews, Protestants and Catholics alike were all considered part of the same locality. However, despite the cohesiveness of the village, the network of which Smits was the anchor point was not completely immune to betrayal. On two occasions, Kurt Falkenstein, a Jewish boy in hiding, was betrayed by neighbors and had to be taken to a new shelter.[4]

While local-level isolation and cohesion compensated for the lack of minority commitment and empathy in Weerselo and Haaksbergen, the majority organization of Protestants in Nijverdal was nudged toward resistance by outside forces. Ankie Stork was a member of an organization of students that secretly moved Jews from the university city of Utrecht to other parts of the country (Flim 1997). In 1943, Stork was asked by her coworkers to look for shelter addresses in Nijverdal, where she grew up. Stork decided to call Pastor Berkhoff in the neighboring town of Lemele, who had revealed himself as anti-German in several student magazines before the war broke out. She was aware of his sympathies because he had often preached in the Dutch Reformed church she attended. Stork motivated Berkhoff to shelter Jews. Via Berkhoff, Stork was able to get a list of five Protestant families who were willing to help. It is important to emphasize that not all the addresses provided by Berkhoff were equally safe; the twelve Jews housed by the Groten family were soon arrested by local bounty hunters.[5]

Overtime, Berkhoff's network slowly expanded as the five original families started recruiting among their close friends (Flim 1997). It is telling that these majority rescuers did not blindly trust their fellow church members and were afraid to bring sheltered Jews to church, something that, as we have seen, was common practice among minority churches.[6] Rescuers realized that their Jewish guests had to be kept away from some fellow churchgoers, who were believed to be members of the Dutch Nazi party. Another indication that, compared to minority congregations, levels of trust were lower in majority groups was that Reverend Berkhoff himself was arrested after parish members leaked information about him reading an anti-German text from the pulpit.[7] Instead of relying on church commitment, rescuers in Nijverdal were motivated and

---

[4] *Purification police file 5, National Archives, Den Haag.*
[5] *Yad Vashem file A. Knappert in Michman et al.*
[6] *Archive Flim NIOD 471 11 B, Amsterdam.*
[7] *Yad Vashem file A. Stork in Michman et al.*

helped to overcome initial collective action problems by Stork, who provided them with food and illegal paperwork in the early stages of the operation. It was only later that the "Lemeler Convent," the name the Protestant rescuers had adopted, became largely self-sufficient.

Berkhoff collaborated with his colleague, Reverend Hijmans. Hijmans had personal reasons to help persecuted Israelites as he himself was of Jewish descent. Despite his leading position in the community, sheltering Jews in this Protestant town proved to be quite difficult. Out of fear of betrayal by fellow parish members, a Jewish couple sheltered by two of his followers had to be constantly hidden from the outside world.[8] Other houses were raided[9] and one of his key organizers was arrested.[10] It is therefore not surprising that Hijmans decided to use his interregional networks to place other Jews in Catholic Hengelo, where his mainstream Protestant followers formed a minority, so that Jews could be encapsulated by a small group of committed helpers.[11]

Taken together, these four exceptional cases reveal that majority groups driven by motives unrelated to empathy were able to sustain clandestine resistance against genocide when they operated in a cohesive or isolated environment that compensated for lower levels of secrecy and identification;[12] or received help and motivation from interregional resistance entrepreneurs.

To assess whether these factors travel beyond the borders of Twente, I also investigated whether these factors were present among majority rescue missions in the provinces of Friesland, Groningen, Limburg and Brabant that were discussed as shadow cases in the previous chapter. I marked all majority networks that operated in villages outside of the county seat as well as those for which help came from resistance organizers who were themselves based elsewhere.

Figures 8.2 and 8.3 present the outcomes of this analysis. When we look at the predominantly Catholic provinces in the south, we see that twenty-three out of twenty-eight majority networks were either rooted in a geographically isolated enclave or embedded in interregional networks

---

[8] *Yad Vashemfile Scheffer in Michman et al.*

[9] *Yad Vashem file A. Knappert in Michman et al.*

[10] *Yad Vashem file A. Stork in Michman et al.*

[11] *Yad Vashem A. Hijmans in Michman et al.*

[12] That geographical isolation is a precondition for resistance is a well-established insight from resource mobilization theory (Tilly 1978) and can be traced back to Marx's ideas on how concentration in factories enhances the organizing capacity of the proletariat (Marx and Engels 1906).

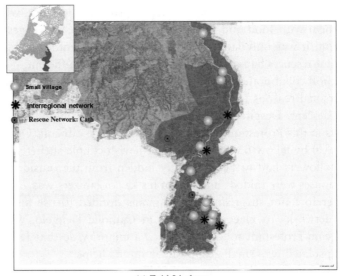

(a) Zuid-Limburg

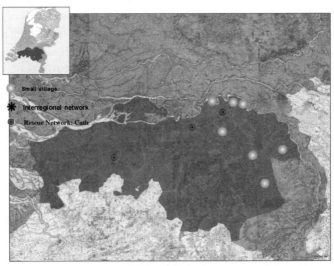

(b) Noord-Brabant

FIGURE 8.2 Majority networks in southern provinces. A black-and-white version of this figure will appear in some formats. For the colour version, please refer to the plate section.

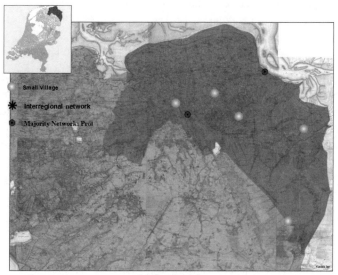

(a) Groningen

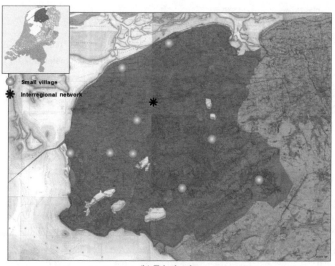

(b) Friesland

FIGURE 8.3 Majority networks in northern provinces. A black-and-white version of this figure will appear in some formats. For the colour version, please refer to the plate section.

(Figure 8.2), while the same is true for fifteen out of the seventeen majority operations active in the northern provinces (Figure 8.3).

8.3 PROXIMITY AND SURVIVAL

To which extent is the striking pattern of minority mobilization in Twente discussed in the previous chapters reflected in a relationship between the presence of minority congregations and evasion more broadly? In Figures 8.4 and 8.5 evasion rate is plotted against the average proximity of Jews to minority congregations for all counties in Twente for

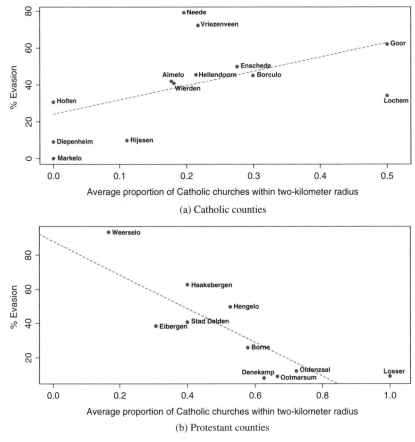

(a) Catholic counties

(b) Protestant counties

FIGURE 8.4 Evasion and proximity to Catholic churches in Twente (counties Jews>10). A black-and-white version of this figure will appear in some formats. For the colour version, please refer to the plate section.

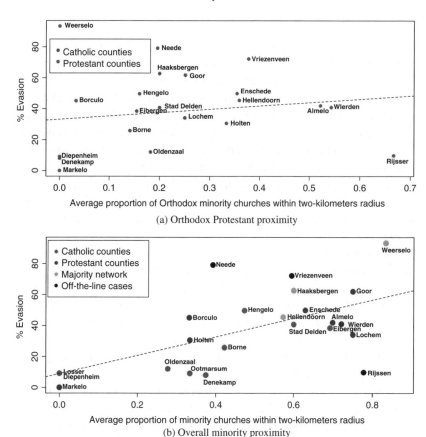

FIGURE 8.5 Evasion and proximity to minority churches in Twente (counties Jews>10). A black-and-white version of this figure will appear in some formats. For the colour version, please refer to the plate section.

which registration lists were available. Figures 8.4a and 8.4b show the relationship between evasion and proximity to Catholic Churches for Protestant and Catholic counties, respectively. As is revealed, proximity to Catholic churches did indeed increase evasion of Jews in western Twente, while the opposite effect is seen in eastern Twente. Figure 8.5a reveals that there is a positive, albeit weak, relationship between proximity to Orthodox communities and the chance that a Jew was able to avoid deportation. The weakness of the relationship is somewhat surprising, given the strong presence of Orthodox rescue operations in the region. However, the absence of a strong association can be explained by one outlier: the town of Rijssen. As I elaborate later, this town is a somewhat unique case where developments in the local police apparatus hampered the ability of clandestine organizations to remain covert. Removing the Rijssen case increases the correlation between Orthodox Protestant church proximity and evasion to r=0.3.

Figure 8.5b combines the Figures 8.4a, 8.4b and 8.5a and plots the overall proximity to all minority churches against the average survival rate. Again, we see a positive slope. Three cases have a standardized residual larger than 1.5 and do not seem to fit the regression line. First, the case of Weerselo, marked in the top right, is where, as discussed earlier, a majority network was able to produce a rescue organization because of its geographical isolation and small community size. The other three outliers, marked in blue, are Neede, Rijssen and Vriezenveen.

Measurement error could explain why Neede is an off-the-line case (high, center). In this town, near the southeastern border of Twente, a rescue network emerged around the liberal protestant minister Assendorp.[13] Although officially part of the mainstream Protestant Church, this denomination has its own church buildings and organizations (Van Eijnatten and van Lieburg 2005). When coding minority churches, however, I was not able to take this information into consideration as both groups were lumped together.

Proximity to minority churches overestimates evasion for Rijssen (bottom right of Figure 8.5). Postwar testimonies leave room for two interpretations of why this might be the case. The first interpretation, draws from testimonies from people within the police commissioner's immediate social circle, is that the Nazis were particularly successful in creating discord between rank and file members of the local police forces. As a result, no collective attempts to sabotage roundups were undertaken, and several Jews were arrested in hiding. In the early years of the occupation, two police troops that had operated independently before the war were merged together and put under the helm of a newly appointed commissioner. The troops did not know what to think of their new leader as he did not openly discuss his attitudes toward the Nazi regime. Consequently, police officers obeyed Nazi orders as they were not sure whether their boss would support their dissent. For his part, the commissioner often tried to warn Jews in hiding and lamented his employees for not taking more risks.[14]

---

[13] *Yad Vashem file J. Assendorp in Michman et al.*
[14] *Purification police file 1, National Archives, Den Haag.*

The second interpretation, which relies more heavily on testimonies of lower-ranked officers, is that the newly appointed commissioner was an opportunistic coward who leaned toward the Nazis in order to advance his career while actively helping advance the genocide. Some suggest he offered help to the SIPO-SD arresting Jews and heard him legitimize obedience toward the Nazis by comparing the police to a "piano that has to make music regardless of who pushes the keys." Two testifiers independently say he recommended officers to volunteer for prison camp when they were not willing to work with the German authorities.[15]

It is remarkable that Haaksbergen and Nijverdal do fit the regression line despite the fact that these villages were home to important majority church operations. For Nijverdal, this is probably due to the fact that, in addition to the Lemeler Convent, four minority groups were active here as well: the Catholic network of Tijhuis, the Orthodox network of bread-baker Flim, the Orthodox network of Reverend Meines and a Baptist network. For Haaksbergen, the picture is less clear. Although a Protestant minority network was active here as well it is hard to believe that this organization had more carrying capacity than the network created by Aleida Smits.[16]

In Vriezenveen, the evasion rate is much higher than one would expect given the overall proximity of Jews to minority churches. Archival documents about Vriezenveen reveal that several Jews were saved by a communist organization. The role that this secular group played in Vriezenveen brings us to the mobilization of nonreligious groups.

8.4 SECULAR GROUPS

Although forty-nine out of the fifty-eight rescue networks could be classified as religious, secular networks also deserve attention. In Figure 8.6, we see that with the exception of a network run by a nobleman who housed Jews on his estate and another network for which the actual organizational base could not be identified, secular groups protecting Jews in Twente all had a radical left profile.

As in most of Western Europe, communists in the Netherlands were political outcasts, resembling small religious sects in combining committed membership with a hierarchal structure (Coser 1974). Much like members of minority congregations, several prominent communist

---

[15] *Purification police file 1, National Archives, Den Haag.*
[16] *Yad Vashem file A. Dijkhuis in Michman et al.*

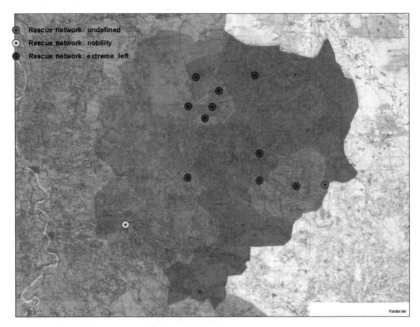

FIGURE 8.6 Secular rescue networks in Twente. A black-and-white version of this figure will appear in some formats. For the colour version, please refer to the plate section.

resistance workers active in Twente were expelled from mainstream organizations and had to pay the costs for their revolutionary ideals.

Across the board, communist organizations had less of an impact on resistance than religious communities because most of their formal infrastructure was taken out by the Nazis. Large numbers of prominent party members were arrested in June 1941. Given that secular left-wing movements included many Jews among their members, intact organizations would have probably been willing to stage a concerted insurgency against the Holocaust (Blom and Cahen 2002).

Communist organizations in Almelo, Hengelo, Enschede and Vriezenveen seemed to be less affected by this wave of repression because they mainly recruited among unknown rank and file members (Hilbrink 1989). After Hilter launched operation Barbarossa, they started organizing themselves in small cells, ressembling the segregated structure of religious minority groups. At the initiative of Wobben a group of neighbors started printing and distributing an illegal communist newspaper, *De Waarheid*, in Almelo. The five men were "sworn friends" and longtime acquaintances from banned Communist youth organizations.

This helped them establish rapport: "we knew each other from way before the war. We were lefties and anti-national socialist, we knew this from each other."[17]

Not long after they set up an illegal printing station, they engaged in more risky activities, secretly helping Jewish and gentile members of their movement evade deportation. They even established an illegal electricity connection with a local brewery to provide their organization with energy resources. One of the men sheltered Jews in his own house, aided by local networks in his left-wing neighborhood. When one of the Jews committed suicide and needed to be buried, all his neighbors were aware of the situation: "everyone in the street knew about the Jews," but "the whole street could be trusted."[18]

Printing also helped radical socialists recruit. Hein Vrind led the legal office of the Nederlands Verbond van Vakverenigingen (Dutch Union of Labor Associations). He published several protests against anti-Jewish legislation in the illegal newspaper *De Vonk*. Through his work, he created a distribution network of laborers who distributed *De Vonk* in their neighborhoods. Via this network, Vrind, together with his colleague Te Riet, recruited between six and eight radical socialists who engaged in rescue operations for Jewish socialists. In total, forty Jews were provided for. Much like its Christian and Communist counterparts, the *De Vonk* group remained a purely socialist group insulated from outside influences (Cornelissen 2006).

Another left-wing network formed around Henk Hoften, an employee of the provincial employment office. He was inspired by a series of lectures given by radical socialist Scheps at meetings of the socialist youth movement Arbeiders Jeugd Centrale (Labor Youth Center), in which Hoften, together with his brother, played a leading role. On at least twenty occasions, Scheps lamented the passive attitude of the Social Democrat's party leadership during the war: "what is the use of the SDAP-party if it loses its soul, Germany might have won a military battle but it will lose the cultural-historical war." This strengthened Hoften in his conviction that one should refuse to cooperate with the German occupiers (Hilbrink 1989).

Together with several other members of the AJC, he started distributing illegal left-wing magazines. Similar to the case of *De Vonk*, this network formed a strong base for an illegal shelter organization. An

[17] *SVB-file 48, DOCDIRECT, Winschoten.*
[18] *SVB-file 45, DOCDIRECT, Winschoten.*

alternative source of recruits was provided by youngsters, who refused to work for the German compulsory labor programs and relied on the socialist youth association for financial support.[19] Via his work, Hoften had contacts with census offices and agencies for food distribution, guaranteeing a steady supply of illegal documents and food coupons. Like what was seen for religious minority operations, mutual distrust between socialist and religious organizations often prevented the formation of a unified rescue organization in Almelo. According to Hoften, Orthodox Protestants were not careful enough as they organized too many meetings and even left an extensive paper trail of their operations.[20]

This section has given an overview of all secular rescue organizations active in Twente. Strikingly, almost all of these groups comprised political minorities. When looking at how these networks operated, some remarkable similarities with religious minorities emerged. Like their religious counterparts, political minorities formed isolated hubs of commitment, operating independently of other resistance organizations. They were often motivated to provide protection because Jewish members of their own movements were under threat.

8.5   BACK TO THE QUANTITATIVE DATA

The in-depth analysis of Twente uncovered some cases of religious majority networks, secular operations and other off-the-line cases that contradict the minority hypothesis. Further investigation of these cases helped identify four additional factors that potentially affect evasion: 1) activation of resistance facilitated by geographical rather than social isolation; 2) interregional entrepreneurs who prompt religious leaders in the countryside to undertake rescue activities (often these entrepreneurs were former residents or recent immigrants who were able to take care of initial collective action problems and funneled Jews to and from other localities); 3) the capacity of marginalized (secular) political factions to setup clandestine networks for their Jewish members; and 4) negatively, the ability of the Nazis to exploit the police apparatus either due to internal discord between officers and superiors or the presence of opportunistic commissioners.

In this section, I again utilize the geocoded database presented in Chapter 6 to assess whether these factors affected evasion rates for Dutch

---

[19] *SVB-file 18, DOCDIRECT, Winschoten.*
[20] *SVB-file 18, DOCDIRECT, Winschoten.*

Jews more generally. I construct six additional quantitative measures to do so. Based on historical land-use data, I recovered the overall size of residential areas to capture geographical isolation. The historical land-use data is collected by Alterra at the Univeristy of Wageningen and provides information on how land has historically been used for raster cells of 25×25 meters (Kramer, van Dorland and Gijsbertse 2010). One of the coded categories is residential development. This category is exploited to create patches of connected residential cells that are used to proxy for the overall size of living communities.

Figure 8.7 illustrates the stepwise process through which this is done for the Twente localities of Weerselo, where a majority rescue network emerged, and Oldenzaal, where this was not the case. We see that the residential area of Weerselo, in the top-left corner, is very small compared to the city of Oldenzaal. Unfortunately, no land-use data is available for the war period. Instead, I take the average score of the last land-use survey before (1900) and after the war (1960). As this measure is skewed, I use logged valued.

To operationalize links with interregional networks, I construct two measures. The first measure is the number of sheltered Jews per capita that lived in a different county before the war broke out. Information is obtained from lists created by the Jewish Coordination Commission (JCC) after the war, which were digitalized by Flim (Michman et al. 2004). The JCC was a government-funded agency that aimed to restore Jewish family relationships by mapping where different relatives had gone underground during the war. It is important to note that these data are far from complete as it only provides information on 10,807 sheltered Jews (around 33 percent of the total number). This is largely due to the fact that Jews during the war had become reluctant to provide address information to government bureaucracies.

Second, I use migration to and from the county in the five years preceding the war to capture potential interregional linkages.[21] The logic behind this operationalization is that recent immigrants and emigrants often played an important role in forging linkages with other communities. Data is obtained from Beekink et al. (2003).

To measure the presence of left-wing minorities, I utilize the percentage of radical left voters in the 1937 election, the last election before the war broke out. Data are obtained from the Central Bureau for Statistics (CBS 1939). Finally, I exploit unique German administrative records to

---

[21] Alternative time frames are used. Results are consistent with the ones presented later.

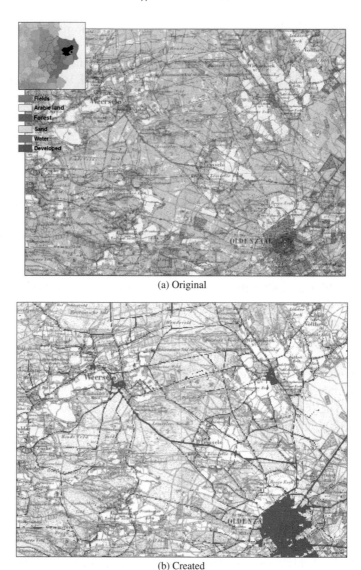

(a) Original

(b) Created

FIGURE 8.7 Example land-use data: Weerselo and Oldenzaal, 1960. A
black-and-white version of this figure will appear in some formats. For the
colour version, please refer to the plate section.

create two measures that tap the overall level of collaboration within the
Dutch police forces. During the war, the Nazis monitored the reliability
of Dutch police operatives and created lists of anti-Nazi officers. Based on
these lists, they identified policemen who needed to be replaced. I use the

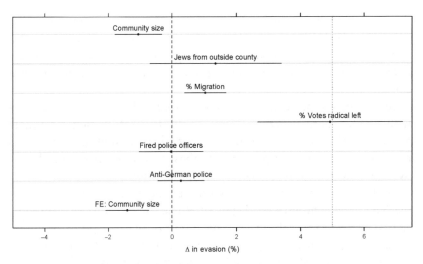

FIGURE 8.8 The change in predicted probability of evasion as variable is increased one standard deviation with 90 percent confidence intervals.

number of anti-Nazi police officers per 1,000 inhabitants in a county as a first proxy for (non-)collaboration. Secondly, I use the number of officers actually fired by the Nazis per 1,000 inhabitants. Both these measures are created from lists stored in the Dutch National Archives.[22]

In the analysis, I reproduce the main statistical model presented in Chapter 6 and add the six measures described earlier. The results of the analysis are visualized in Figure 8.8. Increasing the size of a residential area with one standard deviation reduces the likelihood of evasion by 1 percent. This suggests that evasion is indeed slightly more frequent in small living communities, where everyone, gentiles as well as Jews, knows each other. Because counties contain multiple villages, I also include county-level fixed effects. Taking into account county-level omitted variable bias, increases the effect of community size, with a one standard deviation change increasing evasion by 1.5 percent.

The analysis provides mixed support for the importance of interregional ties. There seems to be no relationship between evasion and the placement of Jews from outside the county. This could of course be due to the fact that the data on sheltered Jews is far from complete. The level of migration to and from a county before the war, however, does have a

[22] *Purification police 2.2.1 51, National Archives, Den Haag. Purification police 2.2.1 66, National Archives, Den Haag.*

significant and positive effect on the chance that a Jew survived the war. A one standard deviation increase in migration results in a 1.5 percent higher evasion rate. This indicates that Jews were somewhat more likely to be sheltered in places where people had more contacts outside the local community.

Increasing the percentage of votes for radical left parties in a county with one standard deviation increases the level of evasion by almost 5 percent. This supports the notion that, that in addition to religious minorities, marginalized political factions were motivated and able to overcome the clandestine collective action dilemma.

Neither of the two measures that tap police (non-)collaboration with the Nazis seems to have a substantial impact on evasion. This could be caused by the fact that the measurement is too crude to capture the underlying processes. In Rijssen, we saw that mutual distrust between rank and file and leadership prevented coordinated resistance to the Nazis. It is likely that Nazis intelligence was not able to pick up on these subtle processes. Moreover, successful police moles working for the resistance were probably never detected and, consequently, did not end up in Nazi records.

All in all, the quantitative analysis confirms that interregional ties, small tight-knit residential communities and nonreligious minorities also played an important role in producing clandestine collective action against the Holocaust. In short, this shows that rescue was more likely to take place in areas where non empathy-related motives were embedded in underlying network structures resembling those of religious minority congregations.

8.A APPENDIX

TABLE 8.A1 *Auto-logistic regression of Jewish evasion: Additional factors*

	Auto-logistic	OLS
	(1)	(2)
	Evasion	
Community size (logged)	−0.056**	−0.014***
	(0.023)	(0.004)
Jews from outside county per 1,000 inhabitants	0.077	
	(0.063)	
% Migration (previous five years)	0.053**	
	(0.020)	

TABLE 8.A1 *(continued)*

	Auto-logistic	OLS
	(1)	(2)
	Evasion	
% Votes radical left	0.257***	
	(0.070)	
Fired police officers per 1,000 inhabitants	64.602	
	(61.336)	
Anti-German police per 1,000 inhabitants	9.300	
	(18.110)	
Catholic proximity	1.241***	0.510***
	(0.294)	(0.118)
Catholic strength	1.748***	
	(0.445)	
Catholic proximity × Catholic strength	−2.062***	−1.110***
	(0.574)	(0.289)
Orthodox proximity	0.883*	0.233**
	(0.414)	(0.080)
Number of Jews/1,000	−0.018***	−0.002*
	(0.003)	(0.001)
Number of churches/1,000	−5.794***	−2.796***
	(1.057)	(0.380)
Constant	−2.745***	0.781***
	(0.331)	(0.124)
Autocovariate	Y	Y
Controls	N	Y
County FEs	N	Y
Buffer	2 km	2 km
Counties	439	439
Jews	122,694	122,694
Log-likelihood	−69, 727.186	−70, 046.791

M1: Entries are logistic regression coefficients.
M2: Entries are unstandardized regression coefficients.
County clustered standard errors are in parentheses.
*p<0.05; **p<0.01; ***p<0.001.

9

Christian Rescue in Belgium

9.1 INTRODUCTION

This chapter explores Christian rescue operations in largely Catholic Belgium. In support of the minority hypothesis, I similarly turn to geocoded evasion data, postwar surveys and secondary literature to show that Protestant enclaves in Belgium were more likely to protect Jews. Once again, their minority status imbued networks with a willingness to protect victims of mass persecution and facilitated clandestine collective action by producing isolated hubs of commitment.

The chapter then moves to off-the-line cases to explain Belgium's Catholic rescue missions. According to the minority hypothesis, we would expect to see relatively few Catholic rescue organizations in Belgium as Catholics formed the majority everywhere. Yet, Catholic protection of Jews was not uncommon. How can this pattern, which at first sight contradicts the central arguments of this book, be explained? Catholic rescue in Belgium took two forms. First, Catholic rescue was more likely to emerge in religious institutions such as convents, monasteries or health colonies that provided an alternative form of isolation, making any minority position redundant (Teitelbaum-Hirsch 2006; Vromen 2010). Second, Catholics mobilized against genocide when their local leaders had idiosyncratic motives to shelter Jews and, at the same time, could exploit isolated hubs of religious commitment created by secularization. In predominantly secular towns, Catholics formed a social minority vis-à-vis a secular majority, creating network structures comparable to those of minority Protestants. Similar to communist cells and tight-knit majority congregations in Twente, Catholics in secular parts of Belgium were able to combine motives unrelated to pluralism with social isolation to produce clandestine rescue operations for threatened neighbors. As such, majority churches that engaged in rescue operations mimicked the social structure of minority congregations.

The empirical analysis establishing these patterns proceeds in four steps. After describing the positions of Protestant and Catholics elites toward pluralism and Jews, I provide illustrative examples of Protestant rescue operations. I then explore more systematically whether Protestant communities were indeed more likely to engage in the protection of Jews than their Catholic counterparts by making use of a postwar survey conducted among both Protestant and Catholic clerics. Section 9.4 introduces a geocoded database of Jewish evasion, similar to the one used in Chapter 5 for the Netherlands, to assess whether Jews living in the vicinity of Protestant enclaves were indeed more likely to evade. Finally, I use case studies, postwar surveys, individual-level evasion data and information on religious institutions to investigate the relationship between secularization and Catholic rescue operations.

9.2 CHRISTIAN EMPATHY BEFORE THE WAR

Anecdotal evidence indicates that throughout the nineteenth and twentieth century Belgian Protestantism was immune to anti-Semitism (Phillip 1970). At the turn of the century, James Hocart, a minister of a Protestant church in Brussels, organized five seminars addressing the relationship between Protestants and Jews that rejected Christian anti-Jewish sentiments, such as beliefs of Jews as deicides or ideas expressed by notorious French anti-Semite Drumont. During these meetings, Hocart linked his defense of Jews to the general importance of tolerance, brotherhood and pluralism: "beware, sons of free thinking; you deny your origins and principles when you refuse the Jews the title of brothers, simply by difference in belief ... What would you say yourselves if the same happened to you in Catholic countries? Would you not then call upon your freedom of conscience?" (Hocart 1899). Like what we saw in the Netherlands, Protestant minorities empathized with Jews because they themselves were dependent on pluralism for survival.

Hocart was not alone in his condemnation of anti-Semitism. Throughout the nineteenth century, Protestant newspapers rejected the idea of the blood libel and expressed strong support for Alfred Dreyfus, a Jewish captain in the French army who was unfairly sentenced to life in prison for treason (Saerens 2007a).

The pluralist defense of Jews came to the surface right before the outbreak of World War II. Despite, or perhaps because of, their own marginal status, Protestant churches in Belgium repeatedly and openly supported Jews throughout the 1930s, distancing themselves from anti-Semitism. Numerous Protestant communities expressed their sympathy with Jews in letters to the central Jewish Church and public gatherings. In 1938, Reverend Schyns, the vice-president of the synod for the union of Protestant churches, directly condemned anti-Jewish legislation in Nazi Germany during a protest meeting. Although Catholic political party members also attended the same meeting, the church never sent a representative. In that same year, Schyns went on to become the chairman of a Brussels-based aid committee for refugees that provided help to Jews fleeing Germany. At around the same time, a similar committee was founded in the Flemish port city Antwerp by Gerriet Vanderriet of the local Belgian Evangelical mission church (Saerens 2007a).

The contrast to the Catholic response in Belgium is stark. Neither political nor clerical elites took a stance against the slow and steady increase of anti-Jewish sentiments, which, as a result, developed freely throughout the early twentieth century. Cardinal Van Roey, the primate of the Belgian church, never spoke out on behalf of the Jews, because, in his view, others had not done the same for Catholics when they were discriminated against in Russia, Mexico and Spain. In addition, he feared that an active fight against anti-Semitism would bring Catholics into contact with Jewish communists and Freemasons. Instead, he preferred to convert all Jews through prayer. In line with this attitude, the cardinal forbade the World Alliance for Combating Anti-Semitism from giving a series of lectures in Antwerp and Brussels and dismantled the Catholic Office for Israel, an association that was established a few years earlier to create atonement between Jews and Catholics (Saerens 2005).

Religious anti-Semitism in Belgium got an enormous boost during the late twenties and early thirties. This upsurge in anti-Semitism was driven by an interplay of religious anti-Semitism, economic scapegoating and rising levels of nationalism among Christian elites. The connection between Catholicism and nationalism was in large part made possible by the fact that Catholicism was considered a constitutive part of both the Belgian and Flemish identities (Witte 2008; De Smaele 2009). Consequently, both Flemish and Belgian nationalist movements grew out of Catholic networks (Van Haver 1983; Gerard 1985). Religion and exclusionist nationalism were brought together through a dual process: while nationalist politicians started combining religious anti-Semitism with nationalism to appeal to Catholic constituencies (Gerard 1985; Wils 2009), elites within mainstream Catholic parties embraced mild forms of nationalism paired with political and economic anti-Semitism to fend off attacks from new right-wing movements (Caestecker 1993).

The former process is illustrated in a series of articles written by Jan Brans, chief editor of *De Schelde*, the party newspaper of the Flemish Nationalist Association (VNV). As a devout Catholic, he considered the gap between the Bible and "the degenerated laws of the Jewish priests" an "abyss." He linked this difference to the inability of Jews to ever become part of the Belgian nation. In order to do so, one had to "penetrate the soul" of the people, "and this was exactly what the Jews have always been incapable of." He combined this religious nationalism with economic and political forms of anti-Semitism, as he believed that the Jewish "Talmud-spirit" found its expression in "commercial corruption," "speculative materialism" and "a relentless lust to overrule others" (Saerens 1991, pp. 258–267).[1]

It is important to note that this phenomenon was not unique to Flanders. Much like their Dutch-speaking counterparts, Francophone Belgian nationalists also incorporated religious stereotypes about Jews into their ideology. The *Action National* wrote in 1924 that "the Jews are Asian, strangers [...] in Europe, in Christian civilization ... They are Talmudists, enemies of our race, our traditions our culture" (Saerens 2005, p. 241). Following this line of reasoning, the Belgian nationalist movement REX started in the mid-1930s to propose policies that forbade trade with Jews at a local level to protect the economic interests of real "Belgians," who could not work on Sundays (Saerens 2005). Thus, despite their diametrically opposed interests, Belgian and Flemish nationalists shared the view that Jews were a threat to the Christian nation, regardless of what form it would take (Meir 1987; Verbeke 2003).

Articles in the Catholic magazine *Het Vlaamsch Heelal* reveal how Catholics incorporated nationalist and economic sentiments into their anti-Jewish discourse. According to senior editor Johan Leemans, who on an earlier occasion had described Jews as "poor and dirty," adding that "there is something wrong with Jewish lifestyle as they are not willing to adjust to the law and order of a society that has opened its doors to them," "many Jews insult Belgian religious practices, especially regarding the Sunday as a day of rest," thereby connecting religious, economic

---

[1] Similar blends of nationalism and religious anti-Semitism can also be found within Verdinaso and other militant nationalist movements (Saerens 1991).

and political threat frames (Saerens 1991, p. 260). This convergence of Catholic and nationalist discourse melded exclusive nationalism with exclusive Catholicism to create a dualistic notion of in- and out-siders. Jews were increasingly depicted as "aliens" and "Christ killers" who contradicted the nature of both Flemish and Belgian society (Saerens 1991, p. 260).

Instead of protecting group rights, Catholic elites in Belgium insisted that Judaism had to disappear. This was expressed most clearly in claims about conversion. Catholic professors and journalists alike contend that Jews "had to unite in the real Israel: the Catholic Church"[2] and that the Roman Catholic Church is "the real Zion,"[3] while bishops organized prayers dedicated to conversion[4] and celebrated every notable conversion in public ceremonies.[5]

As a result of this discourse, Catholics also emphasized the differences between Jews and Christians when talking about religious persecutions, which prevented them from staging a forceful protest against Nazi or Soviet policies. Instead of unequivocally rejecting Nazi violence against Jews, editorials in the Catholic *Gazet van Antwerpen*, repeatedly attacked socialists, liberals and others for expressing outrage about anti-Jewish legislation while not standing up for Roman Catholics undergoing a similar fate. In response to a denunciation of Nazi violence by socialist parliament member Jules Destree, the paper wrote: "the Jews are important to him, but he does not care about Catholics. In the view of socialists, Catholics stand outside the law. Everywhere socialists rule, Catholics get persecuted."[6]

As the last sentence reveals, these critiques often included an implicit reference to a secret coalition between secular political movements and Jews, invoking a political threat frame. According to the Flemish Catholic press, Freemasons, socialists and liberals only protested anti-Semitic legislation for opportunistic reasons[7] or because they let the Jewish part of their heart speak too much.[8] Sometimes this notion took extreme forms. For instance, after religious persecution of both Catholics and Jews in the Soviet Union were well under way, the *Gazet* could not recognize the

---

[2] *Dagblad Gazet van Antwerpen 25/3/31.*
[3] *Dagblad Gazet van Antwerpen 29/7/31.*
[4] *Dagblad Gazet van Antwerpen 7/2/1931.*
[5] *Dagblad De Standaard 25/1/39.*
[6] *Dagblad Gazet van Antwerpen 9/9/1935.*
[7] *Dagblad Gazet van Antwerpen 4/10/1933.*
[8] *Dagblad Gazet van Antwerpen 7/3/1937.*

shared fate of both groups and kept referring to the Russia's political elites as a "large heap of Jews" who were threatening Catholicism.[9] Even in 1938, when knowledge of Jewish persecution in the Soviet Union was widespread, an editorial written by the Francophone Tharaud brothers – active Catholic commentators on Palestine – kept highlighting the powerful role that Jews played in Russian politics.[10]

Throughout the 1930s, the Francophone Catholic newspaper *La Libre Belgique* also explicitly criticized the role of Jews in both domestic and international politics when discussing the Jewish persecutions. These critiques were sometime accompanied by pictures of socialist marches depicting Jews carrying Hebrew Banners, reminiscent of stereotypes of Jews as political revolutionaries threatening Catholic order.[11]

At times, economic forms of anti-Semitism were blended in as well. A rather extreme example comes from an editorial in *Gazet van Antwerpen* in which the author claimed that Nazis sent Jews to Belgium so that they could destroy the economy from within.[12] The columnist Wannes in turn incorporated religious threat frames in his comments: "liberals and socialists refused to denounce religious persecutions elsewhere but do pretend to be defenders of the Jews who tortured the lord and crucified him."[13]

When the *Gazet* did reject anti-Jewish persecutions, it did so conditionally and not without highlighting the economic and cultural threats posed by Jews: "even though Jews rule the press and other elements of our cultural plus financial world, even though it is fair to speak of cheaters, usurers and blood suckers, this does not justify the cruelties perpetrated against them."[14] In a similar vein, *La Libre Belgique* kept emphasizing "Jewish problems" and their perceived disproportionate political influence when distancing itself from Jewish persecutions.[15] This resulted in an overall rejection of help to Jewish refugees in the Catholic press, which did not shy away from using pejorative terms such as "untouchables," "wandering Jews"[16] and "vagabonds" when describing

---

[9] *Dagblad Gazet van Antwerpen 10/6/1939.*

[10] *La Libre Belgique 28/1/1938.*

[11] *La Libre Belgique 9/5/1938.*

[12] *Dagblad Gazet van Antwerpen 27/9/1934. La Libre Belgique 17/5/1938.*

[13] *Dagblad Gazet van Antwerpen 8/2/1934.*

[14] *Dagblad Gazet van Antwerpen 14/11/1938.*

[15] *La Libre Belgique 18/3/1938. La Libre Belgique 21/11/1938.*

[16] Referring to the legend that Jews were destined to wander around the world until the second coming of Christ.

fleeing Jews seeking shelter in Belgium (Caestecker 1993).[17] Catholic elites simply deemed more exposure to Jews undesirable, going so far as to say that it was a threat to indigenous culture (Van Loo 2010).[18]

Comparing Protestant and Catholic responses to anti-Semitism in Belgium reveals a striking difference. Protestant minority elites, on the one hand, emphasized similarity between Jews and Christians and highlighted the importance of pluralism. This in turn created empathy and motivated protests against anti-Jewish legislation. Catholic elites in Belgium, on the other hand, refused to recognize that Jews and Catholics were both facing persecution and stressed the unfair treatment that Catholics received relative to their Jewish counterparts. This prevented the emergence of a coherent narrative of empathy and acted as an anchor point for other forms of anti-Semitism to latch on to.

9.3 PROTESTANT RESCUE NETWORKS

During the German occupation, Protestant Reverends Schyns and Vanderriet (introduced in the previous section) were able to translate their pro-Semitic dispositions into clandestine collective action in Brussels and Antwerp, respectively. In Brussels, numerous Jews were allowed to convert to Protestantism during the early years of the war (Hellemans 2007).[19] When the deportations started, Schyns exploited the willingness of his "entire" parish to help Jews and found shelter for numerous persecuted neighbors among parish members.[20]

A special role in Protestant networks in Brussels was played by the Visser family, who ran a Methodist orphanage. In total, thirty Jews were sheltered with the Vissers. The entire Methodist congregation was aware of the operation, and whenever Germans threatened to enter the orphanage, all Jews were lifted over the garden fences and temporarily taken in by neighbors.[21] Due in part to the fact that a large number of small Protestant enclaves were located in Brussels, around 63 percent of all Jews living in the Belgian capital were able to go underground.

---

[17] *La Libre Belgique 16/10/1938. La Libre Belgique 18/6/1939.*

[18] *La Libre Belgique 16/10/1938. La Libre Belgique 21/11/1938.*

[19] Much like Schyns, Vandenbroeck from the Evangelical Mission Church used parish members in his Brussels congregation to shelter Jews (Hellemans 2007).

[20] *Schyns in de l'enquete Paul Bouffier sur les Eglises Protestantes de Belgique (CEGE-SOMA AA 1205).*

[21] *Visser in de l'Enquete Paul Bouffier sur les Eglises Protestantes de Belgique (CEGE-SOMA AA 1205).*

Relative to Brussels, Jews in the city of Antwerp had an extremely small chance of evasion. In total, 65 percent of the roughly 14,000 Jews living in the city were deported to extermination camps in Eastern Europe. Given this high deportation rate, it is not surprising that help for Jews in Antwerp was extremely rare. The Protestant community, under the helm of Pastor Vanderriet, formed a positive exception to this rule. When the war broke out, Vanderriet was able to continue the activities of his aid committee in a secretive fashion and used it to shelter numerous Jews.[22] Thus, although overall evasion in Antwerp was extremely low, 57 percent of all Jews living around Vanderriet's community escaped deportation.

The contrast with Catholics in Antwerp is stark. Given the presence of numerous Catholic churches in districts populated by Jews, many clergy must have witnessed the brutal roundups of Jews. Nevertheless, no organized Catholic rescue mission emerged in the city. Developments in the Saint Joseph parish, located in the middle of the Jewish district, near Antwerp's central train station, reveal that the inability of cells rooted in majority congregations to stay underground might be the cause of this glaring absence. Initially, the deputy pastors of the Saint Joseph congregation were open to resistance. Edward Salman, for instance, recruited contacts within the military hospital of Antwerp to obtain information that could be useful for resistance cells. Soon after establishing this connection, however, Salman was arrested because of involvement in resistance operations. A few months later, his immediate colleague deputy Pastor Cassiers, met a similar fate (Saerens 2000).

Much like what we saw in Twente, minority enclaves were also able to exploit interregional ties with similar enclaves elsewhere in the region to funnel Jews from one locality to another. Several Jews from Brussels and Antwerp were sheltered in rural Protestant enclaves in Hainaut, Belgium's most southern province. These communities also helped local Jews escape deportation, as 65 percent of all Jews living around Protestant communities in this area were able to find shelter.

These anecdotes indicate that Protestants networks were imbued with pluralist values because they formed local religious minorities. Moreover, Protestant enclaves were able to transform their tolerance into clandestine collective action during the war because they could activate local and interregional network ties, much like what we saw in the Netherlands. To

---

[22] *Vanderriet in de l'Enquete Paul Bouffier sur les Eglises protestantes de Belgique (CEGESOMA AA 1205).*

explore more systematically whether Protestant communities were indeed more likely to provide assistance to Jews compared to their Catholic counterparts, I turn to postwar survey data collected by the Belgian Institute of War Documentation (SOMA).

9.4 QUANTITATIVE ANALYSIS

In the 1970s, SOMA conducted a survey among both Protestant and Catholic communities in Belgium. This survey reveals developments during the war in different congregations. The survey provides information on thirty-two Protestant[23] and 808 Catholic clerics.[24] The survey asked whether someone in the congregation had provided help to Jews during the war. The answers to this question are summarized in Figure 9.1. The difference between Protestant and Catholic answers is striking. Fewer than 30 percent of all Catholic clerics reported to have saved Jews, while 70 percent of all Protestant respondents answered the question positively. It is of course possible that we are comparing Protestant and Catholic clerics who were active in completely different areas and hence had

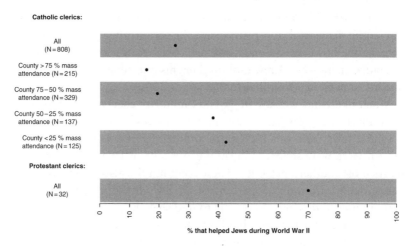

FIGURE 9.1 Percentage of clerics that self-report to have helped Jews.

---

23 *De l'enquete Paul Bouffier sur les Eglises Protestantes de Belgique (CEGESOMA AA 1205).*

24 I include information on monks, priests, chaplains and religious teachers, but excluded information on students and priests who were not in Belgium during the war (*Fonds Enquete Eglise (AA 1448–1449)*).

TABLE 9.1 *Rescue, resistance and new order during World War II:*
Matched clerics

	Protestant	Catholic	Difference	T-Stat
% Rescuing Jews (unmatched)	73.333	21.632	51.702	6.73
% Rescuing Jews (matched w R)	73.333	20	53.333	4.09
% Rescuing Jews (matched w/o R)	73.333	23.333	50	4.40
% Resistance (unmatched)	65.217	25.498	39.719	4.29
% Resistance (matched w R)	65.217	34.783	30.434	1.91
% Resistance (matched w/o R)	65.217	30.435	26.0870	1.79
% Support new order (unmatched)	9.091	5.619	3.471	0.69
% Support new order (matched w R)	9.091	0	9.091	1.45
% Support new order (matched w/o R)	9.091	4.545	4.545	0.59

Based on thirty-two pairs matched on county.

completely different opportunities to rescue Jews. To account for these differences, I will limit the comparison to Protestant and Catholic clerics living in the same locality.

The analysis takes a binary dependent (help to Jews versus no help) and independent variable (Protestant versus Catholic). Traditionally, scholars would analyze this data in a regression framework with country fixed effects to keep local context constant. This is not the ideal solution for this type of data for two reasons. First, rescue activities are rare, and a statistical model could result in perfect separation when including fixed effects and religious denomination. Second, given the small number of cases, it is likely that the outcomes of the analysis will be driven by the parametric assumptions made in the model.

Instead, I rely on matching. This strategy consists of pairing each Protestant cleric with a Catholic cleric in the same locality to keep local factors constant. This eliminates large contextual differences and guarantees that I am comparing relatively similar clerics who only differ in denomination. I rely on exact matching, both with and without replacement. A simple difference-in-means test is used to estimate the average treatment effect.

Table 9.1 reports the average treatment effect. Protestants were 50 percent more likely to protect Jews than their Catholic counterparts. It is, of course, possible that these effects are driven by an unobserved confounding variable. Therefore, I calculate Rosenbaum bounds to determine how sensitive these results are to potential omitted variable bias. These bounds show the extent to which the results still hold if we vary the correlation between being a Protestant cleric and an unobserved

TABLE 9.2 *Rosenbaum bounds sensitivity analysis: Effect of Protestantism on helping Jews (matching without replacement)*

Gamma	Upper bound P-value	Lower bound P-value
1	0	0
1.1	0.001	0
1.2	0.001	0
1.3	0.002	0
1.4	0.003	0
1.5	0.004	0
1.6	0.006	0
1.7	0.008	0
1.8	0.010	0
1.9	0.013	0
2	0.016	0
2.1	0.020	0
2.2	0.024	0
2.3	0.029	0
2.4	0.033	0
2.5	0.038	0
2.6	0.044	0
2.7	0.050	0

confounder. Tables 9.2 and 9.3 present the Rosenbaum bounds for matching with and without replacement, respectively. The first column presents the gammas; typical studies using observational data maintain statistical significance between a gamma of one and two. A gamma of one indicates that matched clerics who rescued have the same chance of being in the treatment group, while a gamma of two indicates that matched clerics who rescued are twice as likely to receive the treatment.

The Rosenbaum bounds in Tables 9.2 and 9.3 show that even if the odds of a cleric who saved Jews being a Protestant were between 2.7- and 3-times higher because of the effect of an unobserved confounder, the inference regarding the effect still holds at the 0.05 confidence level.

The SOMA survey also asked questions about other types of resistance activities and whether or not there was support within the congregation for new order movements, which advocated for supporting the Nazi occupiers in order to create a unified and pure state. Comparing resistance and new order support among Catholic and Protestant congregations could potentially shed light on the mechanisms underlying

TABLE 9.3 *Rosenbaum bounds sensitivity analysis: Effect of Protestantism on helping Jews (matching without replacement)*

Gamma	Upper bound P-value	Lower bound P-value
1	0	0
1.1	0	0
1.2	0.001	0
1.3	0.001	0
1.4	0.001	0
1.5	0.002	0
1.6	0.003	0
1.7	0.004	0
1.8	0.006	0
1.9	0.008	0
2	0.010	0
2.1	0.013	0
2.2	0.016	0
2.3	0.019	0
2.4	0.023	0
2.5	0.027	0
2.6	0.032	0
2.7	0.037	0
2.8	0.042	0
2.9	0.048	0
3	0.055	0

the minority hypothesis. If it is indeed clandestine capacity that is driving the minority advantage, we would expect to find a positive relationship between minority status and other secretive resistance activities. If the minority advantage is driven by a disposition to protect pluralism, we would expect minorities to be less likely to encapsulate supporters of new order movements, which idealized a racially pure state.

Table 9.1 reveals that in line with a capacity mechanism, Protestants were more likely to engage in other resistance activities that required clandestine collective action. Compared to Catholics, Protestants were 30 percent more involved in resistance networks. This result is more sensitive to omitted variable bias, however, as seen in Tables 9.4 and 9.5. The results no longer hold at the 0.05 confidence level when the odds of a resisting cleric being a Protestant are between 1.3- and 1.6-times higher because of the effect of an unobserved confounder.

TABLE 9.4 *Rosenbaum bounds sensitivity analysis: Effect of Protestantism on resistance (matching with replacement)*

Gamma	Upper bound P-value	Lower bound P-value
1	0.033	0.033
1.1	0.044	0.022
1.2	0.058	0.016

TABLE 9.5 *Rosenbaum bounds sensitivity analysis: Effect of Protestantism on resistance (matching without replacement)*

Gamma	Upper bound P-value	Lower bound P-value
1	0.010	0.010
1.1	0.013	0.006
1.2	0.019	0.004
1.3	0.026	0.002
1.4	0.035	0.001
1.5	0.045	0.001
1.6	0.056	0.001

There seems to be no relationship between support for the new order in a congregation and minority status. To some extent, this sheds doubt on the importance of pluralist values for minority rescue. However, it remains likely that clerics reporting wartime behavior postwar might not have been fully open about collaborationist tendencies in their parishes, truncating the overall level of variation on the dependent variable. In addition, the fact that the minority advantage is stronger for Jewish rescue than for other resistance activities suggests that pluralist values on top of clandestine capacity did actually factor into the decision to stand up to the purification campaigns initiated by the Nazis.

Needless to say, the data presented in this section suffers from several biases, as church leaders have incentives to misrepresent their help to Jews in order to make their communities look better than they actually were. It is not entirely implausible that minority communities have a stronger motivation to do so as they alway try to prove themselves vis-à-vis dominant groups (Durkheim 1897). In the next section, I therefore turn to administrative data compiled by the Nazis to assess whether Jews living in the vicinity of Protestant churches were more likely to evade deportation.

9.5 PROTESTANT PROXIMITY AND JEWISH EVASION

Following the same strategy deployed for the Netherlands in Chapter 5, I construct a geocoded database of Jewish evasion based on German registrations and deportation lists to determine whether Jews living close to Protestant churches were more likely to evade deportation. Much like in the Netherlands, the German occupying regime conducted a registration of all Jews in collaboration with local authorities. The first registration was conducted in October 1940 and only focused on Jews older than fifteen years (Delplancq 2003). The census provided information on 42,500 Jews. Postwar calculations suggest that around 2,000 Jews, less than 5 percent, evaded registration (Van Doorslaer et al. 2004).

Substantial Jewish migration from Antwerp to Brussels likely motivated the German regime to update the 1940 registration. In the summer of 1941, municipality governments were again ordered to conduct a census of all Jews in the country. The updated lists recorded the names, date of birth, nationality, profession and address of 42,392 Jews older than fifteen years old. Similar to what we saw for the Netherlands, the SIPO-SD coordinated the second registration (Saerens 2006a).

In December 1941, a third registration took place. This time, information was collected in light of the establishment of the AJB, a German front organization whose goal was to stimulate and coordinate Jewish "migration" to the east. As part of this registration, information was collected for 31,472 Jews in Belgium, regardless of age (Saerens 2006a). The third registration also provided information on names, professions and street addresses.

I combine the updated 1941 registration with the lists compiled by the AJB for two reasons. First, there is considerable debate among historians over which lists were more reliable and used more frequently by the Nazis (Meinen 2009). On the one hand, Saerens argues that the AJB lists were more reliable because they were most recent (Saerens 2000). On the other hand, Schram suggests that the Nazis relied more heavily on the first registrations because it included information on more Jews (Schram 2004). Instead of taking sides in this debates I combine aforementioned strengths of both registrations. Second, the two registrations complement each other in terms of coverage. As mentioned, the first two registrations only included information on Jews older than fifteen, while the AJB lists had no age restriction. For the AJB lists, however, registrations for certain streets in Antwerp has gone missing.[25] Hence, whereas the AJB lists provides information on Jews younger than fifteen, the second registration includes information on all streets.

After digitalizing all registrations, I paired them to delete doubles and update information on Jews that was available in one registration but not in another.[26] This resulted in a database of 51,570 Jews. This is remarkably close to the 52,000 Jews that the occupiers believed to be in the country in 1940 (Steinberg 2004).[27]

For the Dutch case, I collected data on people who died and survived in camps to obtain information on the evasion of deportation. In Belgium, however, all deportation lists are complete and intact, making the construction of an evasion database more straightforward (Steinberg and Schram 2008).[28] Deploying the matching strategy introduced and vetted in Chapter 4, I match the Jewish registrations to the deportation list based on first and last name and date of birth. Street addresses provided by the registrations were then used to geocode the location of all Jews (Braun 2011).

Information on Protestant churches is obtained from the Catholic yearbook of 1950, the year closest to World War II for which this information is available.[29] Surprisingly, Catholic yearbooks did not include detailed street information for Catholic church buildings.[30] Street

---

[25] In particular, the two folders with street names starting with M–P and W–Z in Antwerp have disappeared. These streets, however, are included in the earlier registrations (Saerens 2006a).

[26] I use the same matching procedure described and tested in Chapter 5. I use information from the more recent AJB lists if a Jew showed up in both registrations.

[27] The first two registrations can be found at the Jewish Museum of Belgium, while the AJB lists are stocked at the Belgian Center for the Study of War and Society: *CEGESOMA Archive Pierre Beeckmans (AA1314 nr. 300–500)*. I would like to thank Laurence Schram and Dorien Styven from the Kazerne Dossin – Memorial, Mechelen for providing me with digitalized spreadsheets of these registrations. Nationality, street addresses and legal status were coded manually from scanned files also provided by the Kazerne Dossin – Memorial.

[28] Lists are available at the newly opened Holocaust Museum Kazerne Dossin. I would like to thank Laurence Schram and Dorien Styven for providing me with digital versions of these lists.

[29] *Katholiek jaarboek van Belgie. 1950. Brussels.*

[30] For the Flanders region I was able to compile a list of Catholic churches based on information from the Centre for Religious Art and Culture and inventories provided by the Inventory for Heritage. These data will be analyzed later in this chapter.

addresses were utilized to obtain fine-grained coordinates of Protestant church buildings. As in Chapter 4, I draw circular buffers around each Jew, varying in size between 1.25 and 2 km. Within each buffer, I then count the number of Protestant churches to construct a measure of the overlap between Jewish and Protestant networks. The counts are logged to address the skewness of the measure. A variogram suggests that spatial autocorrelation is present among observations 3.5 km apart. I therefore included an autocovariate that measures the percentage of Jews that evaded deportation within a 3.5-km radius. Mirroring the analysis in Chapter 4, I control for distance to the county center, nearest SIPO-SD office and dummies that mark whether a Jew converted to Christianity, had Belgian nationality or was married to a gentile. In the main analysis, I regress whether a Jew evaded deportation against the logged number of Protestant churches within a specific radius while controlling for spatial autocorrelation and the set of controls already specified. All standard errors are clustered at the county level to make sure that interdependence of Jews living in the same county is not introducing a downward bias in standard errors. Results of a logistic regression analysis are presented in Figure 9.2.

Regardless of which buffer is used, increasing the logged number of Protestant churches by one standard deviation results in around a 1.5 percent higher chance of evasion. The positive correlation between

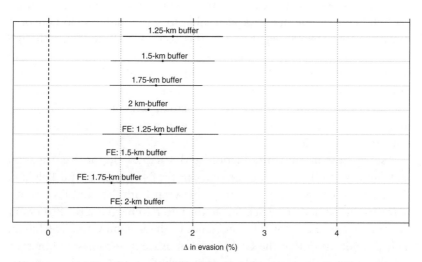

FIGURE 9.2 The change in predicted probability of evasion with 90 percent confidence intervals if the number of Protestant Churches increases with one standard deviation.

Protestant proximity and evasion indicates that Jews were more likely to survive the war if their networks overlapped with those of religious minorities. The overall effect, however, is relatively small. This makes sense given the fact that Protestants in Catholic Belgium constituted such a small group and only had a limited capacity to take in Jews.

To make sure that the relationship between Protestant proximity and evasion is not driven by county-level omitted variable bias, I also reran the models with county-level FEs. These models are estimated using OLS to allow for the inclusion of a large number of dummy variables. The results are presented in the lower half of Figure 9.2. As we can see, the overall results remain remarkably similar when we include FEs. The effect only disappears when using a 1.75-km buffer. All in all, this suggests that the correlation between Protestant proximity and evasion is robust to local-level omitted variable bias.

9.6 OFF-THE-LINE CASES

The previous section established that in line with the minority hypothesis Protestants were more likely to protect Jews than were Catholics. This, of course, does not imply that Catholic communities did not rescue at all. As a matter of fact, there is a common understanding in Belgian public discourse that the Catholic Church played a crucial role in resistance against the Nazis in general and the Holocaust in particular (Lagrou 1997).

How is it possible that, despite the absence of a minority advantage, Catholic church communities were able to setup clandestine networks to protect threatened neighbors? In this section, I show that, although Catholics formed religious majorities everywhere, they did not form social majorities as broadly, due to the strong secularizing forces present in Belgian society. Exactly in these more secular regions, where Catholic church communities were relatively isolated, religious elites, driven by idiosyncratic motives, were at times able to produce secretive mobilization against genocide.

As we saw in the Introduction and Chapter 3, the Reformation had fundamentally different outcomes in the Netherlands and Belgium. Whereas it created a strong cleavage between Catholics and Protestants in the former, it had no such effect in the latter. In Belgium, the Protestant uprising failed to destroy the dominance of the Roman Catholic Church. This did not mean that the Catholic Church went uncontested however. On the contrary, as in other homogeneously Roman Catholic countries, Belgian nation builders produced a deep division between a unified group of Christians who defended their religious rights and secularists who tried to minimize the role of religion in the political and public realm (Lipset and Rokkan 1967; Urwin 1970).

Contrary to the Netherlands, where early waves of secularization sparked by the French Revolution only touched small pockets of Freemason and Humanist lodges, anti-clerical attitudes in Belgium became a driving force behind a broader liberal movement that possessed an enormous mobilizing potential (Lesthaeghe and Lopez-Gay 2013). This early trend was amplified by the fact that Belgium was the second country to industrialize after Britain in the nineteenth century (Landes 2003).

During the following century, strong liberal and, later, socialist parties started forming anchors of secularism throughout the country. However, not all regions within Belgium were affected by secularism in the same way. Figure 9.3 displays local-level mass attendance in 1950[31] and voting for the Catholic party in the parliamentary election of 1925.[32]

When we take a close look at the local strength of Catholicism, it appears that secularism was more prevalent in urban and industrial centers located in the center of the country, but, others have observed that no strong relationship between urbanization and secularization actually exists (De Smaele 2009; Lesthaeghe and Lopez-Gay 2013). This makes it possible to assess the effect of secularization and Catholic strength independently of industrialization and urbanization (Lesthaeghe and Lopez-Gay 2013).

Historically, secularization was particularly strong in the Liege region (Lesthaeghe 1991), an original hotbed of free thinkers (Witte and Craeybeckx 1983). Strikingly, Liege was also home to the most famous Catholic rescue organization in Belgium, which was led by Monseigneur Kerkhofs, the local bishop. Before the German occupation, Kerkhofs was part of an organization that aimed to convert Jews to Catholicism. His prewar activities shaped the ways in which he perceived the German

[31] Because Protestantism was so rare in Belgium, it is safe to see secularization and Catholic strength as each other's reverse. Mass attendance data for each county is based on Collard (1952). Digital files are provided by LOKSTAT at Ghent University. I would like to thank Sven Vrielinck for all his help with obtaining the data.

[32] I make use of voting data from 1925 because it was the last election before the Flemish movements splintered the Catholic voting bloc. Since I am interested in all Catholics, regardless of party preference and nationalist sentiment, I prefer this measure over measures from later elections. The statistical data analysis was are also executed with later election data. Results are consistent with the ones presented later. Data are obtained from www.ibzdgip.fgov.be/result/nl/main.html. Data was only available at the kanton level, a geographical unit that on average includes ten counties.

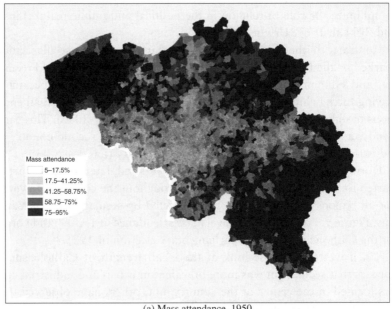

(a) Mass attendance, 1950

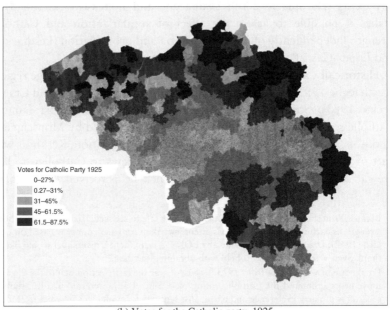

(b) Votes for the Catholic party, 1925

FIGURE 9.3 Local strength of Catholicism.

occupation. In particular, he conceived of anti-Jewish legislation as an opportunity created by God to prostelytize.[33] This motivated him to call on his followers to open their doors to persecuted Jews. He himself took in a Jew and personally encouraged local clergy and Catholic institutions to do the same. Like Archbishop Van Roey he never openly rejected in the deportations from the pulpit. However, in October 1942, shortly after the deportations started, he used a sermon to subtly motivate people to help the children of those most in need (Saerens 1998).

His message of *conversion through protection* resonated with his immediate followers. In Banneux, a pilgrimage site right outside Liege, several Jews from Kerkhofs' network were sheltered. The charismatic chaplain of this small parish, Jamin, was rather hostile toward Jews, whom he considered cowards and Christ killers. The chance to "cure" Semitic souls, however, made Jamin take in Jews. According to Jamin, protecting Jews: "was of vital importance for the Christian apostolate. For the children, a stay in Banneux must leave a indelible impression, a memory that they will experience time and time again, regardless of their future" (Hellemans 2007). The presence of this conversion motive in a Catholic island surrounded by seculars had an enormous impact on the opportunities to evade. Seventy percent of all Jews living around Kerkhofs' church escaped deportation.

Kerkhofs' clandestine operations reached far outside of Liege. The most successful rescue operation the bishop of Liege activated was coordinated by Father Bruno from the Emperors Abbey in the city of Leuven, again a city where Catholicism's influence was waning (Torfs 1984). After working for the bishop's group, Father Bruno decided to split off and protect local Jews whom he funneled to localities in seven of the eleven Belgian provinces. This had a enormous impact on the survival chances of Jews, as 87 percent of all Jews living around the abbey were able to go underground and avoid deportation.

In building his network, Bruno relied on individual Catholic families living in other localities. Historian Hellemans has collected local-level information of shelters for this Louvain network based on the administrative records of Father Bruno. It is revealing that there is a strong negative correlation between the presence of Jews sheltered with individual families and the local strength of Roman Catholicism (r=−0.76 and P=0.024, n=11) (Hellemans 2007). This suggests that a Catholic minority position was important for setting up clandestine operations among Catholic households (Vromen 2010).

---

[33] *Dagblad Gazet van Antwerpen 7/2/1931.*

The minority operations in Louvain and Liege seem to be representative of a more general pattern. Almost all famous Catholic rescue
networks that made use of parish structures in Belgium were located in
areas where secularism was widespread, such as Namur (Thyange 1995),
and, of course, Brussels (Inghelram 1992). The only exception to this rule
seems to be the rescue operation active in the town of Mechelen (Nowak
2000). Here, however, the main base of operation was located in a small
castle about ten kilometers outside of the city's residential center, confirming that geographical isolation could substitute for minority group
status.

In all these cases, idiosyncratic or locally induced motives unrelated
to pluralism activated rescue operations. These motives often saw the
persecution of Jews as an opportunity to convert through protection,
something that was quite uncommon in the Netherlands (Evers-Emden
and Flim 1996). However, other motives played a role as well. The
Namur network, for instance, was setup by Pastor Andre, who had personal ties to Judaism. Before the war, he was close friends with a Jewish
couple and he had employed a Jewish convert as a chaplain in his parish
(Thyange 1995). The Catholics responsible for rescue in Mechelen were
friends with deserters from the German army who were extremely hostile
toward the Nazi regime (Hellemans 2007). In Brussels, Catholic helpers
were located in the middle of the Jewish district and confronted with
waves of help requests from their Jewish neighbors (Saerens 2015), which
induced their assistance (Varese and Yaish 2000). It is instructive to contrast the rise and success of this network with what we earlier this chapter
saw happen to clerics residing in the Jewish district of Antwerp. In this
Catholic bulwark, clerics were also triggered to engage in resistance
activities, but were arrested during the early years of the war.

9.7 BACK TO THE QUANTITATIVE DATA

Taken together, these illustrations provide suggestive evidence for the
argument that religious resistance emerged in places where rescue
motives unrelated to pluralism converged with overall isolation due to
secularization (Saerens 2000). The survey of Catholic clerics introduced
in Section 9.4 makes it possible to determine whether the relationship
between Catholic isolation due to secularization and parish mobilization
holds true across a wider range of congregations. In Figure 9.3, I
disaggregated the percentage of clerics who said they helped Jews during
the war by the overall attendance at mass in the county in which their
parish was located. There seems to be a linear and negative relationship

between clerics' self-reported help and the overall strength of Catholicism in their region. Whereas 20 percent of the 215 clerics active in areas where Catholicism was still dominant helped Jews, more than twice as many did the same in regions where Catholicism was practiced by a minority of the population.

Of course, it is possible that this relationship is simply picking up the fact that secularization was stronger in urban areas with distinct social dynamics that were home to larger Jewish populations that required help from neighboring parishes. To take this into account, I conduct a multivariate analysis that conditions on Jewish population and other socioeconomic background variables. In particular, I control for the logged 1939 population size, the percentage of the population that was Jewish in 1941, the level of unemployment in 1936, the level of urbanization in 1938, the percentage of the population working in industry and agriculture in 1910 and whether a parish was located in Flanders.[34] In addition, I include province-level fixed effects to limit regional-level omitted variable bias.

The negative correlation between Catholic strength, proxied by mass attendance, and rescue by clerics is still in place after we control for Jewish presence and other socioeconomic background characteristics. Increasing mass attendance with one standard deviation decreases self-reported rescue operations by Catholic clerics by 6 percent (Figure 9.4). As with Protestant clerics, we can also compare other resistance activities and support for new order movements to get closer to the actual mechanisms underlying the minority hypothesis. Mass attendance has a negative effect on (self-reported) resistance activities and no effect on support for new order movements. It is interesting to note that contrary to what we saw for Protestant clerics, the effect of Catholic strength is somewhat stronger for other resistance activities than for helping Jews. Together, these correlations suggest that for Catholic rescue organizations' clandestine capacity played a more important role in explaining the minority advantage than ideological factors. This confirms that it was the personal motives of local elites, unrelated to pluralism, that were instrumental in activating protection. Figure 9.5 demonstrates that results remain largely unchanged if we use the strength of the Catholic party in 1925 instead of mass attendance as a proxy for Roman Catholic dominance.

---

[34] Data on unemployment is obtained from NDAW 1936. I would like to thank Guy Vanthemsche for sharing digital scans. Data on the Jewish population is culled from the sources described in Section 9.5. All other measures are from Ghent University's LOKSTAT. Urbanization is measured as a five-category ordinal variable.

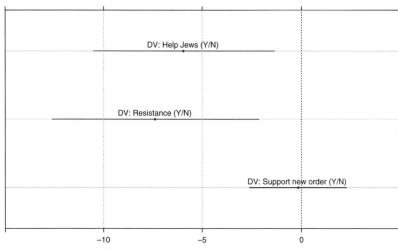

FIGURE 9.4 Effect of increasing mass attendance one standard deviation.

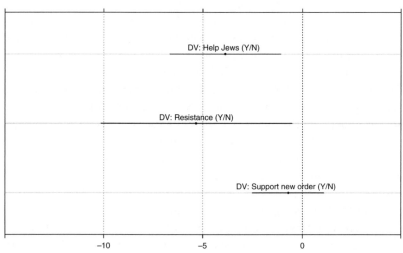

FIGURE 9.5 Effect of votes for the Catholic party, 1925.

Did Catholic mobilization in secular areas result in higher rates of evasion? Unfortunately, I have not been able to find systematic data on the exact location of Catholic churches for the whole of Belgium during World War II. However, I have been able to compile such data for the northern region of Flanders based on information made available by

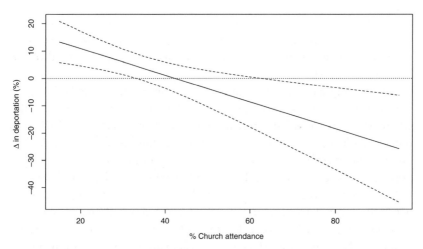

FIGURE 9.6 The change in predicted probability of evasion with 90 percent
confidence intervals as Catholic proximity moves from its minimum to its
maximum value conditional on Catholic church attendance
using a 1.25-km buffer.

the Centre for Religious Art and Culture (Religieuze Kunst en Cultuur
2014) and lists provided by the Inventory for Heritage (Onroerend Erfgoed 2014).[35] Following a similar approach as was used with the Dutch
data in Chapter 4, I calculate Jewish proximity to Catholic churches by
taking the percentage of Catholic churches of all churches located around
each Jew. I then interacted this measure with overall church attendance
in the corresponding municipality.

Results are presented in Figure 9.6. In line with the qualitative and
survey data, we can see that proximity to Roman Catholic churches had
a positive effect on evasion rates in secular parts and a reversed effect
in Catholic parts of Flanders. Increasing Catholic proximity from its
minimum to its maximum value in the most secular regions increased
evasion by 10 percent, while it reduced evasion in areas that are almost
completely Catholic.

9.8 CONCLUSION

In this chapter, we have taken a closer look at Christian rescue operations in Belgium. In line with the minority hypothesis, we saw that in
this almost completely Catholic country, Protestant church communities
were more likely to initiate and sustain rescue operations as they were

---

[35] I would like to thank Joris Colla from the Catholic Documentation Center (KADOC) at
the Catholic University of Leuven for his help with the data.

more sensitive to attacks on pluralism and could insulate their networks from uncommitted defectors. As a result, Jews were more likely to evade deportation if their networks spatially overlapped with those of Protestant enclaves.

This finding has important implications, as it demonstrates that both minority mechanisms also operate in religiously homogenous settings where the persecuted are recent immigrants, national church leaders remained silent and the strength of the persecuting agents was checked by other authorities. In addition, this chapter reveals that the Catholic rescue networks that did emerge did so in places where local religious leaders with rescue motives unrelated to pluralism were able to exploit isolated networks created by secularism. This finding dovetails nicely with the previous chapter, which revealed that alternative forms of social isolation can compensate for a lack of minority status. Like communist sects and majority congregations embedded in geographically isolated towns, Catholic communities in Belgium that formed social minorities vis-à-vis secular majorities, produced the isolated hubs of commitment that are required to produce clandestine assistance to threatened neighbors.

9.A APPENDIX

TABLE 9.A1 *Regression of Jewish evasion in Belgium*

	Autologistic regression			
	(1)	(2)	(3)	(4)
		Evasion		
Prot churches	0.022*	0.020*	0.018*	0.017*
	(0.005)	(0.005)	(0.005)	(0.004)
Number of Jews/1,000	−0.024*	−0.020*	−0.019*	−0.017*
	(0.006)	(0.005)	(0.005)	(0.005)
Constant	1.528*	1.564*	1.581*	1.605*
	(0.093)	(0.096)	(0.093)	(0.094)
Autocovariate	Y	Y	Y	Y
Controls	Y	Y	Y	Y
County FEs	N	N	N	N
Buffer	1.25 km	1.5 km	1.75 km	2 km
Counties	327	327	327	327
Jews	51,570	51,570	51,570	51,570
Log-likelihood	−33,707.084	−33,715.940	−33,718.718	−33,722.212

Entries are logistic regression coefficients.
County clustered standard errors are in parentheses.
*p<0.05; **p<0.01; ***p<0.001.

TABLE 9.A2 *Auto-logistic regression of Jewish evasion in Belgium: County FEs*

	OLS			
	(5)	(6)	(7)	(8)
		Evasion		
Prot churches	0.005***	0.004*	0.003	0.002*
	(0.002)	(0.002)	(0.002)	(0.001)
Number of Jews/1,000	−0.008***	−0.007***	−0.006***	−0.006***
	(0.001)	(0.001)	(0.001)	(0.001)
Constant	0.658***	0.672***	0.684***	0.694***
	(0.030)	(0.036)	(0.039)	(0.040)
Autocovariate	Y	Y	Y	Y
Controls	Y	Y	Y	Y
County FEs	Y	Y	Y	Y
Buffer	1.25 km	1.5 km	1.75 km	2 km
Counties	327	327	327	327
Jews	51,570	51,570	51,570	51,570
Log-likelihood	−35,151.535	−35,166.548	−35,172.608	−35,177.264

Entries are unstandardized regression coefficients.
County clustered standard errors are in parentheses.
*p<0.05; **p<0.01; ***p<0.001.

TABLE 9.A3 *Clerics rescue behavior in Belgian counties: The effect of Catholic strength*

	Logit		
	(9) Save Jews	(10) Resistance	(11) New order
% Mass attendance	−0.018*	−0.017*	−0.001
	(0.009)	(0.007)	(0.014)
Population (log)	−0.058	−0.200**	−0.149
	(0.117)	(0.083)	(0.192)
% Jews	9.780	12.693	18.643
	(8.608)	(8.253)	(14.429)
% Unemployment	1.398	2.242	−6.951
	(2.582)	(2.200)	(5.275)
% Industry	−3.423*	−2.374*	1.255
	(1.796)	(1.313)	(2.601)
% Agriculture	−0.023	−0.007	0.023
	(0.014)	(0.012)	(0.025)

(continued)

TABLE 9.A3 *(continued)*

	Logit		
	(9) Save Jews	(10) Resistance	(11) New order
Flanders	−1.324**	−0.328	0.728
	(0.565)	(0.419)	(1.246)
Constant	2.900*	2.172**	−1.749
	(1.301)	(0.818)	(1.776)
Province FEs	Y	Y	Y
Urbanization FEs	Y	Y	Y
Clerics	808	803	782
Counties	326	325	319
Log-likelihood	−345.122	−420.447	−157.442

Entries are logistic regression coefficients.
County clustered standard errors are in parentheses.
*p<0.05; **p<0.01; ***p<0.001.

TABLE 9.A4 *Jewish evasion in Belgian counties: The effect of Catholic strength*

	Logit		
	(12) Save Jews	(13) Resistance	(14) New order
% Votes for the Catholic party 1925	−0.019*	−0.019*	−0.010
	(0.009)	(0.010)	(0.015)
Population (log)	0.045	−0.115	−0.140
	(0.111)	(0.091)	(0.186)
% Jews	12.606	14.582*	17.549
	(8.165)	(8.571)	(13.535)
% Unemployment	1.246	2.203	−6.866
	(2.604)	(2.255)	(5.274)
% Industry	−3.053*	−2.007	1.214
	(1.835)	(1.285)	(2.758)
% Agriculture	−0.019	−0.003	0.030
	(0.015)	(0.012)	(0.023)
Flanders	−1.414**	−0.385	0.850
	(0.559)	(0.461)	(1.237)
Constant	1.073	0.523	−1.781
	(1.224)	(1.087)	(2.429)

TABLE 9.A4 *(continued)*

| | *Logit* | | |
	(12) Save Jews	(13) Resistance	(14) New order
Province FEs	Y	Y	Y
Urbanization FEs	Y	Y	Y
Clerics	808	803	782
Counties	326	325	319
Log-likelihood	−346.221	−421.262	−157.233

Entries are logistic regression coefficients.
County clustered standard errors are in parentheses.
*p<0.05; **p<0.01; ***p<0.001.

TABLE 9.A5 *Regression of Jewish evasion in Flanders*

| | *Autologistic regression* |
	(1) Evasion
Catholic proximity	0.206***
	(0.060)
Catholic proximity × church attendance	−0.005**
	(0.002)
Number of Jews/1,000	−0.004***
	(0.001)
Number of churches/1,000	6.284
	(4.968)
Constant	0.355*
	(0.199)
Autocovariate	Y
Controls	Y
County FEs	Y
Buffer	1.25 km
Observations	19922
Municipalities	130
Log-likelihood	−14,025.782

Entries are unstandardized regression coefficients.
County clustered standard errors are in parentheses.
*p<0.05; **p<0.01; ***p<0.001.

10

Conclusion: Minority Protection across Time and Space

10.1 INTRODUCTION

The previous chapters demonstrated the importance of religious minorities for the production of rescue networks for threatened outsiders during the Holocaust in the Low Countries. In this concluding chapter, I will explore whether the minority hypothesis travels to other countries under Nazi occupation as well as to other episodes of mass killing to identify the scope conditions of my theory. Drawing on secondary literature, postwar testimonies and microlevel data on Jewish as well as Tutsi victimization, this analysis reveals the robustness of the minority hypothesis across space and time. Furthermore, the chapter sheds light on several scope conditions that limit the portability of my theory.

A striking pattern emerges when we look at resistance to the Final Solution outside the Low Countries. Religious minorities were overrepresented among rescuers in all but five of the occupied countries: Denmark, Bulgaria, Hungary, Poland and Lithuania. Closer inspection of these countries reveals that the theory does not seem to travel to places where rescue missions were highly individualized, minority interests were aligned with those of the persecutor or where national elites could openly cooperate with leaders of majority congregations to safeguard victims of mass persecution. Put otherwise, the theory does not work in cases where resistance to genocide was neither collective nor clandestine.

There is suggestive evidence that the dynamics described in this book also operate in other genocides. The Rwandan case is particularly interesting because religious cleavages did not reinforce ethnic differences in

216

the predominantly Catholic country. Yet again, there is evidence that minority communities, such as the Pentecostals, Abarokore, Adventists and Muslims, actively opposed mass killings. Islam, on the other hand, was a driving force in the Armenian Genocide, where the Young Turks used religion to mobilize the majority of the population against a small group of Christians. Consistent with what we saw in our analysis of the Low Countries, help for persecuted Armenians often came from Kurdish sects, Western missionaries and small patches of Syrian Christians. In the US context, Quaker and Methodist congregations were central to the Underground Railroad, providing shelter to runaway slaves.

On top of this, evidence from ethnically divided Belgium suggests that the minority mechanisms might also operate for nonreligious groups, as Flemish citizens were more likely to protect in Wallonia and Walloons were more likely to protect in Flanders. All in all, this provides suggestive evidence that the minority thesis travels beyond its unique geographical landscape and time period as well as the realm of religion.

10.2 RESCUE OF JEWS IN NAZI-RULED EUROPE

The comparison of religious rescue patterns within the Netherlands and Belgium already assures us that the minority mechanisms operate independently of whether countries have a military or civil occupation regime, whether national church leaders openly protest persecutions, whether victims of mass persecution are largely immigrants or natives and whether the overall levels of resistance against the Holocaust were high or low. Despite large differences in elite behavior, Jewish population and occupation regime, the Netherlands and Belgium also had numerous characteristics in common that could act as scope conditions. Both countries were liberal democracies with pillarized societies where foreign occupiers conducted mass murder through well-organized deportation campaigns.

To explore whether these commonalities somehow triggered minority mobilization, making my finding unique to the Low Countries, I cull testimonies of 6,407 religious rescuers living in twenty countries with different political traditions where the Final Solution took different forms. I divide the share of minority rescuers in the body of testimonies through the percentage of minority believers in a particular country to assess whether religious minorities were under- or over-represented among rescuers. An overview of these ratios are presented for each country separately in Figure 10.1.

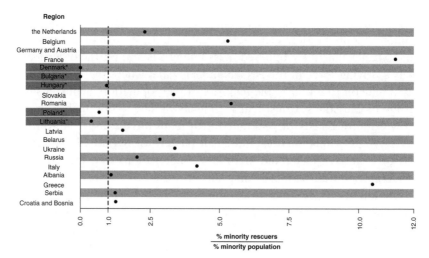

FIGURE 10.1 Over- and under-representation of religious minorities among rescuers in other Nazi-ruled countries.

I discuss each of these countries in more detail later. I start with the Low Countries' southern neighbor, France, which lacked the pillarized societal structures that characterized religious groups in the Netherlands and Belgium, before moving on to Germany, where mass killings were initiated by natives instead of foreign occupiers, and then to other countries with different democratic traditions where mass killing took place through organized deportations. I lastly examine the more chaotic bloodlands of Eastern Europe, where mass shooting rather than deportation was the modal form of murder.

10.2.1 France

A first important commonality between the Netherlands and Belgium is that both countries were segmented societies characterized by what Lijphart dubbed pillarization. Despite elite coordination at the top, local populations of different denominations lived in separation. Forced segregation might have increased the costs of minority membership and as such activated isolated hubs of commitment that could be exploited for clandestine collective action. France provides a first test of the minority hypothesis absent of pillarization. In this country, pillars failed to emerge because divisions between republicans and monarchists had a strong disorganizing effect on the Catholic community. The hope for monarchical restoration among religious elites delayed the independent mobilization of laymen into unions and political parties, inhibiting the formation of a strong faith-based mass organization (Kalyvas 1996).

Despite the absence of pillars, but in line with the minority hypothesis, Protestant groups were strongly overrepresented among rescuers in Catholic stronghold France. Although Protestants made up only 2 percent of the French population, they made up more than 10 percent of all who resisted the Holocaust. Protestant mobilization had already started before the German occupation, when Cimade, a consortium of Protestant youth movements mainly for women, starting helping refugees from Alsace Lorraine, which had just fallen to the Nazis (d'Aubigné, Fabre and Mouchon 1989). Solidarity with Jews continued after the occupation began, with Protestant, Unitarian and Quaker welfare organizations coming together to organize help for interned Jews in prison camps (Grynberg 2013).[1]

Initially, Protestant elites condoned the collaborating Vichy regime. This, however, changed when the deportation of Jewish children was ordered. Although Marc Boehner, president of the Protestant Reformed Church, had enormous respect for state institutions and was attracted to the national revolution advocated by the Vichy regime, he empathized with Jews early on. Already in 1933, he wrote the chief rabbi of France: "The spiritual sons of the Huguenots are stirred with emotion and sympathy whenever a religious minority is persecuted ... May god help your sorely tried co-religionists to find in Him their strength and consolation, as did our frequently persecuted ancestors." He repeated this message during a series of protest meetings, including one in Paris in 1935: "I should say that in light of what is going on in Germany – whether it be the persecutions of Jews or of Christians – it is impossible for us not to add our most energetic protests ... Once you believe in Christ, whatever one's denomination may be, it is impossible not to subscribe fully to the words of that Jew of olden times, Saint Paul the Apostle, who having plumbed the depths of Christ's thought exclaimed: There is neither Jew nor Greek, there is neither male nor female for all are one in ChristJesus" (Snoek 1969).

When deportations were extended to those younger than sixteen, Boehner staged a public protest meeting and secretly summoned leaders from Cimade to setup rescue networks for Jewish children in Protestant

---

[1] The Quaker organization, the American Friends Service Committee, won the 1947 Nobel Peace prize for the relief that it provided Jews in France and other countries during the war (Benz and Wetzel 1998).

enclaves in the Ardeche and Cevennes region. In this part of the country, generations of Huguenots, Ravenists and Darbyists had retreated in silence in the face of threats to non-Catholics. The secluded nature of these communities gave this region its nickname *pays de silence*, or land of silence (Moorehead 2014).

Protestant sects were not only silent, but also defiant, especially when confronted with the Shoah. Huguenots, Ravenists and Darbyists had always likened themselves to the persecuted people of Israel, as they were all willing to die for their faith. Historically, Protestant minorities and Jews had frequently supported each other. Republicanism was widespread among members of both communities, as the French Revolution had granted them legal status and recognition. During the Dreyfuss affair, most Protestants sided with the Jewish captain because they understood all too well what discrimination felt like. Consequently, they empathized with Jews when the Nazis rose to power and drew strong parallels between anti-Semitic persecutions and the revocation of the Edict of Nantes, which unleashed clerical attacks on Protestants near the turn of the seventeenth century (Cabanel 2008). For instance, Pastor Idebert Exbrayat, a Protestant minister in Rodez, expressed his motivation to help the Jews by saying: "As a Calvinist, I understood the meaning of persecution. That is why I understood the persecution of the Jews and opened my doors to the Rabbi" (Paldiel 1993).

Protestant minorities, like their fellows in the Low Countries, were characterized by striking group commitment.[2] In Chambon-sur-Lignon, without doubt the most famous example of a Protestant community protecting Jews in France, Pastor Trocme organized all his parishioners into daily Bible study meetings, during which he underlined the importance of providing asylum to outsiders: "You will love the stranger, for you have been strangers in Egypt." Similar to what we have seen in the Low Countries, this combination of silence, empathy and commitment provided fertile ground for the interregional welfare workers from Cimade. Throughout the land of silence, a large number of rescue networks, which involved twenty-four Huguenot pastors, along with several Ravenist and Darbyist leaders, emerged, saving the lives of between 500 and 800 Jews (Moorehead 2014).[3]

[2] Suzanne Babut, for instance, was the widow of a Protestant pastor and gave dozens of Jews refuge in her boarding house. The home was close to the local Gestapo headquarters. Her high esteem in the community, however, prevented people from reporting her (Paldiel 1993).

[3] There is also suggestive evidence that Muslims played an important role in protecting Jews in France. It has been claimed that the head of what one could consider the most

10.2.2 Germany and Austria

To assess whether the minority hypothesis also operates in cases where genocide is not driven by a foreign occupier, but rather by domestic authorities, I turn to Germany. The religious landscape in Germany closely resembles that of the Low Countries in that it consists of Catholic- and Protestant-dominated areas. On October 31, 1517, a relatively unknown monk, Martin Luther, protested a series of practices of the Catholic Church in the Saxony town of Wittenberg. Due to the recent invention of the printing press as well as conflicts between the German emperor, the pope and local princes, his protest spread through Germany like wildfire. At the time, Germany was a loose federation of states in which the Roman emperor and local lords vied for sovereignty. Several princes adopted Lutheranism in an attempt to break Catholic hegemony, making the right to choose a territory's religious denomination an extremely salient part of these power struggles.

This conflict was resolved temporarily in 1555 with the Peace of Augsburg, which sanctioned local lords with the authority to impose the religion of their choice on their subjects. This state ended, however, when the newly elected Emperor Ferdinand II forced all territories to convert back to Catholicism, culminating in the Thirty Years War. The war ended in 1648 with the Peace of Westphalia, which declared that the religious choice of citizens had to be accepted, forbidding forced conversion. As the war had failed to deliver a clear winner, the country was split into a Catholic southwest and a Protestant northeast, located closer to Wittenberg, the original source of religious division. The ban on forced conversion, however, resulted in the survival of minority enclaves everywhere (Dixon 2008).

This landscape provides us with a similar research design to that used for the Netherlands. If the minority hypothesis travels to Germany, we would expect to see Catholic rescue in the northeast and Protestant rescue in the southwest. I utilize local deportation data for all German villages collected by Voigtländer and Voth (2012) to see whether this is

---

important Muslim institution in Western Europe, the Great Mosque of Paris, saved the lives of many Jews by huddling them in the mosque's main sanctuary and providing them with certificates of Muslim identity. If true, this would be extremely important evidence in favor of the minority hypothesis, as Muslim leaders, as well as followers, were eager to participate in anti-Semitic violence, plunder and propaganda in French colonies where they were the dominant religious group (Satloff 2006). It would also reinforce the notion that the minority mechanisms operate for non-Christians as well.

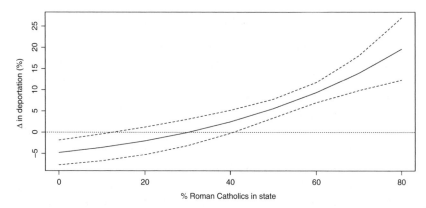

FIGURE 10.2 The change in predicted probability of deportation with 90 percent confidence intervals as a Catholic village increases one standard deviation conditional on Catholic strength in a German state.

indeed the case. I reproduce their main model, with the addition of three variables. First, I add village-level percentages of Catholics in 1925. I then interact this variable with the percentage of Catholics living in the given village's state to assess its minority or majority status. Finally, I add fixed effects for each of the twenty-four German states to reduce omitted variable bias.[4]

Results of the analysis are visualized in Figure 10.2. In line with the minority hypothesis, Catholicism has a negative effect on levels of deportation in Protestant German states but a positive effect in Catholic areas. A one standard deviation increase in Catholic strength reduces deportations by 5 percent in the Protestant northeast, but increases deportations by almost 20 percent in the southwest of the country.

In line with this correlational evidence, both Protestant and Catholic minority leaders were among the first to protest anti-Jewish legislation. The first Protestant bishop to openly express his concerns about the Jewish plight was Hermann Diem, from Bavaria, a southern region dominated by Catholicism. Despite his efforts, his colleagues from Protestant

---

[4] Three additional changes to the model are made. First, I include all German villages, while Voigtländer and Voth's main analysis focused on those who had a Jewish community in 1349. Second, I take out the variable of the proportion of Protestants in a county, as this is almost the same measure as the Catholic percentages used in this analysis. Lastly, I take out all measures that capture legacies of anti-Semitism. Since our empathy mechanism operates by reducing levels of anti-Semitism, these measures would effectively act like post-treatment controls.

areas failed to follow his example (Bank 2015). Following Diem's lead, several small Protestant rescue networks emerged throughout Catholic Bayern (Kosmala and Schoppmann 2002).

While none of the Catholic bishops in Germany openly protested the introduction of the anti-Semitic Nuremberg Laws or the violence of *Kristallnacht*, one prominent Catholic did step up: Bernard Lichtenberg, the provost of the Saint Hedwig Cathedral in Protestant Berlin. Right after the outburst of anti-Jewish violence, he pointed out that there is no difference between a church and synagogue as both are houses of God. This was followed by a weekly prayer for persecuted Jews on Sundays, in which he encouraged parish members to "love thy neighbor" (Gilbert 2010).[5] Although Lichtenberg was arrested in October 1941, Berlin remained a hotbed of Catholic rescue activities, built around dense networks of the Catholic Charitas (Phayer 1993), the Women's League and the nuns of the Elizabeth Foundation (Phayer 1990).

The prevalence of Catholic rescue in Berlin dovetails nicely with the claim that Catholics in eastern Germany were in general more tolerant toward Jews due to their minority position, especially compared to their coreligionists in predominantly Catholic Austria, where anti-Semitism was remarkably influential (Pulzer 1988). At the turn of the century, Austria had witnessed the successful rise of the Christian Social Party, a movement backed by local clergy that was both Catholic and anti-Jewish. Under German occupation, Catholic bishops deemed anti-Semitism acceptable and lamented the "vile inherited characteristics" of "diseased Jews" who were responsible for the death of Christ (Bank 2015). Although Cardinal Innitzer expressed concerns about the Jewish plight and provided some help to converted Jews, his collegium of bishops never spoke out against the deportations and Catholic rescue was rare. Instead, Jews in Austria had to rely on support from minority confines of Quaker, Lutheran and Swedish Church communities (Benz and Wetzel 1998).

10.2.3 Other Deportation Territories

There are striking similarities between Austria and homogeneously Catholic areas in Eastern Europe, such as Slovakia and Croatia. In

---

[5] Leaders of smaller religious communities, such as the Quakers, Jehovah's Witnesses and the Swedish Church, went much further than their Protestant and Catholic counterparts, making Jewish rescue part of official church policy (Paldiel 1993).

both these regions, political regimes emerged that combined Catholic piety with nationalism, which blended cultural and religious forms of anti-Semitism into an explosive mix of xenophobic violence (Steinberg 1994). The Ustasa movement that ruled Croatia has been referred to as a "Croat Catholic brand of fascism" (Hory and Broszat 1964), with the group actively endorsing the removal of foreign elements, including the Jews. Slovakia in turn was led by the Catholic priest Tiso, who was responsible for ordering Jewish persecutions in 1941 and 1944 (Phayer 2000).

This process, however, is not unique to Catholicism. A comparable fusion of xenophobic nationalism and religious anti-Semitism emerged among majority congregations in Orthodox Romania. Although some individual Orthodox leaders helped Jews (Friling et al. 2004), the Patriarchs called upon the nation to "fight the Jewish parasites" (Snoek 1969). A large numbers of helpers belonged to the much smaller Roman Catholic Church (Benz and Wetzel 1996), which, as we just learned, was one of the driving forces behind persecution in nearby Croatia and Slovakia, where it was Orthodox communities that were overrepresented among rescuers alongside other minority enclaves of Lutherans, Baptists (Gilbert 2010) and Greek Orthodox (Snoek 1969).[6]

In both Orthodox and Catholic parts of Eastern Europe, Muslims displayed empathy with Jews. The Archives of Military History in Belgrade are filled with protest letters by Muslim dignitaries invoking Ottoman tolerance. These letters complained about bloodshed and stressed that, under Ottoman rule, tolerance for religious minorities, including Catholics and Orthodox believers was the norm. Now, the same groups who had benefited from tolerance in the past were violating these norms in their treatment of Jews. Others expressed fear that the dominant groups would turn on them once they had finished off the Jews (Jelinek 1990). At a local level, "Bosnian angels of mercy" frequently came to the rescue of Jews (Paldiel 1993).

The Albanian case reinforces this, further suggesting that the empathy mechanism is not distinctively Christian, but instead operates the same for other types of minority religions. The population of this majority

---

[6] The ways in which the dominant Orthodox and Catholic Churches legitimized violence against Jews in the Balkans during World War II bears resemblance to the role they played during the Bosnian Genocide fifty years later. This time, not Jews, but Muslims were depicted as Christ killers who threatened the nation (Sells 1996).

Muslim country staged the most successful resistance operation against the Holocaust, saving almost all Jews living on Albanian soil.[7] This remarkable assistance to Jews is often explained by the existence of a strong ethical code in Albania named *Besa*, prescribing neighboring love, help to refugees and compassion for those in need (Sarner and Weinstein 1998). However, religious minority mobilization seemed to have played an equally important role, as the largest rescue operations in this country were produced by the Bekthasi movement, a small and secretive sect grounded in Shia traditions (Gershman 2008).

Returning to Figure 10.1, when we look at the parts of Europe where the Final Solution was carried out through deportations, a striking pattern emerges. Religious minorities were overrepresented among rescuers in all countries but Denmark, Bulgaria and Hungary. Although these countries are very different in terms of anti-Semitic traditions and political culture, they do seem to have one thing in common: for most of the war they were granted some form of autonomy by the Nazis (Hilberg 2003). Denmark was exceptional in that it operated relatively independently of the German Reich, had a low SIPO-SD presence and was, at the same time, reluctant to execute anti-Jewish destruction. As a result, majority church leaders could easily cooperate with national elites to safeguard the Jewish population, limiting the importance of clandestine collective action. In the absence of full foreign occupation, the congruence of majority religion and nation created a unified front against the Nazis instead of reinforcing boundaries with outsiders. The rescue of Jews as such was in part a manifestation of a broader national revolt that aimed to limit the influence of a somewhat remote foreign power (Yahil 1983).

Hilberg, arguably the most prominent social scientist of the Holocaust, dubbed Bulgaria and Hungary "opportunistic satellites." The fate of the Jews in these countries was always connected to overall enthusiasm for the war effort. In exchange for territorial enlargement, both countries had joined the German war effort against the allied forces *and* the Jews. Military setbacks and conflicts over time, however, ate away at the loyalty for the National Socialist cause. As a result, Jewish extermination tended to be erratic and was characterized by procrastination, interruptions, reversals and delays. Pro-German leaders and reluctant collaborators in these countries divided the ruling elites,

---

[7] Note that Jews living in Albania-ruled Macedonia were not protected (Gutman 2007).

producing political opportunities (McAdam, Tarrow and Tilly 2001) for the institutional interruption of mass murder (Hilberg 2003).[8]

This was very similar to what happened in Italy, another clear example of a somewhat reluctant ally. Although, a very small number of Waldensian rescuers in this completely Catholic country obscures the large role of majority rescue in Figure 10.1, it is generally believed that Italy was the only country where the mobilization potential of Catholic networks was fully exploited to protect Jewish citizens. While hatred toward Germans provided the motivation to rescue, the knowledge that everyone was sheltering Jews nullified the clandestine collective action dilemma (Zuccotti 1987). As a result, minority empathy and capacity were less important for the production of rescue operations.

10.2.4 The Bloodlands

Mass killing did not take the same form throughout occupied Europe. Whereas Jews in the countries discussed earlier were mostly annihilated through deportation to extermination camps, the "bloodlands" of Eastern Poland and the Soviet Union witnessed a "Holocaust by bullets" (Snyder 2012). Territory brought under Nazi control was ruled through terror and plunder. Local authorities were brushed aside and large parts of the native populations were deemed racially inferior species that, together with the Jews, had to make room to secure "*Lebensraum*" for the Germanic race. The war against Stalin unleashed a violent energy that was at first directed at the Red Army, but was later turned on local populations, in particular Jews, who were seen as natural allies of the Bolsheviks. Through a process of controlled escalation, Himmler and Heydrich provided incentives to Einsatztruppen and local gentiles to engage in mass violence against the sons of Israel (Browning 2014).

Despite differences in the method of killing, minority rescue was not unique to Western Europe and is confirmed by evidence from Orthodox Ukraine, where a large number of survivor records collected after the war came from people hidden by Evangelicals (Berkhoff 2009), Catholic Poles, Christian Czechs (Spector 1990), Jehovah's Witnesses, Seventh Day Adventists (Brandon and Lower 2008) and Baptists (Gilbert 2010). This defiance stands in stark contrast with the behavior of the dominant

---

[8] This is not to say that these countries did not have anti-Semitic traditions or were overall less willing to introduce anti-Jewish legislation. What it implies is that the Final Solution was implemented in a more erratic fashion.

Orthodox Church leaders who did nothing on behalf of the Jews. At a local level, Orthodox ministers gave blatant anti-Semitic sermons. A priest in Kovel encouraged parishioners to hand all Jews over to the Nazis as they should be erased from the earth. Before going out to murder Jews, Ukrainian police officers prayed in church. Priests sprinkled them with holy water and emphasized the importance of the war against Jewish Bolsheviks (Arad 2009).

As Figure 10.1 demonstrates, rescue in the Ukraine seems to reflect a broader pattern. While dominant churches remained silent or embraced anti-Semitism, minority Baptists, Jehovah's Witnesses, Catholics, Russian Orthodox (Cholawski 1998) and Karachay Muslims (Gutman 2007) were overrepresented among rescuers in Latvia, Belarus and other parts of the Soviet Union.[9] This last group is particularly interesting as it again confirms that the minority hypothesis applies to Muslims as well as Christians.

However, if we look at Figure 10.1, we see minority rescuers were not overrepresented in Lithuania and Poland. This is surprising given that, similar to what we saw in other parts of the bloodlands, anti-Semitism was quite prevalent among majority Catholics in both countries. Clerics in Poland actively discouraged help to Jews (Tec 1987), while some bishops in Lithuania went even further by forbidding their followers to provide shelter (Arad 2009).[10]

What then explains the absence of minority protection?[11] Inspection of rescuer files in the two countries reveals that rescue missions hardly

---

[9] More than a third of rescuers in Russia were people to whom the Soviet Union had related with great suspicion or actively repressed either for religious reasons or during the collectivization purges. This includes large numbers of national minorities. This, of course, raises the question of whether the minority hypothesis can be applied to nonreligious identity groups as well (Gutman 2007).

[10] However, Gross argues that clergy in general played a conciliatory role. Murders of individual Jews and pogroms taking place right outside the Jedwabne area were stopped by a local priest. Clergy also calmed down anti-Semitic agitation while survivors of the Jedwabne massacre could find a safe shelter at the house of the bishop of Łomża. Contradicting his own conclusions, Gross also cites statements by a Jewish survivor from the pogrom in Raziłów. According to this eyewitness, the priest, Alexander Dogolewski, was asked to prevail on his worshippers to take no part in the persecution of Jews. He simply answered that all Jews were communists and that he had no interest in defending them (Gross 2001).

[11] It needs to be noted that secondary literature provides numerous examples of minority rescue operations that are not included in the files presented in Figure 10.1. This could suggest that the absence of minority rescue is due to measurement error. See, for instance, the rescue operations by the Baptists in Podhajce (Gutman and Krakowski 1986) as well as several Evangelical and Methodist networks (Ringelblum, Kermish and Krakowski 1992).

ever extended beyond one household. A coding of 4,119 testimonies by Linde reveals that only eighty-nine cases involved organized religion. A similar coding of 674 Polish postwar testimonies by Czerniawski indicates that only forty-seven cases involved any form of collective action (Gutman 2005).

The individualist nature of rescue in both countries has been linked to the extremely repressive nature of the Nazi regime, increasing the already high risks involved in helping Jews (Tec 1987).[12] An equally important factor in the absence of minority protection might be that the largest religious minority group in both countries was the Lutheran community. Lutheran congregations were often home to German immigrants who were less inclined to resist the Nazi occupation in general due to a shared ethnic identity (Tec 1987).

Overall, the study of rescue operations for Jews outside of the Low Countries suggests two sets of scope conditions. First, the minority mechanisms do not seem to operate when majority elites openly mobilized and created a national resistance movement that did not require clandestine collective action, turning Jewish rescue into a manifestation of broader discontent with German influence; this was the case in Denmark. Second, minority operations did not emerge when these minority groups, such as the German immigrant communities, identified strongly with the Nazi occupiers and rescue was more individualized, as was the case in Poland and Lithuania.

Looking over Nazi-occupied Europe, the importance of minority protection seems to display a curvilinear relationship with the overall strength of authoritarian rule. At the two extremes, majorities were able to exploit political opportunities in countries that operated relatively autonomously, while high levels of repression prevented any form of collective action. However, in the large middle area of the curve, the combination of clandestine capacity and empathy turned minority congregations into hotbeds of resistance against the Holocaust. For a particularly striking example, we briefly return to Paris, where a strong religious network around the Dalian family was imbued with a very distinct form of empathy. The oldest son explained: "since we ourselves

---

[12] Interestingly, Poles did step up to provide collective assistance to fellow Catholics (Gross 2001). At first sight this seems to undermine the link between high levels of repression and collective action. However, it is important to highlight that saving majority members poses fewer clandestine collective action problems, since the immediate environment as a whole is more likely to indentify with the victims, posing less of a threat.

came from the Armenian community, an ethnic community which in other times had gone through comparable misfortunes, it was only natural and our duty to help those who would suffer" (Ménager 2005). This brings us to the role of minority communities in other genocides.

10.3 RESISTANCE IN OTHER EPISODES OF MASS PERSECUTION

There is suggestive evidence that the mechanisms described in this book also operate in episodes of mass killing that were rooted in different types of cleavages and that involved different forms of violence. A particularly interesting case is Rwanda where religious cleavages did not reinforce ethnic differences, as Hutus and Tutsis belonged to both Protestant and Catholic Church communities. Yet again, there is evidence that sects, such as Pentecostals and the born-again Abarokore actively opposed mass killings in the majority Catholic country.

Several postwar testimonies cite membership in one of these two church communities as a reason for why individuals provided assistance to threatened Tutsis. In Butare, for instance, a Pentocostal policeman charged with instigating violence refused to cooperate and transported several Tutsi children to a Red Cross sanctuary from where they were taken to Burundi (Longman 2010). In the northern prefecture Ruhengeri, a group of Seventh Day Adventists harbored Tutsis in their church buildings, putting themselves between potential victims and genocidaires. They were able to funnel the Tutsis to safe territory with the help of the Rwandan Patriotic Front (RPF), the Tutsi liberation army (Fujii 2011).

In line with the minority hypothesis, Muslims also staged a coordinated challenge to killers in northern Mabare, a region dominated by Christians. The small group differentiated themselves from their neighbors through distinctive headgear and frequented Islamic stores and restaurants. These dense networks were imbued with preferences to resist genocide as purification rested on the same absolutist foundations that had marginalized them previously. The day the attacks started, Muslims confronted armed Hutus and blocked their way. While the Muslims in Mabare resisted genocide, coreligionists a few miles to the north in Gahengeri did not protect their Tutsi neighbors. Here, the Muslim community was much closer to dominant, providing further support for the importance of a minority status (Viret 2008).

By combining information on the pre-genocide population, surviving Tutsi population, Gacaca courts and projections of natural death

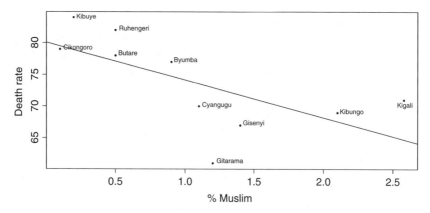

FIGURE 10.3 Death rate prefectures in rural Rwanda by percentage of the population that is Muslim.

rates, Verpoorten has compiled local-level data on Tutsi victimization (Verpoorten 2012). Figure 10.3 plots provincial death rates against the percentage of Muslims. As we can see, a strong negative correlation exists (r=0.67), suggesting that the presence of Islamic minority communities indeed had a dampening effect on violence. Of course, it is possible that other factors were driving this relationship. The eastern provinces, where Islam was relatively stronger, were also more isolated, ethnically mixed and less populated, all factors that can be plausibly linked to lower death rates (Verpoorten 2012). Therefore, I also conducted multivariate analysis of sector-level death rates and religious composition, controlling for population density, RPF strength, distances to the nearest roads and towns, ethnic intermarriage and the size of the Tutsi population. In line with what we saw in Figure 10.3, the presence of Muslims is negatively and significantly related to local death rates. In a multivariate setting, increasing the percentage of Muslims by 1 percent reduces killings by almost 13 percent. In support of the minority hypothesis, the presence of Seventh Day Adventists and other Protestant churches also has a negative effect on violence. However, their coefficients do not reach conventional levels of statistical significance.

Although Muslims protected victims of mass persecution during the Rwandan Genocide and the Holocaust, Islam was a driving force in the Armenian Genocide. Although the Young Turks were primarily motivated by secular nationalism, they used the country's dominant religion to mobilize large groups of the population against small groups of Christians at the local level. Armenians were often referred to as infidels, depicted as spies trying to destroy the empire from within or as serving the interests of Christian European powers. This religiously inspired dehumanization increased acceptance of the mass brutalities. Often perpetrators performed Islamic rites while killing in order to bestow religious legitimacy on acts of murder (Dadrian 2003).

Given this religious legitimization of violence, it is not surprising that very few Muslims were willing to sacrifice their lives to help Armenians (Tevosyan 2008). Consistent with what we saw in our analysis of the Low Countries, help for persecuted Armenians often came from minority congregations. Postwar testimonies from the Sassoun province repeatedly refer to Kurds helping Armenian families evade deportation, while those who miraculously escaped the death camps and desserts were often taken in by Bedouin communities, Orthodox Greeks, Gregorian groups, small patches of Syrian Christians, Evangelicals and Arabs. All these groups sympathized with the suffering Armenians because of their own precarious position within the Ottoman Empire (Hovannisian 1992; Tevosyan 2008). In Marash, similar sentiments motivated the Protestant pastor Eskidjian to build a large Christian network of underground workers providing relief for Armenian deportees with the help of Swiss missionaries who, together with their American, German and Scandinavian counterparts, activated rescue organizations throughout the whole empire (Kieser 2008).

The Armenian region of Mardin deserves special attention. This region was a religious hodgepodge of Yezidi sects, Syriac Christians, Jacobites and Armenians whose pasts had been fraught by Ottoman persecution and conflict with mainstream Muslims. This shared memory of maltreatment created a strong bond between the different minority groups and, when the genocidaires came for the Armenians, a unified front emerged. The Jacobites refused to partake in any killing and helped Armenians flee, the Syriac bishop was able to spare his local community from persecutions and Yezidi sects created a safe haven for the persecuted in the surrounding Sinjar mountain range (Ternon 2008; Gaunt 2015).

In the United States, we find evidence for the fact that religious minorities also provided assistance to victims of other forms of mass persecution. Quaker congregations played a critical role in organizing abolitionist societies and running the Underground Railway to places in ante-bellum America. Secretive cells, stretching northwards from southern Pennsylvania all the way through upstate New York to Canada, made it possible to funnel fugitives who had crossed the Mason–Dixon line. Although there was no official statement from any Quaker body saying that followers had to help, slavery's illegitimacy was clear to all members as a violation of the individual right to freedom of expression (Foner 2015).[13]

It is important to note that minority membership does not insulate everyone from engagement in mass persecution. Kurdish sects played an enormously important part in the Armenian massacres as organized killing squads (Suny 2015), while some important killings in Rwanda were facilitated by Presbyterian and Adventist pastors who, under the false guise of shelter, lured Tutsis to killing sites within their church buildings (Gourevitch 1998). Looking at minorities who did partake in violence more closely suggests that minority perpetrators were often entrenched in elite networks and had an interest in defending the status quo. As a consequence, genocidal regimes have occasionally been capable of incorporating minority congregations into their repressive killing machines when violence broke out.

For example, before the outbreak of the Armenian massacres of 1915, Sunni Kurds had long been deployed as allies of the state to police lands contested by Shi'a groups and other dissident groups, including Armenians. Through this role, several Kurdish tribal leaders had gained powerful positions in eastern parts of the Ottoman empire where a lot of Armenians lived. More informally, Turks often pitted Kurds against Armenians in local conflicts over land. As a result, Kurds had a lot to gain by Armenian persecution and were natural allies of the Young Turk movement. The spoils of plunder provided additional motivation for the Kurds to remove Armenian neighbors from their properties (Suny 2015).

Similarly to the Kurds in the Ottoman Empire, some Protestant elites in Rwanda relied on the Hutu regime to maintain power. They had used state resources to fend off attacks from democratization movements within their own congregations. When Rwandan elites turned to ethnic politics to regain public support, these church leaders associated with the regime were willing to go along and affiliated themselves with Hutu nationalism despite the presence of Tutsis among their flock (Longman 2010).

10.4 SECULAR MINORITIES

When looking at rescue networks for Armenians embedded in communities of Syriac Christians, Iranian Sects and Greek Orthodox,

---

[13] Interestingly, these sentiments were echoed more recently by Hindu and Sikh groups in the United States in response to Muslim persecution in the United States after 9/11 and attacks against minorities in San Bernadino (Hindu Times 2015).

it is striking that religious minority status was often reinforced by an additional minority status. This raises the question of whether the mechanisms outlined in this book also apply to nonreligious minorities such as ethnic groups, immigrants or political factions. Of course, the empathy and clandestine capacity mechanisms limit the value of the minority hypothesis to minority groups that have some form of organizational segregation, self-identify as a group, recognize others as minorities and are dependent on pluralism for survival.

Despite these qualifications, the question still remains whether religious minorities may just be one of many concrete sites through which organized minority status can be studied (Guhin 2014). If this is the case, the empathy and clandestine capacity mechanisms should operate for other minority categories as well. On the other hand, religion's strong organizational infrastructure and defining powers might make it more distinctively robust in the creation of resistance than other organized minority categories (Brubaker 2015).

In the Dutch case, we already saw that radical socialists, communists and immigrants working in the mining industry were also able to setup early evasion networks. Often these groups functioned like religious sects in that they combined discipline with a solemn commitment to the group (Hilbrink 1989; Van Rens 2013). They also relied on pluralism for survival. Communist cells were important for arresting the Holocaust throughout Western Europe (Gutman 2005); in other parts of occupied Europe, there are numerous examples of ethnic minorities stepping up on behalf of the Jews. The afore mentioned Poles in the Ukraine, Hungarians in Romania and Byelorussians in Latvia come to mind along with the Swedish mission churches in Germany and Austria.

The Belgian case provides a unique opportunity to explore the importance of ethnic minorities more systematically. After its secession from the Netherlands in 1830, nation builders in Belgium were confronted with two large ethnolinguistic groups, the French-speaking Walloons in the south and the Dutch-speaking Flemish in the north. The Belgian capital, Brussels, was more mixed but dominated by those who spoke French, the official language of the administrative services (Urwin 1970). Even though the language division largely coincided with a geographical north–south divide, intra-country migration created small pockets of ethnic minorities in both parts of the country, as one can see in Figure 10.4.

To explore whether minority mechanisms also operate for nonreligious minorities, I first assess whether evasion rates were indeed higher in

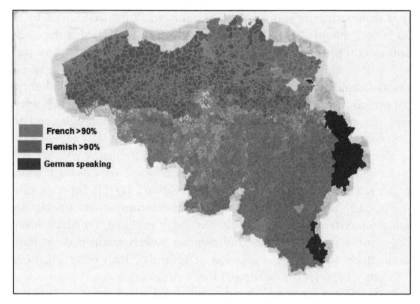

FIGURE 10.4 Geographical distribution of the French and Flemish in Belgium,
1930 (Vanhaute and Vrielinck 2013). A black-and-white version of this
figure will appear in some formats. For the colour version, please
refer to the plate section.

places with more ethnoreligious outsiders. In order to do so, I reproduce
the main spatial regression model from the previous chapter and add
an interaction between percentage of the county's population that spoke
Flemish in 1930 and a dummy marking whether a county is located in
Flanders or Wallonia.[14]

The results are presented in Figure 10.5. In line with the minority
hypothesis, increasing the percentage of Flemish speakers in Flanders
by one standard deviation decreases Jewish evasion by 3 percent; the
reverse is true in Wallonia. This suggests that proximity to the Flemish
protected Jews in French-speaking parts of the country, while proximity
to the Walloons had the same effect in Dutch-speaking parts of Belgium.

To ascertain whether ethnolinguistic rescue networks could be plausibly linked to these evasion patterns, I turn to earlier analyzed testimonies

---

[14] In the analysis, I exclude the twenty Jews living in German-speaking territory. In addition, I add a dummy that marks the city of Brussels to make sure that the unique
position of the Belgian capital is not driving the results. Data on language composition
is obtained from LOKSTAT (Vanhaute and Vrielinck 2013).

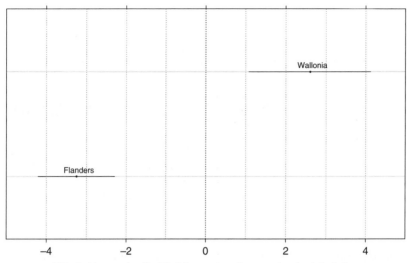

FIGURE 10.5 The change in evasion with 90 percent confidence intervals when the percentage of Dutch speakers increases by one standard deviation, Belgium.

collected by Yad Vashem. For each rescuer mentioned in these files I code whether his or her last name was Flemish (Germanic/Dutch) or Walloon (Romanic/French) and whether rescue activities took place in Flanders, Wallonia or Brussels.

I then assessed whether ethnolinguistic minorities were overrepresented among rescuers by dividing the share of minority rescuers in the body of testimonies by the percentage of minority believers for each of the three regions. As Figure 10.6 reveals ethnic minorities were strongly overrepresented among those whose provided shelter to Jews. Whereas Flemish citizens were three and six times more likely to protect Jews in Francophone Brussels and Wallonia, Walloons were strongly overrepresented among rescuers in Flemish-speaking territory. Taken together, these results indicate that ethnolinguistic and religious minorities alike played a crucial role in the resistance to genocide and that the minority mechanisms might operate beyond the realm of religion.

10.5 A MULTILEVEL THEORY

This chapter has revealed that the central thesis of this book, that religious minorities are more likely to resist genocide because they are better

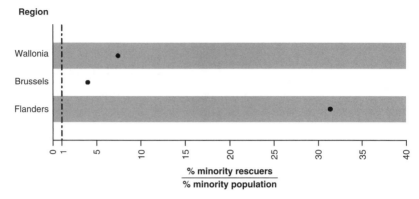

FIGURE 10.6 Overrepresentation of ethnic minorities among rescuers in Belgium.

able to setup clandestine organizations imbued with pluralism and empathy for victims of mass persecution, travels outside the borders of the Low Countries to France, Germany and Yugoslavia during the Holocaust as well as beyond the Holocaust to other episodes of mass persecution such as those that have occurred in the Ottoman Empire, Rwanda and the United States. All in all, there seems to be considerable evidence that the empathy and clandestine capacity mechanisms are broadly applicable in a wide range of contexts. However, the exploration also brought to light three important sets of scope conditions that limit the theory's portability. First, the minority hypothesis does not travel to contexts where majority elites, both secular and religious, openly object to persecution and cooperate to arrest its implementation. In this case, a general resistance mentality and ability to resist in the open make both the clandestine capacity and empathy advantages of minority congregations redundant for resistance against genocide. Second, the minority argument does not operate in situations where rescue behavior is so individualistic that it does not require coordination. Third, minority mobilization against killing does not take off if the minorities in question are closely aligned with the repressive apparatus undertaking the violence.

These scope conditions notwithstanding, this book makes a strong call for a multilevel perspective on resistance to genocide that interrogates the interactions between microlevel factors, local community structures and national processes to better understand how, when and where social relations can be translated into protection networks for threatened neighbors. The data presented throughout the book illustrates the importance of such an approach. First, it provides powerful evidence that the influence of microlevel factors, such as an individual's availability, motivation and adventurousness, are conditional on minority capacity. My analysis shows that adventurous individuals in minority communities were able to join successful clandestine operations and rescue hundreds of Jews while those in majority congregations with the same traits failed to have a similar impact. It also reveals that moral outrage was not sufficient for clandestine collective action. Many individuals were shocked by anti-Jewish legislation but refrained from clandestine collective action because they were not assured that the production of rescue networks was feasible. Only outraged individuals embedded in minority networks had the ability to translate their sentiments into effective underground networks. In addition, altruistic religious majority leaders who mobilized on behalf of Jewish refugees before the war were unable to continue their activities illegally once the occupation began because their networks were immediately exposed or because they could not recruit the right people to overcome the clandestine collective action dilemma. Hence, whether adventurous, available and outraged individuals with strong identities and values are able to mobilize in secret is dependent on the local-level structures in which they are embedded.

Second, national forces affect clandestine mobilization differently depending on whether communities form minority enclaves. Several instances of rescue revealed that national church leaders played an important role in motivating Christians to engage in rescue. Others believed that the persecution of Jews did not belong in a plural society. However, most sympathetic citizens were not able to translate their motivations into action because they considered the risks too high. Gentiles who did try, saw their attempt thwarted early on by the Nazi security apparatus. It was citizens embedded in minority enclaves who could not only see an opportunity to act on national norms or obey elite calls to action, but could also circumvent the challenges of a wartime repressive context. As with microlevel factors, the impact of national leadership, pluralistic norms and repressive contexts was conditioned by the availability of distinct local networks. This book thus suggests that if we want to better understand clandestine operations in times of mass repression, we need to take into consideration the local challenges of clandestine collective action and explain when, where and how social networks can be appropriated for underground mobilization, in addition to studying micro motives and national conditions.

Local group position does not only mediate micro and macro forces by shaping the capacity to overcome the clandestine collective action

dilemma, it also imbues networks with the norms and values that motivate resistance to genocide to begin with. Individual-level dispositions to
rescue are not distributed randomly, but in part reflect the underlying
structure of civic life, as members of minority groups are more likely
to display empathy with outsiders. As a result, national-level calls to
resist attacks on pluralism resonated much stronger among local minority
groups that were benefiting from peaceful coexistence on a daily basis,
revealing how national messages, individual motivations and local networks interact to produce both the form and content of political action
(McVeigh, Myers and Sikkink 2004; Charnysh 2015).

Different levels of analysis can also strengthen each other. The Dutch
data presented in the second part of this book suggest that the minority
effect was stronger for Catholics in Protestant areas than for Protestants
in Catholic areas. It seems plausible that the more hierarchical structure
of the Catholic Church (Croes and Tammes 2004) reinforced the mobilization capacity of more empathetic minority communities. In doing so,
macrolevel factors created an asymmetric minority effect by condition-
ing the impact of mesolevel processes. Further research should further
specify these cross-level interactions.

10.6 CONCLUSION

This book started with the ambivalence of the sacred, discussing the
strong role that religion has played in both producing and impeding violence. My research has identified an important underlying factor that
under certain conditions shapes which side of the sacred prevails by
studying religious resistance against genocide. This book reveals that
local minorities in general and religious minorities in particular are more
likely to resist violence because their leaders are attached to pluralism, emphasize with victims of mass persecution and have the networks
to translate defiant norms into the collective action required to arrest
aggression.

This leads to the sobering conclusion that in most cases exceptional
behavior is only displayed by exceptional communities, which are rare
by definition. Mainstream society hardly ever steps up in times of
need. Heroes in times of crisis, on the contrary, are often the dissi-
dents, deviants and marginalized outsiders, who, in normal times, are
ridiculed, looked down on or persecuted. What makes people successful in peacetime is exactly what makes them unsuccessful in times of
crisis and vice versa. As such, this book is not as much a story of
hope as of tragedy. The theory reveals how strong, rapid collective

mobilization in the face of genocide depends on relatively strong social ties among well-screened community members with strong moral values. The necessity to restrict channels of recruitment to trusted ties, however, prohibits the expansion of collective rescue efforts beyond a narrow set of like-minded actors who take exceptional positions in society. In other words, being a religious minority not only explains mobilization against mass killing, but also its disjointed nature as segregated networks only have limited carrying capacity to provide assistance. This highlights both the potential and the inefficiencies of minority groups, which, much like tight-knit neighborhood movements, require interregional ties to really transform society (Gould 1995). While deviants try to mobilize but eventually fail to have an impact because they lack mainstream access and legitimacy, the majority that can really make a difference often remains passive when confronted with human suffering. This explains why, despite the presence of minority enclaves throughout the Low Countries, close to a 140,000 Dutch and Belgian Jews, including my ancestors, found their tragic death in the monstrous hands of a mass-killing machine.

Future studies should try explain why and how some disjointed covert activities percolate upward and forge these connections while others do not, exploring how reactive mobilization interacts with broader political opportunities, broader institutional coalitions or broader issue networks (Loveman 1998) in producing the broad multigroup coalitions necessary for the transformation of society (Erikson and Occhiuto 2017). If this book accomplishes anything, I hope that it draws attention to the responsibility we all have in producing the broad-based coalitions that are required for the protection of pluralism. We might need them sooner than we would like to think.

10.A APPENDIX

TABLE 10.A1 *Religious minorities and deportations in Germany*

	Poisson
	(1) Deportations
Population, 1933 (log)	0.047 (0.079)
Jews, 1933 (log)	1.011** (0.075)

(continued)

TABLE 10.A1 *(continued)*

	Poisson
	(1) Deportations
% Jewish, 1933	−0.047
	(0.038)
% Catholics in village, 1925	−0.272*
	(0.146)
% Catholics in village 1925* % Catholics in state 1925	0.009**
	(0.002)
Constant	−2.053**
	(0.429)
State FE	Y
Villages	1,080
States	24
Log-likelihood	−3,007.248

Entries are unstandardized regression coefficients.
Stare clustered standard errors are in parentheses.
*p<0.05; **p<0.001.

TABLE 10.A2 *Religious minorities and death rate in rural Rwanda*

	OLS
	(1) Death rate
% Muslim, 1991	−12.799*
	(5.207)
% Protestant, 1991	−0.076
	(0.171)
% 7th Day Ad., 1991	−51.705
	(65.027)
% Other minorities, 1991	13.557
	(8.232)
% Secular, 1991	−1.082
	(0.714)
# days under RPF	0.101**
	(0.027)
Population density, 1991	1.467**
	(0.491)
% Tutsi, 1991	61.392*
	(23.043)

TABLE 10.A2 *(continued)*

	OLS
	(1) Death rate
Population, 1991 (log)	−2.774 (3.418)
Distance from town km (log)	2.007 (2.681)
Distance from road km (log)	5.294* (2.809)
% Mixed households, 1991	−4.091 (11.857)
Constant	69.338* (25.871)
Sectors	1,294
Provinces	10
Log-likelihood	−6,052.739

Entries are unstandardized regression coefficients.
Province clustered standard errors are in parentheses.
*p<0.05; **p<0.01.

TABLE 10.A3 *Regression of Jewish evasion in Belgium*

	Autologistic regression
	(1) Evasion
% Dutch speakers, 1930	0.696* (0.263)
Flanders	0.237** (0.071)
% Dutch*Flanders	−1.505** (0.321)
Prot churches	0.050** (0.013)
Number of Jews/1,000	−0.019** (0.004)

(continued)

TABLE 10.A3 *(continued)*

| | Autologistic regression |
	(1) Evasion
0 Constant	1.237**
	(0.072)
Autocovariate	Y
Controls	Y
County FE	N
Buffer	1.25 km
Observations	51,570
Municipalities	327
Log-likelihood	−33,644.980

Entries are unstandardized regression coefficients.
County clustered standard errors are in parentheses.
*p<0.01; **p<0.001.

Bibliography

Primary Sources

Archive Flim NIOD 471 11 B, Amsterdam.
Archive Flim NIOD 471 13 B, Amsterdam.
Archive Flim NIOD 471 13 D, Amsterdam.
Archive Flim NIOD 771 12D, Amsterdam.
Archive LOKP NIOD 853, Amsterdam.
Archive NIOD, 251a 61.
Archive NIOD, 251a 119.
Archives Stokman Collection, Katholiek Documentatie Centrum Nijmegen (Stokman 939).
CEGESOMA Archive Pierre Beeckmans (AA1314 nr. 300–500).
Dagblad De Standaard 25/1/1939.
Dagblad De Tijd 3/4/1930.
Dagblad De Tijd 23/12/1930.
Dagblad De Tijd 4/7/1931.
Dagblad De Tijd 14/6/1933.
Dagblad De Tijd 31/8/1933.
Dagblad De Tijd 7/11/1937.
Dagblad De Tijd 14/11/1938.
Dagblad De Tijd 3/12/1938.
Dagblad De Tijd 3/10/1939.
Dagblad Gazet van Antwerpen 7/2/1931.
Dagblad Gazet van Antwerpen 25/3/1931.
Dagblad Gazet van Antwerpen 29/7/1931.
Dagblad Gazet van Antwerpen 4/10/1933.
Dagblad Gazet van Antwerpen 8/2/1934.
Dagblad Gazet van Antwerpen 27/9/1934.
Dagblad Gazet van Antwerpen 9/9/1935.
Dagblad Gazet van Antwerpen 7/3/1937.

Dagblad Gazet van Antwerpen 14/11/1938.
Dagblad Gazet van Antwerpen 10/6/1939.
Dagblad Het Limburgs Dagblad 24/9/1930.
Dagblad Het Limburgs Dagblad 1/10/1932.
Dagblad Het Limburgs Dagblad 27/10/1932.
Dagblad Het Limburgs Dagblad 6/7/1933.
Dagblad Het Limburgs Dagblad 23/12/1933.
Dagblad Het Limburgs Dagblad 17/6/1936.
Dagblad Het Limburgs Dagblad 1/8/1938.
Dagboek Douwes, NIOD 244 1065, Amsterdam.
De l'enquete Paul Bouffier sur les Eglises Protestantes de Belgique (CEGESOMA
    AA 1205).
Diary Theresa Wertheim, www.joodscheraadenschede.nl.
Fonds Enquete Eglise (AA 1448–1449).
Interview Flim, Archive Flim NIOD 471 13C.
Interview Grunningman. Archive NIOD 251a-117, Amsterdam.
Interview kapelaan Van Der Brink, NIOD, Amsterdam.
Katholiek jaarboek van Belgie. 1950. Brussels.
La Libre Belgique 28/1/1938.
La Libre Belgique 18/3/1938.
La Libre Belgique 9/5/1938.
La Libre Belgique 17/5/1938.
La Libre Belgique 16/10/1938.
La Libre Belgique 21/11/1938.
La Libre Belgique 18/6/1939.
NIOD 020, 2122: Uitreksels Meldungen aus den Niederlanden.
NIOD 077, 353-357: Meldungen aus den Niederlanden.
Purification police 2.2.1 51, National Archives, Den Haag.
Purification police 2.2.1 66, National Archives, Den Haag.
Purification police file 1, National Archives, Den Haag.
Purification police file 2, National Archive, Den Haag.
Purification police file 3, National Archives, Den Haag.
Purification police file 5, National Archives, Den Haag.
Purification police file 6, National Archives, Den Haag.
Schyns in de l'enquete Paul Bouffier sur les Eglises Protestantes de Belgique
    (CEGESOMA AA 1205).
SVB-file 1, DOCDIRECT, Winschoten.
SVB-file 2, DOCDIRECT, Winschoten.
SVB-file 3, DOCDIRECT, Winschoten.
SVB-file 4, DOCDIRECT, Winschoten.
SVB-file 5, DOCDIRECT, Winschoten.
SVB-file 6, DOCDIRECT, Winschoten.
SVB-file 7, DOCDIRECT, Winschoten.
SVB-file 8, DOCDIRECT, Winschoten.
SVB-file 9, DOCDIRECT, Winschoten.
SVB-file 10, DOCDIRECT, Winschoten.
SVB-file 12, DOCDIRECT, Winschoten.

SVB-file 13, DOCDIRECT, Winschoten.
SVB-file 14, DOCDIRECT, Winschoten.
SVB-file 17, DOCDIRECT, Winschoten.
SVB-file 18, DOCDIRECT, Winschoten.
SVB-file 19, DOCDIRECT, Winschoten.
SVB-file 20, DOCDIRECT, Winschoten.
SVB-file 22, DOCDIRECT, Winschoten.
SVB-file 23, DOCDIRECT, Winschoten.
SVB-file 23, DOCDIRECT, Winschoten.
SVB-file 24, DOCDIRECT, Winschoten.
SVB-file 25, DOCDIRECT, Winschoten.
SVB-file 28, DOCDIRECT, Winschoten.
SVB-file 29, DOCDIRECT, Winschoten.
SVB-file 30, DOCDIRECT, Winschoten.
SVB-file 32, DOCDIRECT, Winschoten.
SVB-file 33, DOCDIRECT, Winschoten.
SVB-file 34, DOCDIRECT, Winschoten.
SVB-file 35, DOCDIRECT, Winschoten.
SVB-file 36, DOCDIRECT, Winschoten.
SVB-file 37, DOCDIRECT, Winschoten.
SVB-file 39, DOCDIRECT, Winschoten.
SVB-file 40, DOCDIRECT, Winschoten.
SVB-file 41, DOCDIRECT, Winschoten.
SVB-file 42, DOCDIRECT, Winschoten.
SVB-file 43, DOCDIRECT, Winschoten.
SVB-file 45, DOCDIRECT, Winschoten.
SVB-file 46, DOCDIRECT, Winschoten.
SVB-file 47, DOCDIRECT, Winschoten.
SVB-file 48, DOCDIRECT, Winschoten.
SVB-file 49, DOCDIRECT, Winschoten.
SVB-file 50, DOCDIRECT, Winschoten.
SVB-file 51, DOCDIRECT, Winschoten.
SVB-file 52, DOCDIRECT, Winschoten.
SVB-file 53, DOCDIRECT, Winschoten.
SVB-file 54, DOCDIRECT, Winschoten.
SVB-file 55, DOCDIRECT, Winschoten.
Tijdschrift De Klok 4/5/34.
Tijdschrift De Klok 10/6/38.
Tijdschrift De Klok 8/9/39.
*Vanderriet in de l'Enquete Paul Bouffier sur les Eglises protestantes de Belgique
    (CEGESOMA AA 1205).*
*Visser in de l'Enquete Paul Bouffier sur les Eglises Protestantes de Belgique
    (CEGESOMA AA 1205).*
Yad Vashem A. Hijmans in Michman et al.
Yad Vashem file A. Dijkhuis in Michman et al.
Yad Vashem file A. Knappert in Michman et al.
Yad Vashem file A. Stork in Michman et al.

Yad Vashem file A. Ten Tije in Michman et al.
Yad Vashem file B. Oskam, in Michman et al.
Yad Vashem file C. Moulijn in Michman et al.
Yad Vashem file C. Staal in Michman et al.
Yad Vashem file D. Somsen in Michman et al.
Yad Vashem file D. Spoelstra in Michman et al.
Yad Vashem file F. Pakker in Michman et al.
Yad Vashem file G. Haveman in Michman et al.
Yad Vashem file G. Hustinx in Michman et al.
Yad Vashem file G. Olink in Michman et al.
Yad Vashem file H. Bockma in Michman et al.
Yad Vashem file H. Dijkhuis in Michman et al.
Yad Vashem file J. Assendorp in Michman et al.
Yad Vashem file J. Hofstra in Michman et al.
Yad Vashem file J. Musch in Michman et al.
Yad Vashem file J. Tabak in Michman et al.
Yad Vashem file L. Gerritsen in Michman et al.
Yad Vashem file M. Coelingh in Michman et al.
Yad Vashem file N. Talsma in Michman et al.
Yad Vashem file R. Hamming in Michman et al.
Yad Vashem file S. Vis in Michman et al.
Yad Vashem file Scheffer in Michman et al.
Yad Vashem file T. Velsing in Michman et al.

Secondary Sources

Abicht, Ludo. 2006. *Geschiedenis van de Joden van de Lage Landen*. Brussels: Manteau.

Adorno, Theodor W., Else Frenkel-Brunswik, Daniel J. Levinson et al. 1950. *The Authoritarian Personality*. Oxford: Harpers.

Aldrich, Howard. 1999. *Organizations Evolving*. Thousand Oaks, CA: Sage.

Allport, Gordon W. 1966. "The Religious Context of Prejudice". In: *Journal for the Scientific Study of Religion* 5.3, pp. 447–457.

Appleby, Scott. 1999. *The Ambivalence of the Sacred: Religion, Violence, and Reconciliation*. Lanham, MD: Rowman & Littlefield Publishers.

Arad, Yitzhak. 2009. *The Holocaust in the Soviet Union*. Lincoln: University of Nebraska Press.

Aukes, Hendrikus. 1956. *Kardinaal de Jong*. Utrecht: Spectrum.

Autesserre, Séverine. 2010. *The Trouble with the Congo: Local Violence and the Failure of International Peacebuilding*. Vol. 115. New York: Cambridge University Press.

Bail, Christopher. 2012. "The Fringe Effect: Civil Society Organizations and the Evolution of Media Discourse about Islam since the September 11th Attacks". In: *American Sociological Review* 77.6, pp. 855–879.

Baker, Wayne and Robert Faulkner. 1993. "The Social Organization of Conspiracy: Illegal Networks in the Heavy Electrical Equipment Industry". In: *American Sociological Review* 58.6, pp. 837–860.

Bank, Jan. 2015. *God in Oorlog. De rol van de Kerk in Europa 1939–1945.* Amsterdam: Balans.

Bank, Wim. 1985. *Kennemerland hongert naar zijn bevrijding.* Haarlem: Haarlems Dagblad.

Barkey, Karen and Ronan Van Rossem. 1997. "Networks of Contention: Villages and Regional Structure in the Seventeenth-Century Ottoman Empire". In: *American Journal of Sociology* 102.5, pp. 1345–1382.

Batson, C. Daniel. 1991. *The Altruism Question: Toward a Social-Psychological Answer.* New York: Psychology Press.

Bauer, Yehuda and Nili Keren. 2001. *A History of the Holocaust.* Danbury, CT: Franklin Watts.

Bazuin, Jantje. 2008. *Theesurrogaat voor Sneek.* Leeuwarden: Penn Communicatie.

Bearman, Peter. 1995. *From Relations to Rhetorics.* New Brunswick, NJ: Rutgers University Press.

Beekink, Erik, Onno Boonstra, Theo Engelen and Hans Knippenberg. 2003. *Nederland in verandering: maatschappelijke ontwikkelingen in kaart gebracht.* Amsterdam: Aksant.

Bekkenkamp, Alfred. 2000. *Leendert Overduin. Het Levensverhaal van Pastor Pimpernel (1900–1976).* Enschede: Van De Berg.

Benz, Wolfgang and Juliane Wetzel. 1996. *Solidarität und Hilfe für Juden während der NS-Zeit: Regionalstudien 1. Polen, Rumänien, Griechenland, Luxemburg, Norwegen, Schweiz.* Berlin: Metropol.

—— 1998. *Solidarität und Hilfe für Juden während der NS-Zeit: Regionalstudien 2.* Berlin: Metropol.

Berkhoff, Karel. 2009. *Harvest of Despair: Life and Death in Ukraine under Nazi Rule.* Cambridge, MA: Harvard University Press.

Berman, Eli and David Laitin. 2008. "Religion, Terrorism and Public Goods: Testing the Club Model". In: *Journal of Public Economics* 92.10, pp. 1942–1967.

Berry, Marie. 2017. "Barriers to Womens Progress After Atrocity: Evidence from Rwanda and Bosnia-Herzegovina". In: *Gender & Society* 31.6, pp. 830–853.

Birnbaum, Pierre. 1992. *Anti-Semitism in France: A Political History from Leon Blum to the Present.* Oxford: Blackwell.

Blaschke, Olaf. 1997. *Katholizismus und Antisemitismus.* Gottingen: Vandenhoeck & Ruprecht.

Blasnik, Michael. 2010. "RECLINK: Stata Module to Probabilistically Match Records". https://ideas.repec.org/c/boc/bocode/s456876.html, accessed 10/10/2018.

Blom, Hans. 1987. "De vervolging van de joden in Nederland in internationaal vergelijkend perspectief". In: *De Gids* 6/7, pp. 494–506.

—— 2006. *History of the Low Countries.* New York: Berghahn books.

Blom, Hans and Joel Cahen. 2002. "Jewish Netherlanders, Netherlands Jews, and Jews in the Netherlands, 1870–1940". In: *The History of the Jews in the Netherlands,* ed. by Hans Blom, Rena Fuks-Mansfeld and Ivo Schoffer. Portland, OR: The Littman Library of Jewish Civilization, pp. 245–310.

Bloxham, Donald. 2005. *The Great Game of Genocide: Imperialism, Nationalism, and the Destruction of the Ottoman Armenians*. Oxford: Oxford University Press.

Bosma, Ewart. 2015. *Oude Waarheid Nieuwe Orde*. Apeldoorn: de Banier.

Brandon, Ray and Wendy Lower. 2008. *The Shoah in Ukraine: History, Testimony, Memorialization*. Bloomington: Indiana University Press.

Braun, Robert. 2011. "The Differential Deportation Rates of Jews in Occupied Belgium: Toward a Micro-Level Dataset of Genocide Victimization". In: *Perspectives on Europe* 41.2, pp. 121–124.

—— 2016. "Religious Minorities and Resistance to Genocide: The Collective Rescue of Jews in the Netherlands during the Holocaust". In: *American Political Science Review* 110.1, pp. 127–147.

Brewer, Marilynn and Michael Silver. 2000. "Group Distinctiveness, Social Identification, and Collective Mobilization". In: *Self, Identity and Social Movements*, ed. by Sheldon Stryker, Timothy Owens and Robert White. Twin Cities: University of Minnesota Press, pp. 153–171.

Bronzwaer, Paul. 2010. *Maastricht en Luik bezet: een comparatief onderzoek naar vijf aspecten van de Duitse bezetting van Maastricht en Luik tijdens de Tweede Wereldoorlog*. Hilversum: Uitgeverij Verloren.

Browning, Christopher. 2014. *The Origins of the Final Solution*. New York: Random House.

Brubaker, Rogers. 2015. "Religious Dimensions of Political Conflict and Violence". In: *Sociological Theory* 33.1, pp. 1–19.

Bruinsma, Gerben and Wim Bernasco. 2004. "Criminal Groups and Transnational Illegal Markets". In: *Crime, Law and Social Change* 41, pp. 79–94.

Brustein, William. 2003. *Roots of Hate: Anti-Semitism in Europe before the Holocaust*. New York: Cambridge University Press.

Burt, Ronald. 2009. *Structural Holes: The Social Structure of Competition*. Cambridge, MA: Harvard University Press.

Cabanel, Patrick. 2008. "Protestantismes minoritaires, affinités judéo–protestantes et sauvetage des juifs". In: *La résistance aux génocides: de la pluralité des actes de sauvetage*, ed. by Jacques Semelin, Claire Andrieu and Sarah Gensburger. Paris: Presses de Sciences Po, pp. 445–456.

Caestecker, Frank. 1993. *Ongewenste gasten. Joodse vluchtelingen en migranten in de dertiger jaren*. Brussels: VUB Press.

Cammaert, Alfred. 1994. *Het Verborgen Front: Geschiedenis van de Georganiseerde Illegaliteit in de Provincie Limburg tijdens de Tweede Wereldoorlog*. Leeuwarden: Eisma.

Campbell, Bradley. 2010. "Contradictory Behavior During Genocides". In: *Sociological Forum* 25.2, pp. 296–314.

Capellen, W. and H. Oolders-Jurjens. 2008. "Het leven in de Groninger pastorie in oorlogstijd". In *Kerkblad voor het Noorden, editie* 2.5, p. 4.

Carroll, James. 2002. *Constantine's Sword: The Church and the Jews – A History*. Boston: Houghton Mifflin Harcourt.

CBS. 1931. *Census 1930*. Den Haag: CBS.

—— 1937. *Uitslagen verkiezingen 1918–1937*. Voorschoten: CBS.

—— 1939. *Uitslagen provincial staten verkiezingen 1939*. Den Haag: CBS.

Charnysh, Volha. 2015. "Historical Legacies of Interethnic Competition: Anti-Semitism and the EU Referendum in Poland". In: *Comparative Political Studies* 48.13, pp. 1711–1745.

Cholawski, Shalom. 1998. *The Jews of Bielorussia During World War II*. London: Taylor & Francis.

Clemens, Elisabeth. 2007. "Toward a Historicized Sociology: Theorizing Events, Processes, and Emergence". In: *Annual Review of Sociology* 33, pp. 527–549.

Coleman, James. 1988. "Social Capital in the Creation of Human Capital". In: *American Journal of Sociology* 94, S95–S120.

Collard, Emile. 1952. *Carte de la Pratique Dominicale en Belgique, par Commune*. Mons: Mons Editions, Dimanche.

Cornelissen, Cor. 2006. *Onvoltooid verleden tijd*. Oldenzaal: Twents-Gelderse Uitgeverij De Bruyn.

Coser, Lewis. 1956. *The Functions of Social Conflict*. New York: Routledge.

—— 1974. *Greedy Institutions: Patterns of Undivided Commitment*. New York: Free Press.

Croes, Marnix and Peter Tammes. 2004. *"Gif Laten wij niet Voortbestaan": een Onderzoek naar de Overlevingskansen van Joden in de Nederlandse Gemeenten 1940–1945*. Amsterdam: Aksant.

Crossley, Nick, Gemma Edwards, Ellen Harries and Rachel Stevenson. 2012. "Covert Social Movement Networks and the Secrecy–Efficiency Trade Off: The Case of the UK Suffragettes (1906–1914)". In: *Social Networks* 34.4, pp. 634–644.

Daalder, Hans. 1974. "The Consociational Democracy Theme". In: *World Politics* 26.4, pp. 604–621.

Dadrian, Vahakn. 2003. *The History of the Armenian Genocide: Ethnic Conflict from the Balkans to Anatolia to the Caucasus*. New York, NY: Berghahn Books.

Darden, Keith. 2015. *Resisting Occupation in Eurasia*. New York: Cambridge University Press.

d'Aubigné, Jeanne Merle, Emile Fabre and Violette Mouchon. 1989. *Les Clandestins de Dieu: CIMADE 1939–1945*. Geneva: Labor et Fides.

della Porta, Donatella. 1988. "Recruitment Processes in Clandestine Political Organizations: Italian Left-Wing Terrorism". In: *International Social Movement Research* 1, pp. 155–169.

—— 2013. *Clandestine Political Violence*. New York: Cambridge University Press.

Delleman, Thomas. 1949. *Opdat wij niet vergeten. De bijdrage van de gereformeerde kerken, van haar voorgangers en leden, in het verzet tegen het nationaal-socialisme en de Duitse Tyrannie*. Kampen: Kok.

Delplancq, Thierry. "Des paroles et des actes. L'administration bruxelloise et le registre des Juifs, 1940–1941". *Cahiers d'Histoire du Temps Présent/Bijdragen tot de Eigentijdse Geschiedenis* 12 (2003): 141–179.

Demant, Froukje. 2015. *Verre Buren: Samenleven in de Schaduw van de Holocaust*. Amsterdam: University of Amsterdam.

Des Forges, Alison. 1999. *Leave None to Tell the Story: Genocide in Rwanda.* New York: Human Rights Watch.

Dhooge, Jan. 1985. "Het Belgisch protestantisme". In: *Kerken, religieuze groeperingen en lekenbewegingen: Belgie en zijn goden.* Leuven: Cabay.

Dixon, C. Scott. 2008. *The Reformation in Germany.* Hoboken, NJ: John Wiley & Sons.

Dovidio, John. 1984. "Helping Behavior and Altruism: An Empirical and Conceptual Overview". In: *Advances in Experimental Social Psychology* 17, pp. 361–427.

Dovidio, John, F., Jane Allyn Piliavin, David A. Schroeder and Louis A. Penner. 2006. *The Social Psychology of Prosocial Behavior.* New York: Psychology Press.

Duffhues, Ton, Albert Felling and Jan Roes. 1985. *Bewegende Patronen: een Analyse van het Landelijk Netwerk van Katholieke Organisaties en Bestuurders, 1945–1980.* Nijmegen: Katholiek Documentatie Centrum.

Durkheim, Emile. 1897. *Suicide. A Study in Sociology.* New York: The Free Press.

Einwohner, Rachel and Thomas Maher. 2011. "Threat Assessment and Collective-Action Emergence: Death-Camp and Ghetto Resistance during the Holocaust". In: *Mobilization: An International Quarterly* 16.2, pp. 127–146.

Elster, Jon. 1979. *Ulysses and the Sirens: Studies in Rationality and Irrationality.* New York: Cambridge University Press.

—— 1989. *The Cement of Society: A Survey of Social Order.* Cambridge: Cambridge University Press.

Enders, Walter and Xuejuan Su. 2007. "Rational Terrorists and Optimal Network Structure". In: *Journal of Conflict Resolution* 51.1, pp. 33–57.

Entman, Robert. 2004. *Projections of Power: Framing News, Public Opinion, and US Foreign Policy.* Chicago: University of Chicago Press.

Erickson, Bonnie. 1981. "Secret Societies and Social Structure". In: *Social Forces* 60.1, pp. 188–210.

Erikson, Emily and Nicholas Occhiuto. 2017. "Social Networks and Macrosocial Change". In: *Annual Review of Sociology* 43, pp. 229–248.

Evers-Emden, Bloeme and Bert-Jan Flim. 1996. *Ondergedoken Geweest: een Afgesloten Verleden? Joodse Kinderen over hun Onderduiken Vijftig Jaar Later.* Amsterdam: Kok.

Fein, Helen. 1979. *Accounting for Genocide: National Responses and Jewish Victimization during the Holocaust.* New York: Free Press.

Ferree, Myra Marx. 2003. "Resonance and Radicalism: Feminist Framing in the Abortion Debates of the United States and Germany". In: *American Journal of Sociology* 109.2, pp. 304–344.

Ferris, Elizabeth. 2005. "Faith-Based and Secular Humanitarian Organizations". In: *International Review of the Red Cross* 87.858, pp. 311–325.

Fine, Gary and Lori Holyfield. 1996. "Secrecy, Trust, and Dangerous Leisure: Generating Group Cohesion in Voluntary Organizations". In: *Social Psychology Quarterly* 59.1, pp. 22–38.

Finkel, Evgeny. 2015. "The Phoenix Effect of State Repression: Jewish Resistance during the Holocaust". In: *American Political Science Review* 109.2, pp. 339–353.

—— 2017. *Ordinary Jews: Choice and Survival during the Holocaust*. Princeton, NJ: Princeton University Press.

Flap, Henk, Kathy Geurts and Wout Ultee. 1997. "De Jodenvervolging in lokaal perspectief". In: *De organizatie van de bezetting*, ed. by Henk Flap and Wil Arts. Amsterdam: Amsterdam University Press, pp. 31–54.

Flim, Bert-Jan. 1997. *Omdat hun hart sprak: geschiedenis van de georganiseerde hulp aan Joodse kinderen in Nederland, 1942–1945*. Kampen: Kok.

—— 1998. "The Possibilities for Dutch Jews to Hide from the Nazis, 1942–1945". In: *Dutch Jews as Perceived by Themselves and by Others. Proceedings of the Eighth International Symposium on the History of the Jews in the Netherlands, Jerusalem*, pp. 289–305.

Fogelman, Eva. 1994. *Conscience and Courage: Rescuers of Jews during the Holocaust*. New York: Random House.

Foner, Eric. 2015. *Gateway to Freedom: The Hidden History of the Underground Railroad*. New York: WW Norton & Company.

Fox, Nicole and Hollie Nyseth Brehm. 2018. "I Decided to Save Them: Factors that Shaped Participation in Rescue Efforts during Genocide in Rwanda". In: *Social Forces*, 96(4), pp. 1625–1648.

Franzosi, Roberto. 1987. "The Press as a Source of Socio-historical Data: Issues in the Methodology of Data Collection from Newspapers". In: *Historical Methods: A Journal of Quantitative and Interdisciplinary History* 20.1, pp. 5–16.

Friedlander, Saul. 1997. *Nazi Germany and the Jews, Volume 1: The Years of Persecution, 1933–1939*. London: Phoenix Giant.

Friling, Tuvia, Radu Ioanid, Mihail E. Ionescu et al. 2004. *Final Report of the International Commission on the Holocaust in Romania*. Bucharest: International Commission on the Holocaust in Romania.

Fujii, Lee Ann. 2008. "Sauveteurs et sauveteurs-tueurs durant le génocide Rwandais". In: *La résistance aux génocides: de la pluralité des actes de sauvetage*, ed. by Jacques Semelin, Claire Andrieu and Sarah Gensburger. Paris: Presses de Sciences Po, pp. 445–456.

—— 2011. *Killing Neighbors: Webs of Violence in Rwanda*. Ithaca, NY: Cornell University Press.

Gamson, William. 1992. *Talking Politics*. New York: Cambridge University Press.

Ganz, Marshall. 2000. "Resources and Resourcefulness: Strategic Capacity in the Unionization of California Agriculture, 1959–1966". In: *American Journal of Sociology* 105.4, pp. 1003–1062.

Gaunt, David. 2015. "The Complexity of the Assyrian Genocide". In: *Genocide Studies International* 9.1, pp. 83–103.

Gerard, Emmanuel. 1985. *De Katholieke Partij in Crisis: Partijpolitiek Leven in Belgie (1918–1940)*. Leuven: Kritak.

Geritz-Koster, Rieky. 1999. *Dorp in deMediene. De Geschiedenis van de Joodse Gemeenschap in Haaksbergen*. Zutphen: Walburg Pers.

Gershman, Norman H. 2008. *Besa: Muslims Who Saved Jews in World War II*. Syracuse, NY: Syracuse University Press.

Gevers, Lieve. 2006. "Bisschoppen en bezetting: De Kerk in de Lage Landen tijdens de Tweede Wereldoorlog". In: *Trajecta* 13, pp. 372–399.

Gibson, David. 2014. "Enduring Illusions: The Social Organization of Secrecy and Deception". In: *Sociological Theory* 32.4, pp. 283–306.

Gilbert, Martin. 2010. *The Righteous: The Unsung Heroes of the Holocaust*. London: MacMillan.

Gill, Anthony. 2007. *The Political Origins of Religious Liberty*. New York: Cambridge University Press.

Gilman, Sander. 1997. *Smart Jews: The Construction of the Image of Jewish Superior Intelligence*. Lincoln: University of Nebraska Press.

Gilman, Sander and Steven Katz. 1991. *Anti-Semitism in Times of Crisis*. New York: New York University Press.

Goffman, Erving. 1970. *Strategic Interaction*. Philadelphia: University of Pennsylvania Press.

— 1974. *Frame Analysis: An Essay on the Organization of Experience*. Cambridge, MA: Harvard University Press.

Golding, Louis. 1939. *The Jewish Problem*. London: Penguin books.

Gould, Roger. 1993. "Collective Action and Network Structure". In: *American Sociological Review*, 58(2), pp. 182–196.

— 1995. *Insurgent Identities: Class, Community, and Protest in Paris from 1848 to the Commune*. Chicago: University of Chicago Press.

— 1996. "Patron-Client Ties, State Centralization, and the Whiskey Rebellion". In: *American Journal of Sociology* 102.2, pp. 400–429.

Gourevitch, Philip. 1998. *We Wish to Inform You that by Tomorrow We Will Be Killed with our Families*. New York: Farrar, Straus Giroux.

Gramsci, Antonio. 1935. *Further Selections from the Prison Notebooks*. Minneapolis: University of Minnesota Press.

Granovetter, Mark. 1995. "The Economic Sociology of Firms and Entrepreneurs". In: *The Economic Sociology of Immigration*, ed. by Alejandro Portes. New York: Russell Sage Foundation, pp. 128–166.

Greenspan, Henry. 2001. *The Awakening of Memory: Survivor Testimony in the First Years after the Holocaust, and Today*. Washington, DC: United States Holocaust Memorial Museum, Center for Advanced Holocaust Studies.

Greif, Avner. 2006. *Institutions and the Path to the Modern Economy: Lessons from Medieval Trade*. New York: Cambridge University Press.

Griffioen, Pim and Ron Zeller. 2011. *Jodenvervolging in Nederland, Belgie en Frankrijk, 1940–1945. Overeenkomsten, verschillen, oorzaken*. Amsterdam: Boom.

Gross, Jan Tomasz. 2001. *Neighbors: The Destruction of the Jewish Community in Jedwabne, Poland*. Princeton, NJ: Princeton University Press.

Gross, Michael. 1994. "Jewish Rescue in Holland and France during the Second World War: Moral Cognition and Collective Action". In: *Social Forces* 73.2, pp. 463–496.

Grynberg, Anne. 2013. *Les Camps de la Honte: les Internés Juifs des Camps Français (1939–1944)*. Paris: La Découverte.

Guhin, Jeffrey. 2014. "Religion as Site Rather Than Religion as Category: On the Sociology of Religion's Export Problem". In: *Sociology of Religion* 75.4, pp. 579–593.

Gushee, David. 1993. "Many Paths to Righteousness: An Assessment of Research on Why Righteous Gentiles Helped Jews". In: *Holocaust and Genocide Studies* 7, pp. 372–401.

Gutman, Israel. 2005. *The Encyclopedia of the Righteous Among the Nations: Rescuers of Jews during the Holocaust in Poland*. Jerusalem: Yad Vashem.

—— 2007. *The Encyclopedia of the Righteous Among the Nations: Europe (Part II) Rescuers of Jews during the Holocaust*. Jerusalem: Yad Vashem.

Gutman, Israel and Shmuel Krakowski. 1986. *Unequal Victims: Poles and Jews during the Second World War*. New York: Holocaust library.

Habermas, Jürgen. 1993. *Justification and Application: Remarks on Discourse Ethics*. Cambridge: Cambridge University Press.

Hagan, John and Wenona Rymond-Richmond. 2008. *Darfur and the Crime of Genocide*. New York: Cambridge University Press.

Hallie, Philip. 1979. *Lest Innocent Blood Be Shed: The Story of the Village of Le Chambon and How Goodness Happened There*. New York: Harper Collins.

Hamans, Paulus. 2008. *Getuigen voor Christus: Rooms-Katholieke Bloedgetuigen uit Nederland in de Twintigste Eeuw*. Den Bosch: Beleidssector Liturgie van de Nederlandse Bisschoppenconferentie.

Hardin, Russel. 1982. *Collective Action*. Baltimore: Johns Hopkins University Press.

Helbling, Marc. 2014. "Framing Immigration in Western Europe". In: *Journal of Ethnic and Migration Studies* 40.1, pp. 21–41.

Hellemans, Hanne. 2007. *Schimmen met een Ster: het Bewogen Verhaal van Joodse Ondergedoken Kinderen tijdens de Tweede Wereldoorlog in België*. Brussels: Manteau.

Hellemans, Staf. 1988. "Verzuiling en Ontzuiling van de Katholieken in België en Nederland. Een Historisch-Sociologische Vergelijking". In: *Sociologische Gids* 35.1, pp. 43–56.

Herdt, Gilbert. 1990. "Secret Societies and Secret Collectives". In: *Oceania* 60.4, pp. 360–381.

Herzberg, Abel. 1978. *Kroniek der jodenvervolging, 1940–1945*. Amsterdam: Meulenhoff.

Hilberg, Raul. 2003. *The Destruction of the European Jews*. New Haven, CT: Yale University Press.

Hilbrink, Coen. 1989. *De Illegalen: Illegaliteit in Twente en het Aangrenzende Salland 1940–1945*. Nijmegen: SUN.

—— 1998. *De Ondergrondse: Illegaliteit in Overijssel, 1940–1945*. Den Haag: SDU Uitgevers.

—— 2015. *Knokploegen: religie en gewapend verzet*. Amsterdam: Boom.

Hirschfeld, Gerhard. 1991. "Niederlande". In: *Dimension des Volkermords. Die Zahl der Judischen Opfer des Nationalsozialismus*, ed. by Wolgang Benz. Munchen: Munchen Verlag, pp. 52–72.

Hindu Times. 2015. "Hindu, Sikh Groups Join to Protect Religious Pluralism in U.S.". December 20, 2015.

Hocart, James. 1899. *La Question Juive: Cinq Conferences avec un Appendice sure la Charite Juive*. Paris: Fischbacher.

Hoffman, Martin. 2001. *Empathy and Moral Development: Implications for Caring and Justice*. Cambridge: Cambridge University Press.

Holland, Paul. 1986. "Statistics and Causal Inference". In: *Journal of the American Statistical Association* 81.396, pp. 945–960.

Hory, Ladislaus and Martin Broszat. 1964. *Der Kroatische Ustascha-Staat 1941– 1945*. Berlin: Walter de Gruyter.

Houwink ten Cate, Johannes. 1989. "Het jongere deel: Demografische en sociale kenmerken van het jodendom in Nederland tijdens de vervolging". In: *Jaarboek van het Rijksinstituut voor Oorlogsdocumentatie* 1, pp. 52–107.

—— 1999. "Mangelnde Solidaritat gegenuber Juden in den besetzten niederlandischen Gebieten?" In: *Solidaritat und Hilfe fur Juden wahrend der NS-Zeit: Regionalstudien 3*. Vol. 3, ed. by Wolfgang Benz and Juliane Wetzel. Berlin: Metropol, pp. 87–133.

Hovannisian, Richard. 1992. "The Question of Altruism during the Armenian Genocide of 1915". In: Embracing the Other : Philosophical, Psychological, and Historical Perspectives on Altruism, New York: NYU Press, pp. 282– 305.

Hovingh, Jan. 2015. *Predikanten in de Frontlinie*. Barneveld: Vuurbaak.

Iannaccone, Laurence. 1994. "Why Strict Churches are Strong". In: *American Journal of Sociology* 99.5, pp. 1180–1211.

IKGN. 2011. *Inventaris Kerkgebouwen in Nederland*. Amsterdam: VU.

Inghelram, Mieke. 1992. *Joodse Kinderen Opgevangen in een Katholiek Milieu tijdens de Tweede Wereld Oorlog*. Leuven: Leuven Universiteit.

Israel, Jonathan. 1989. "Sephardic Immigration into the Dutch Republic, 1595– 1672". In: *Studia Rosenthaliana* 23.2, pp. 45–53.

Jelinek, Yeshayahu. 1990. "Bosnia-Herzegovina at War: Relations between Moslems and Non-Moslems". In: *Holocaust and Genocide Studies* 5.3, pp. 275–292.

Jenkins, Craig. 1983. "Resource Mobilization Theory and the Study of Social Movements". In: *Annual Review of Sociology*, volume 9, pp. 527–553.

Jong, Loe De. 1969–1991. *Het Koninkrijk der Nederlanden in de tweede wereldoorlog (14 volumes)*. Den Haag: SDU Uitgeverij.

Joosten, Leonardus. 1964. *Katholieken en Fascisme in Nederland, 1920–1940*. Utrecht: HES.

Kahneman, Daniel. 2011. *Thinking Fast, Thinking Slow*. New York: Farrar, Straus, and Giroux.

Kalyvas, Stathis. 1996. *The Rise of Christian Democracy in Europe*. Ithaca, NY: Cornell University Press.

—— 2006. *The Logic of Violence in Civil War*. New York: Cambridge University Press.

Kaplan, Oliver. 2013. "Protecting Civilians in Civil War The Institution of the ATCC in Colombia". In: *Journal of Peace Research* 50.3, pp. 351–367.

Kaplan, Yosef. 1989. "Amsterdam and Ashkenazic Migration in the Seventeenth Century". In: *Studia Rosenthaliana* 23.2, pp. 22–44.

Karylowski, Jerzy. 1976. "Self-Esteem, Similarity, Liking and Helping". In: *Personality and Social Psychology Bulletin* 1.1, pp. 71–74.

Kenny, Anthony. 2013. *Aristotle Poetics*. New York: Oxford University Press.

Kieser, Hans-Lukas. 2008. "Removal of American Indians, Destruction of Ottoman Armenians. American Missionaries and Demographic Engineering". In: *European Journal of Turkish Studies. Social Sciences on Contemporary Turkey* 7, https://journals.openedition.org/ejts/2873, accessed 10/10/2018.

King, Charles. 2012. "Can There Be a Political Science of the Holocaust?" In: *Perspectives on Politics* 10.2, pp. 323–341.

Klandermans, Bert and Sidney Tarrow. 1988. "Mobilization into Social Movements: Synthesizing European and American Approaches". In: *International Social Movement Research* 1.1, pp. 1–38.

Klinken, Geert Johannes van. 1996. *Opvattingen in de Gereformeerde Kerken in Nederland overhet Jodendom, 1896–1970*. Kampen: Kok.

Klokhuis, Gerard. 1982. *De Geschiedenis van Twente*. Hengelo: Twentse Publicaties.

Knippenberg, Hans. 1992. *De religieuze kaart van Nederland: omvang en geografische spreiding van de godsdienstige gezindten vanafde Reformatie tot heden*. Amsterdam: Uitgeverij Van Gorcum.

Koopmans, Ruud and Paul Statham. 1999. "Political Claims Analysis: Integrating Protest Event and Political Discourse Approaches". In: *Mobilization: An International Quarterly* 4.2, pp. 203–221.

Kopstein, Jeffrey and Jason Wittenberg. 2011. "Deadly Communities: Local Political Milieus and the Persecution of Jews in Occupied Poland". In: *Comparative Political Studies* 44.3, p. 259.

Kopstein, Jeffrey, and Jason Wittenberg. *Intimate Violence: Anti-Jewish Pogroms on the Eve of the Holocaust*. Cornell University Press, 2018.

Kosmala, Beate and Claudia Schoppmann. 2002. "Überleben im Untergrund: Hilfe und Rettung für Juden in Deutschland 1941–1945". In: *Solidarität und Hilfe für Juden während der NS-Zeit: Regionalstudien*. Berlin: Metropol, p. 5.

Kossman, Ernst. 1986. *De Lage Landen. Twee Eeuwen Nederland en Belgie*. Amsterdam: Agon.

Kramer, H., G. J. van Dorland and H. A. Gijsbertse. 2010. "Historisch grondgebruik Nederland". In: *Tijd en Ruimte. Nieuwe toepassingen van GIS in de alfawetenschappen*. Utrecht: Uitgeverij Matrijs, pp. 142–153.

Krebs, Dennis. 1975. "Empathy and Altruism". In: *Journal of Personality and Social Psychology* 32.6, p. 1134.

Krippendorff, Klaus. 2004. "Reliability in Content Analysis". In: *Human Communication Research* 30.3, pp. 411–433.

Kroneberg, Clemens, Meir Yaish and Volker Stocké. 2010. "Norms and Rationality in Electoral Participation and in the Rescue of Jews in WWII: An Application of the Model of Frame Selection". In: *Rationality and Society* 22.1, pp. 3–36.

Kuper, Leo. 1990. "Theological Warrants for Genocide: Judaism, Islam and Christianity". In: *Terrorism and Political Violence* 2.3, pp. 351–379.

Kwaasteniet, Marianne de. 1990. *Denomination and Primary Education in the Netherlands (1870–1984): a Spatial Diffusion Perspective.* Florence: European University Institute.

Lagrou, Pieter. 1997. "Victims of Genocide and National Memory: Belgium, France and the Netherlands 1945–1965". In: *Past & Present* 154, pp. 181–222.

Lammers, Cornelis. 1994. "Collaboreren op niveau: een vergelijkende studie van Duitse bezettingsregimes gedurende de Tweede Wereldoorlog". In: *Mens en Maatschappij* 69.4, pp. 366–399.

Landes, David. 2003. *The Unbound Prometheus: Technological Change and Industrial Development in Western Europe from 1750 to the Present.* New York: Cambridge University Press.

Langmuir, Gavin. 1971. "Anti-Judaism as the Necessary Preparation for Anti-Semitism". In: *Viator* 2, p. 383.

Lenin, Vladimir Ilich. 1970. *What is to Be Done?: Burning Questions of Our Movement.* New York: Panther Press.

Lesthaeghe, Ron. 1991. "Moral Control, Secularization and Reproduction in Belgium (1600–1900)". In: *Historiens et Populations.* Louvain-la-Neuve: Acedemia, pp. 259–279.

Lesthaeghe, Ron and Antonio Lopez-Gay. 2013. "Spatial Continuities and Discontinuities in Two Successive Demographic Transitions: Spain and Belgium, 1880–2010". In: *Demographic Research* 28, pp. 77–136.

Liempt, Ad Van. 2002. *Kopgeld: Nederlandse premiejagers op zoek naar joden 1943.* Amsterdam: Balans.

—— 2013. *Jodenjacht.* Amsterdam: Balans.

Lijphart, Arend. 1968. *The Politics of Accommodation: Pluralism and Democracy in the Netherlands.* Berkeley: University of California Press.

—— 1975. "The Comparable Cases Strategy in Comparative Research". In: *Comparative Political Studies* 8.2, pp. 158–177.

—— 1981. *Conflict and Coexistence in Belgium.* Berkeley: University of California Press.

Lindemann, Albert. 1997. *Esau's Tears: Modern Anti-Semitism and the Rise of the Jews.* New York: Cambridge University Press.

Lipset, Seymour Martin and Stein Rokkan. 1967. *Party Systems and Voter Alignments: Cross-National Perspectives.* New York: Free press.

London, Perry. 1970. "The Rescuers: Motivational Hypotheses about Christians Who Saved Jews from the Nazis". In: *Altruism and Helping Behavior*, ed. by Jacqueline Macaulay and Leonard Berkowitz. New York: Academic Press, pp. 241–250.

Longman, Timothy. 2010. *Christianity and Genocide in Rwanda.* New York: Cambridge University Press.

Loo, Pieter van. 2010. *Antisemitisme in de Belgische Franstalige pers? Le Peuple, La Libre Belgique en Le Soir in 1938–1940.* Scriptie: Universiteit van Antwerpen.

Loveman, Mara. 1998. "High-Risk Collective Action: Defending Human Rights in Chile, Uruguay, and Argentina". In: *American Journal of Sociology* 104.2, pp. 477–525.

Luft, Aliza. 2015. "Toward a Dynamic Theory of Action at the Micro Level of Genocide: Killing, Desistance, and Saving in 1994 Rwanda". In: *Sociological Theory* 33.2, pp. 148–172.

Mahoney, James. 2010. "After KKV: The New Methodology of Qualitative Research". In: *World Politics* 62.1, pp. 120–147.

Marwell, Gerald and Pamela Oliver. 1993. *The Critical Mass in Collective Action*. New York: Cambridge University Press.

Marx, Karl and Friedrich Engels. 1906. *Manifesto of the Communist Party*. Chicago: CH Kerr.

McAdam, Doug. 1986. "Recruitment to High-Risk Activism: The Case of Freedom Summer". In: *American Journal of Sociology* 92.1, pp. 64–90.

McAdam, Doug, Sidney Tarrow and Charles Tilly. 2001. *Dynamics of Contention*. Cambridge: Cambridge University Press. ISBN: 05218058800521011876 (pb.)

McCarthy, John and Mayer Zald. 1977. "Resource Mobilization and Social Movements: A Partial Theory". In: *American Journal of Sociology* 82.6, pp. 1212–1241.

McCombs, Maxwell and Donald Shaw. 1993. "The Evolution of Agenda-Setting Research: Twenty-Five years in the Marketplace of Ideas". In: *Journal of Communication* 43.2, pp. 58–67.

McDoom, Omar Shahabudin. 2014. "Antisocial Capital: A Profile of Rwandan Genocide Perpetrators' Social Networks". In: *Journal of Conflict Resolution* 58.5, pp. 866–894.

McGuire, William and Alice Padawer-Singer. 1976. "Trait Salience in the Spontaneous Self-Concept". In: *Journal of Personality and Social Psychology* 33.6, pp. 743–754.

McVeigh, Rory, Daniel Myers and David Sikkink. 2004. "Corn, Klansmen, and Coolidge: Structure and Framing in Social Movements". In: *Social Forces* 83.2, pp. 653–690.

Meershoek, Guus. 1999. *Dienaren van het gezag. De Amsterdamse politie tijdens de bezetting*. Amsterdam: Van Gennep.

Mehra, Ajay, Martin Kilduff and Daniel Brass. 1998. "At the Margins: A Distinctiveness Approach to the Social Identity and Social Networks of Underrepresented Groups". In: *Academy of Management Journal* 41.4, pp. 441–452.

Meinen, Insa. 2009. *Die Shoah in Belgien*. Konstanz: Wissenschaftliche Buchgesellschaft.

Meir, Ephraim. 1987. "The Role of Antisemitism in the Pre-War Rexist Movement". In: *Bulletin Trimestriel de la Fondation Auschwitz* 16, pp. 16–32.

Ménager, Camille. 2005. *Le Sauvetage des Juifs á Paris 1940–1945: Histoire et Memoire*. Paris: Presses de Sciences Po.

Michman, Dan. 1992. "De oprichting van de Joodsche Raad voor Amsterdam vanuit een vergelijkend perspectief". In: *Oorlogsdocumentatie* 40–45.3, pp. 74–100.

Michman, Jozeph, Hartog Beem and Dan Michman. 1999. *Pinkas: Geschiedenis van de joodse gemeenschap in Nederland*. Amsterdam: Contact.

Michman, Jozeph, Bert-Jan Flim, Israel Gutman et al. 2004. *The Encyclopedia of the Righteous Among the Nations: Rescuers of Jews During the Holocaust. The Netherlands.* Jeruzalem: Yad Vashem.

Miller, Robert. 1957. "The Protestant Churches and Lynching, 1919–1939". In: *The Journal of Negro History* 42.2, pp. 118–131.

Monroe, Kristen. 2001. "Morality and a Sense of Self: The Importance of Identity and Categorization for Moral Action". In: *American Journal of Political Science* 45.3, pp. 491–507.

Moore, Bob. 1997. *Victims and Survivors: the Nazi Persecution of the Jews in the Netherlands, 1940–1945.* London: Arnold.

—— 2010. *Survivors: Jewish Self-Help and Rescue in Nazi-Occupied Western Europe.* Oxford: Oxford University Press.

Moorehead, Caroline. 2014. *Village of Secrets: Defying the Nazis in Vichy France.* New York: Random House.

Morris, Aldon. 1981. "Black Southern Student Sit-In Movement: An Analysis of Internal Organization". In: *American Sociological Review* 46.6, pp. 744–767.

—— 1986. *The Origins of the Civil Rights Movement.* New York: Simon and Schuster.

Morris, Aldon and Suzanne Staggenborg. 2004. "Leadership in Social Movements". In: *The Blackwell Companion to Social Movements*, ed. by David Snow, Sarah Soule and Hanspeter Kriesi. Malden, MA: Blackwell, pp. 171–196.

Morselli, Carlo, Cynthia Giguère and Katia Petit. 2007. "The Efficiency / Security Trade-Off in Criminal Networks". In: *Social Networks* 29.1, pp. 143–153.

NDAW. 1936. *Maandblad voor Arbeidsbemiddeling en Werkloosheid.* Brussels: Nationale Dienst voor Arbeidsbemiddeling en Werkloosheid.

Nepstad, Sharon and Clifford Bob. 2006. "When Do Leaders Matter? Hypotheses on Leadership Dynamics in Social Movements". In: *Mobilization: An International Quarterly* 11.1, pp. 1–22.

Noltus, Frank. 1983. *Wierden in Bezettingstijd.* Kampen: Kok.

Nowak, Herman. 2000. *Cyrille Berger. Enfant Cache.* Gennes: La Longue Vue.

Nussbaum, Martha. 1992a. "Human Functioning and Social Justice in Defense of Aristotelian Essentialism". In: *Political theory* 20.2, pp. 202–246.

—— 1992b. "Tragedy and Self-Sufficiency: Plato and Aristotle on Fear and Pity". In: *Oxford Studies in Ancient Philosophy* 107.10, pp. 107–159.

Nyseth Brehm, Hollie. 2017. "Subnational Determinants of Killing in Rwanda". In: *Criminology* 55.1, pp. 5–31.

Oliner, Sam and Pearl Oliner. 1992. *The Altruistic Personality: Rescuers of Jews in Nazi Europe.* New York: Free Press.

Olson, Mancur. 1965. *The Logic of Collective Action: Public Goods and the Theory of Groups.* Boston: Harvard University Press.

Ommeren, Anita Van and Ageeth Scherphuis. 1985. "De onderduikers in de Haarlemmermeer". In: *Vrij Nederland* 11, pp. 1–39.

Onroerend Erfgoed Agentschap. 2014. *Inventaris.* URL: http://inventaris .onroerenderfgoed.be.

Opp, Karl-Dieter. 1997. "Can Identity Theory Better Explain the Rescue of Jews in Nazi Europe than Rational Actor Theory". In: *Research in Social Movements, Conflict and Change* 20.2, pp. 223–253.

Oster, Emily. 2014. "Unobservable Selection and Coefficient Stability: Theory and Evidence". In: *University of Chicago Booth School of Business Working Paper*.

Owens, Peter, Yang Su and David Snow. 2013. "Social Scientific Inquiry into Genocide and Mass Killing: From Unitary Outcome to Complex Processes". In: *Annual Review of Sociology* 39, pp. 69–84.

Paldiel, Mordecai. 1993. *The Path of the Righteous: Gentile Rescuers of Jews during the Holocaust.* Jersey City, NJ: KTAV Publishing House.

Parkinson, Sarah Elizabeth. 2013. "Organizing rebellion: Rethinking high-risk mobilization and social networks in war". *American Political Science Review* 107.3, pp. 418–432.

Pennings, Paul. 1991. *Verzuiling en Ontzuiling: de Lokale Verschillen* Kampen: Kok

Phayer, Michael. 1990. *Protestant and Catholic Women in Nazi Germany.* Detroit, MI: Wayne State University Press.

—— 1993. "The Catholic Resistance Circle in Berlin and German Catholic Bishops during the Holocaust". In: *Holocaust and Genocide Studies* 7.2, pp. 216–229.

—— 2000. *The Catholic Church and the Holocaust, 1930–1965.* Bloomington: Indiana University Press.

Phillip, Franz-Heinrich. 1970. "Protestantismus nach 1848". In: *Kirche und Synagoge: Handbuch zur Geschichte von Christen und Juden.* Stuttgart: Ernst Klett Verlag, p. 341.

Philpott, Daniel. 2007. "Explaining the Political Ambivalence of Religion". In: *American Political Science Review* 101.3, pp. 505–525.

Poorthuis, Marcel and Theo Salemink. 2006. *Een Donkere Spiegel. Nederlandse Katholieken over Joden. Tussen Antisemitisme en Erkenning 1870–2005.* Nijmegen: Valkhof Pers.

Portes, Alejandro. 1995. *The Economic Sociology of Immigration.* New York: Russell Sage Foundation.

Presser, Jacob. 1965. *Ondergang: de vervolging en verdelging van het Nederlandse Jodendom, 1940–1945.* Den Haag: Martinus Nijhoff.

Przeworski, Adam and Henry Teune. 1970. *The Logic of Comparative Social Inquiry.* New York: John Wiley.

Pulzer, Peter. 1988. *The Rise of Political Anti-Semitism in Germany and Austria.* Cambridge, MA: Harvard University Press.

Putnam, Robert. 2000. *Bowling Alone: The Collapse and Revival of American Democracy.* New York: Simon and Schuster.

Raab, Jörg and Brinton Milward. 2003. "Dark Networks as Problems". In: *Journal of Public Administration Research and Theory* 13.4, pp. 413–439.

Ramakers, Jan. 2006. "Conservatisme en antisemitisme". In: *Trajecta* 15.1, pp. 62–75.

Religieuze Kunst en Cultuur, Centrum voor. 2014. *Enquete Vlaamse Kerkgebouwen.* http://crkc.be.

Rens, Herman van. 2013. *Vervolgd in Limburg. Joden en Sinti in Nederlands-Limburg tijdens de Tweede Wereldoorlog.* Hilversum: Verloren.

Riessen, Hendrik van, Rogier van Aerde and A. Algra. 1951. *Het grotegebod: gedenkboek van het verzet in LO en LKP.* Kampen: Kok.

Rigthart, Hans. 1986. *De Katholieke Zuil in Europa: Het Ontstaan van Verzuiling onder Katholieken in Oostenrijk, Zwitserland, België en Nederland.* Amsterdam: Boom.

Ringelblum, Emanuel, Joseph Kermish and Shmuel Krakowski. 1992. *Polish-Jewish Relations during the Second World War.* Evanston, IL: Northwestern University Press.

Roggeband, Conny and Mieke Verloo. 2007. "Dutch Women are Liberated, Migrant Women are a Problem: The Evolution of Policy Frames on Gender and Migration in the Netherlands, 1995–2005". In: *Social Policy & Administration* 41.3, pp. 271–288.

Rogier, Ludovicus. 1964. *Geschiedenis van het katholicisme in Noord-Nederland in de 16de en 17de eeuw.* Amsterdam: Elsevier.

Romijn, Peter. 2002. "The Experience of the Jews in the Netherlands during the German Occupation". In: *Dutch Jewry: Its History and Secular Culture (1500–2000)*, ed. by Jonathan Israel and Reinier Salverda. Leiden: Brill, pp. 253–271.

Rossum, Jan van. 2011. *In de Onderduik: Hoe Steenwijker Joden de Oorlog Overleefde.* Steenwijk: Steenwijks Boekhuis.

Rousseau, Jean-Jacques. [1889] 1979. *Emile, or On Education.* New York: Basic Books.

Saerens, Lieven. 1991. "De Houding van het Vlaams-Nationalisme Tegenover de Joden tijdens de Jaren 30". In: *Extreem rechts in West-Europa*, ed. by Hugo de Schampheleire and Yannis Thanassekos. Brussels: VUBPress, pp. 255–280.

—— 1998. "The Attitude of the Belgian Roman Catholic Clergy toward the Jews Prior to the Occupation". In: *Belgium and the Holocaust: Jews, Belgians, Germans.* Jerusalem: Yad Vashem, pp. 117–159.

—— 2000. *Vreemdelingen in een Wereldstad. Een Geschiedenis van Antwerpen en zijn Joodse Bevolking.* Tielt: Lannoo Uitgeverij.

—— 2005. *Etrangers dans la Cité: Anvers et ses Juifs (1880–1944).* Charleroi: Editions Labor.

—— 2006a. "De Jodenvervolging in België in Cijfers". In: *Bijdragen tot de Eigentijdse Geschiedenis* 30.60, pp. 199–235.

—— 2006b. "De Houding van de Belgische Katholieken tegenover de Joden". In: *Trajecta* 15.1, pp. 76–94.

—— 2007a. "The General Attitude of the Protestant Churches in Belgium Regarding the Jews (from the End of the 19th Century to the Second World War)". In: *Religion under Siege II: Protestant, Orthodox and Muslim communities in occupied Europe (1939–1950)*, ed. by Lieve Gevers and Jan Bank. Leuven: Peeters, pp. 265–281.

—— 2007b. *Jodenjagers van de Vlaamse SS.* Tielt: Lannoo.

—— 2015. *Ongewillig Brussel. Een verhaal over Jodenvervolging en verzet.* Leuven: Davidsfonds.

Sageman, Marc. 2004. *Understanding Terror Networks*. Philadelphia: University of Pennsylvania Press.

—— 2011. *Leaderless Jihad: Terror Networks in the Twenty-First Century*. Philadelphia: University of Pennsylvania Press.

Sarner, Harvey and Jay Weinstein. 1998. "Rescue in Albania: One Hundred Percent of Jews in Albania Rescued from the Holocaust". In: *Michigan Sociological Review* 12, pp. 141–146.

Satloff, Robert. 2006. *Among the Righteous: Lost Stories from the Holocaust's Long Reach into Arab Lands*. New York: Public Affairs.

Scholder, Klaus. 1977. *Die Kirchen und das Dritte Reich: Vorgeschichte und Zeit der Illusionen 1918–1934*. Berlin: Propyläen.

Schram, Laurence. 2004. "De Oproepen voor 'tewerkstelling' in het Oosten". In: *Rudi Van Doorslaer & Jean-Philippe Schreiber (red.), De curatoren van het getto: de Vereniging van de joden in België tijdens de nazi-bezetting*. Tielt: Lannoo Uitgeverij, pp. 247–266.

Sells, Michael. 1996. *The Bridge Betrayed: Religion and Genocide in Bosnia*. Berkeley: University of California Press.

Semelin, Jacques. 1993. *Unarmed against Hitler: Civilian Resistance in Europe, 1939–1943*. Westport, CT: Praeger Publishers.

Semelin, Jacques, Claire Andrieu and Sarah Gensburger. 2008. *La résistance aux génocides: de la pluralité des actes de sauvetage*. Paris: Presses de Sciences Po.

Shapiro, Jacob. 2013. *The Terrorist's Dilemma: Managing Violent Covert Organizations*. Princeton, NJ: Princeton University Press.

Shatz, Adam. 2004. *Prophets Outcast: A Century of Dissident Jewish Writing about Zionism and Israel*. New York: Nation Books.

Sijes, Ben. 1954. *De februari-staking: 25–26 februari 1941*. Amsterdam: Martinus-Nijhoff.

Simmel, Georg. 1906. "The Sociology of Secrecy and of Secret Societies". In: *American Journal of Sociology* 11.4, pp. 441–498.

Simon, Herbert Alexander. 1982. *Models of Bounded Rationality: Empirically Grounded Economic Reason*. Boston: MIT Press.

Sirin, Cigdem, José D Villalobos and Nicholas Valentino. 2016. "Group Empathy Theory: The Effect of Group Empathy on US Intergroup Attitudes and Behavior in the Context of Immigration Threats". In: *The Journal of Politics* 78.3, pp. 893–908.

Smaele, Henk de. 2009. *Rechts Vlaanderen: Religie en Stemgedrag in Negentiende-Eeuws Belgie*. Leuven: Leuven University Press.

Smelser, Neil. 1962. *Theory of Collective Action*. New York: Free Press.

Snoek, Johan. 1969. *The Grey Book: A Collection of Protests against Anti-Semitism and the Persecution of Jews issued by Non-Roman Catholic Churches and Church Leaders during Hitlers rule*. Assen: Van Gorcum.

—— 2005. *De Nederlandse kerken en de Joden*. Kampen: Project Gutenberg.

Snow, David and Robert Benford. 2000. "Framing Processes and Social Movements: An Overview and Assessment". In: *Annual Review of Sociology* 26, pp. 611–639.

Snow, David, Louis Zurcher and Sheldon Ekland-Olson. 1980. "Social Networks and Social Movements: A Microstructural Approach to Differential Recruitment". In: *American Sociological Review* 45.5, pp. 787–801.

Snyder, Timothy. 2012. *Bloodlands: Europe between Hitler and Stalin*. New York: Basic Books.

Spector, Shmuel. 1990. *Holocaust of Volhynian Jews: 1941–44*. Jerusalem: Yad Vashem.

Staniland, Paul. 2014. *Networks of Rebellion: Explaining Insurgent Cohesion and Collapse*. Ithaca, NY: Cornell University Press.

Staub, Ervin. 2003. "Notes on Cultures of Violence, Cultures of Caring and Peace, and the Fulfillment of Basic Human Needs". In: *Political Psychology* 24.1, pp. 1–21.

Steinberg, Jonathan. 1994. "Types of Genocide? Croatians, Serbs and Jews, 1941–5". In: *The Final Solution: Origins and Implementation*, ed. by David Cesarani. New York: Routledge, pp. 175–193.

Steinberg, Maxime. 2004. *La Persécution des Juifs en Belgique (1940–1945)*. Brussels: Editions Complexe.

Steinberg, Maxime and Laurence Schram. 2008. *Transport XX*. Brussel: ASP/VUBPRESS/UPA.

Stemler, Steve. 2001. "An Overview of Content Analysis". In: *Practical Assessment, Research & Evaluation* 7.17, pp. 137–146.

Stokman, Siegfried. 1945. *Het verzet van de Nederlandse bisschoppen. Tegen Nationaal-Socialisme en Duitse tyrannie*. Utrecht: Spectrum.

Straus, Scott. 2012. "Retreating from the Brink: Theorizing Mass Violence and the Dynamics of Restraint". In: *Perspectives on Politics* 10.2, pp. 343–362.

—— 2015. *Making and Unmaking Nations: The Origins and Dynamics of Genocide in Contemporary Africa*. Ithaca, NY: Cornell University Press.

Su, Yang. 2011. *Collective Killings in Rural China during the Cultural Revolution*. Cambridge: Cambridge University Press.

Sullivan, Christopher. 2016. "Political Repression and the Destruction of Dissident Organizations: Evidence from the Archives of the Guatemalan National Police". In: *World Politics* 68.4, pp. 645–676.

Suny, Ronald Grigor. 2015. *They Can Live in the Desert But Nowhere Else: A History of the Armenian Genocide*. Princeton, NJ: Princeton University Press.

Tammes, Peter. 2011. "Residential Segregation of Jews in Amsterdam on the Eve of the Shoah". In: *Continuity and Change* 26.2, pp. 243–270.

Tammes, Peter and Annika Smits. 2005. "De invloed van christenen op de overlevingskansen van joden in Nederlandse gemeenten tijdens de Tweede Wereldoorlog: Een katholieke paradox?" In: *Mens en Maatschappij* 80.4, pp. 353–375.

Tec, Nechama. 1987. *When Light Pierced the Darkness: Christian Rescue of Jews in Nazi-Occupied Poland*. Oxford: Oxford University Press.

Teitelbaum-Hirsch, Viviane. 2006. *Enfants Caches. Les Lames sous le Masque*. Brussels: Editions Luc Pire.

Ternon, Yves. 2008. "L'impossible sauvetage des arméniens de Mardin". In: *La résistance aux génocides: de la pluralité des actes de sauvetage*, ed. by

Jacques Semelin, Claire Andrieu, and Sarah Gensburger. Paris: Presses de Sciences Po, pp. 399–409.

Tevosyan, Hasmik. 2008. "Les Pratiques de Sauvetage Durant le génocides des Arméniens". In: *La Résistance aux génocides: de la Pluralité des Actes de Aauvetage*, ed. by Jacques Semelin, Claire Andrieu and Sarah Gensburger. Paris: Presses de Sciences Po, pp. 163–182.

Thyange, Genevieve. 1995. "L'Abbé Joseph André et l'Aide aux Juifs à Namur". In: *Entre la Peste et le Cholera. Vie et Attitudes des Catholiques sous l Occupation*. Brussels: Arca.

Tiefel, Hans. 1972. "The German Lutheran Church and the Rise of National Socialism". In: *Church History* 41, pp. 326–336.

Tijssen, Henk. 2009. *De Dominee van de NSB: Boissevain en zijn Gang van de Nederlandse Hervormde Kerk*. Kampen: Omnibook.

Tilly, Charles. 1978. *From Mobilization to Revolution*. New York: McGraw-Hill.

Tocqueville, Alexis De. 1840. *Democracy in America*. Garden City, NY: Doubleday.

Torfs, Jan. 1984. *Geschiedenis van Leuven: van den Vroegsten Tijd tot op Heden*. Leuven: Ripova.

Touw, Hendrik. 1946. *Het Verzet der Hervormde Kerk*. Den Haag: Boekencentrum.

Turner, Ralph and Lewis Killian. 1957. *Collective Behavior*. New York: Prentice-Hall.

Urwin, Derek W. 1970. "Social Cleavages and Political Parties in Belgium: Problems of Institutionalization". In: *Political Studies* 18.3, pp. 320–340.

Van Der Boom, Bart. 2012. *We Weten Niets van Hun Lot. Gewone Nederlanders en de Holocaust*. Amsterdam: Boom.

Van Doorslaer, Rudi, Emmanuel Debruyne, Frank Seberechts et al. 2004. *La Belgique Docile*. Brussels: Editions Luc Pire.

Van Doorslaer, Rudi and Jean-Philippe Schreiber. 2004. *De Curatoren van het Getto: de Vereniging van de Joden in België tijdens de Nazi-Bezetting*. Tielt: Lannoo Uitgeverij.

Van Eijnatten, Joris and Frederik Angenietus van Lieburg. 2005. *Nederlandse religiegeschiedenis*. Hilversum: Uitgeverij Verloren.

Van Haver, Griet. 1983. *Onmacht der Verdeelden: Katolieken in Vlaanderen tussen Demokratie en Fascisme. 1929–1940*. Amsterdam: Ekologische Uitgeverij.

Van Klinken, Gert. 2001. "Dutch Jews as Perceived by Dutch Protestants, 1860–1960". In: *Dutch Jews as Perceived by Themselves and by Others*. Leiden: Brill, pp. 125–134.

Van Roon, Gerrit. 1990. *Protestants Nederland en Duitsland 1933–1941*. Kampen: Kok.

Vanhaute, Eric and Sven Vrielinck. 2013. *LOKSTAT: Historische Databank van Lokale Statistieken*. Gent: Universiteit Gent.

Varese, Federico and Meir Yaish. 2000. "The Importance of Being Asked: The Rescue of Jews in Nazi-Europe". In: *Rationality and Society* 12.3, pp. 307–334.

Varshney, Ashutosh. 2003. *Ethnic Conflict and Civic Life: Hindus and Muslims in India*. New Haven, CT: Yale University Press.

Vellenga, Sjoerd. 1975. *Katholiek Zuid Limburg en het Fascisme: een Onderzoek naar het Kiesgedrag van de Limburger in de Jaren Dertig*. Assen: Van Gorcum.

Verbeke, Jasmine. 2003. *Le Pays Réel à l'égard de l'Antisemitisme. Faut-il Chasser les Juifs?: de Pers van Rex ten Aanzien van de Joden (1936–1944)*. Gent: Scriptie Universiteit Gent.

Verdeja, Ernesto. 2012. "The Political Science of Genocide: Outlines of an Emerging Research Agenda". In: *Perspectives on Politics* 10.02, pp. 307–321.

Verkuyten, Maykel and Ali Aslan Yildiz. 2006. "The Endorsement of Minority Rights: The Role of Group Position, National Context, and Ideological Beliefs". In: *Political Psychology* 27.4, pp. 527–548.

Verpoorten, Marijke. 2012. "Leave None to claim the Land A Malthusian Catastrophe in Rwanda?" In: *Journal of Peace Research* 49.4, pp. 547–563.

Viret, Emmanuel. 2008. "Les Musulmans de Mabare pendant le génocide Rwandais". In: *La résistance aux génocides: de la pluralité des actes de sauvetage*, ed. by Jacques Semelin, Claire Andrieu and Sarah Gensburger. Paris: Presses de Sciences Po, pp. 491–504.

Viterna, Jocelyn. 2006. "Pulled, Pushed, and Persuaded: Explaining Womens Mobilization into the Salvadoran Guerrilla Army". In: *American Journal of Sociology* 112.1, pp. 1–45.

Voigtländer, Nico and Hans-Joachim Voth. 2012. "Persecution Perpetuated: the Medieval Origins of Anti-Semitic Violence in Nazi Germany". In: *Quarterly Journal of Economics* 127.3, pp. 1339–1392.

Vreese, Claes de. 2005. "News Framing: Theory and Typology". In: *Information Design Journal & Document Design* 13.1, pp. 51–62.

Vromen, Suzanne. 2010. *Hidden Children of the Holocaust*. New York: Oxford University Press.

Waal, Frans de. 2008. "Putting the Altruism Back into Altruism: The Evolution of Empathy". In: *Annual Review of Psychology* 59, pp. 279–300.

Waller, James. 2007. *Becoming Evil: How Ordinary People Commit Genocide and Mass Killing*. Oxford: Oxford University Press.

Wasserstein, Bernard. 2012. *On the Eve: The Jews of Europe Before the Second World War*. New York: Simon and Schuster.

Weber, Max. [1968] 1978. *Economy and Society*. Berkeley: University of California Press.

—— 1985. "Churches and Sects in North America". In: *Sociological Theory* 3.1, pp. 1–13.

Weiss, John. 1997. *Ideology of Death: Why the Holocaust Happened in Germany*. Chicago: Ivan R. Dee.

Weustink, Gerard. 1985. *Bijdrage tot de Geschiedenis van den Joden van Twente en het Aangrenzende Duitsland*. Oldenzaal: Gemeente Uitgever.

Wielek, Heinz. 1947. *De oorlog die Hilter won*. Amsterdam: Amsterdamse Boek en Courant Maatschappij.

Wijbenga, Pieter. 1995. *Bezettingstijd in Friesland*. Leeuwarden: De Tille.

Wilde, Melissa. 2007. *Vatican II: A Sociological Analysis of Religious Change.* Princeton, NJ: Princeton University Press.

Willink, Bastiaan. 2010. *De textielbaronnen. Twents-Gelders familisme en de eerste grootindustrie van Nederland 1800–1980.* Zuthpen: Walburg Pers Zutphen.

Wils, Lode. 2009. *Van de Belgische naar de Vlaamse natie: Een Geschiedenis van de Vlaamse Beweging.* Leuven: Acco.

Winkel, Lydia and Hans de Vries. 1989. *De Ondergrondse Pers 1940–1945.* Den Haag: Martinus Nijhoff.

Witte, Els. 2008. *La Construction del la Belgique.* Paris: Editions Complexe.

Witte, Els and Jan Craeybeckx. 1983. *Politieke Geschiedenis van Belgie sinds 1830: Spanningen in een Burgerlijke Democratie.* Antwerp: Standaard Wetenschappelijke Uitgeverij.

Wolf, Jan de. 1947. *Getrouw tot in den Dood. Korte Levensbeschrijving ds. Nanne Zwiep.* Enschede: VDMserie XXV.

Wolfson, Manfred. 1975. "Zum Widerstand gegen Hitler: Umriss eines Gruppenporträts deutscher Retter von Juden". In: *Tradition und Neubeginn. Internationale Forschungen zur deutschen Geschichte* 20, pp. 391–408.

Yahil, Leni. 1983. *The Rescue of Danish Jewry: Test of a Democracy.* Philadelphia: Jewish Publication Society of America.

Zondergeld, Gjalt. 1986. *Een kleine troep vervuld van haat.* Houten: De Haan.

Zubrzycki, Geneviève. 2009. *The Crosses of Auschwitz: Nationalism and Religion in Post-Communist Poland.* Chicago: University of Chicago Press.

Zuccotti, Susan. 1987. *The Italians and the Holocaust: Persecution, Rescue, and Survival.* Lincoln: University of Nebraska Press.

Zwerman, Gilda, Patricia Steinhoff and Donatella della Porta. 2000. "Disappearing Social Movements: Clandestinity in the Cycle of New Left Protest in the US, Japan, Germany, and Italy". In: *Mobilization: An International Quarterly* 5.1, pp. 85–104.

Index